BANGL

A Legacy of Blood

Anthony Mascarenhas

HODDER AND STOUGHTON
LONDON SYDNEY AUCKLAND TORONTO

To Yvonne
and our children—
who also have
paid the price

British Library Cataloguing in Publication Data

Mascarenhas, Anthony
  Bangladesh: a legacy of blood.
  1. Bangladesh—History
  I. Title
  954.9'205   DS395.5

ISBN 0 340 39420 X

First published 1986

Printed in Great Britain
for Hodder and Stoughton Educational
a division of Hodder and Stoughton Ltd, Mill Road
Dunton Green, Sevenoaks, Kent by
Richard Clay (The Chaucer Press) Ltd,
Bungay, Suffolk

Contents

List of Plates—Photographs and Documents

(between pages 90 and 91)

Acknowledgements

Photograph 2 reproduced by kind permission of Camera Press Ltd.
Photograph 6 reproduced by kind permission of UPI.
All other photographs and documents reproduced by kind permission of the author.

Preface

This is a true story; in many ways a text book of Third World disenchantment.

On the 16th of December, 1971, the state of Bangladesh (population 70,000,000) was born at the end of a nine-month liberation struggle in which more than a million Bengalis of the erstwhile East Pakistan died at the hands of the Pakistan army. But one of the 20th century's great man-made disasters is also among the greatest of its human triumphs in terms of a people's will for self-determination. The united upsurge of the Bengalis to fashion their own destiny against overwhelming odds captured the imagination of the world. It brought with it an unprecedented outpouring of sympathy and aid from the international community. This ranged from active political and practical support to touching individual acts of generosity and the Concert for Bangladesh by pop stars in New York in 1971 which became the model for Band Aid and Live Aid relief to starving Africa. But the Bengalis gave more than anyone else: their lives in staggering numbers. Those were sacrificed to make a reality of the long-cherished dream of Sonar Bangla or Golden Bengal. This was intended to be a state based on equity, justice, social harmony and cultural effulgence, echoing the sentiments dear to the heart of every Bengali. But it was not to be. The sacrifices were in vain. The dream became a nightmare. Bangladesh got snarled in a legacy of blood.

Few men in history have betrayed the aspirations of their people as did the first leaders of Bangladesh—Sheikh Mujibur Rahman, Khandaker Moshtaque Ahmed and General Ziaur Rahman. When each in turn was called upon to make good, he took the country further along the road to perdition. Once the darling of the independence movement 'in whose magic name all things are done', Sheikh Mujib as Prime Minister and President became the most hated man in Bangladesh within three short years of its founding. He and his family were killed for it. And the hatred lingers. Ten years after Mujib's death his daughter, Hasina, told me that she could not get the agreement of relatives and neighbours in their home village of Tungipara to erect a suitable monument over Mujib's grave. 'People react differently when you are not in power,' Hasina said in what could be an epitaph for both Mujib and General Zia. Moshtaque, who succeeded Mujib, has become a by-word for treachery. General Zia, the next man, was once idolised by the army. But then he showed his true colours and became the target of 20 mutinies and coup attempts in five years. The 21st killed him. As public awareness of the general's real role increases, Zia's memory too has become an embarrassment to his friends.

This book is the unvarnished story of their times, essentially the sad history of the first 10 years of Bangladesh. It is based on my close personal knowledge of the main protagonists; on more than 120 separate interviews with the men and women involved in the dramatic events; and on official archives and documents which I had the privilege to inspect personally. The dialogue, whenever used, is a faithful reproduction of the words which my informants said they actually used during the events in which they were involved. Thus majors Farook and Rashid tell the authentic story of the Why and the How of the killing of Sheikh Mujib; and the mystery is revealed of the slaughter of hapless Tajuddin and his companions in Dhaka jail by the men who planned and executed it. General Zia is exposed by his friends and his critics. His assassins tell how they killed him. And throughout the narrative of the wasted blood of the Bangladesh martyrs cries out the lesson that when hope is extinguished, accountability denied and the people have nothing further to lose, they turn to violence to redress their wrongs.

Shakespeare said: 'The evil that men do lives after them. The good is oft interred with their bones.' So it is with Sheikh Mujib and General Ziaur Rahman who by their headstrong acts and selfish ambition left Bangladesh a legacy of blood. In these circumstances the focus of this book inevitably is on the wrong doing. I make no apology for it. The people must know the truth about their leaders; and may we all take lesson from their mistakes.

November 1985   Anthony Mascarenhas

List of officers convicted by General Court Martial and hanged for the assassination of President Ziaur Rahman:

1. BA-185   *Brigadier Mohsinuddin Ahmed,*
             Commander, 69 Infantry Brigade.
2. BA-200   *Col. Nawzesh Uddin,*
             Commander, 305 Infantry Brigade.
3. BA-212   *Col. Muhammad Abdur Rashid,*
             Commander, 65 Infantry Brigade.
4. BSS-675   *Lt. Col. Shah Mohammad Fazle Hussain,*
             CO, 6 East Bengal Regiment.
5. BA-301   *Lt. Col. A. Y. M. Mahfuzur Rahman,*
             Personal Secretary to President from
             C-in-C Secretariat.
6. BA-400   *Lt. Col. Muhammad Dilawar Hussain,*
             Asst. Director Ordnance Services,
             24 Infantry Division, Chittagong.
7. BSS-722   *Major Gias Uddin Ahmed,*
             2nd in Charge, 11 East Bengal Regiment.
8. BSS-839   *Major Rawshan Iazdani Bhuiyan,*
             Brigade Major, 65 Infantry Division.
9. BA-1167   *Major Mohd. Mujibur Rahman,*
             OC, 112 Signal Coy.
10. BSS-1070 *Captain Mohd. Abdus Sattar,*
             6 East Bengal Regiment.
11. BSS-862 *Major Kazi Mominul Haque,*
             2nd in Charge, 1 East Bengal Regiment.
12. BSS-1526 *Captain Jamil Haque,*
             21 East Bengal Regiment.
13. BSS-1742 *Lt. Mohammad Rafiqul Hassan Khan,*
             6 East Bengal Regiment.

I

Mujib and the Majors

Nobody understands what I do for my country.

—Sheikh Mujibur Rahman.

I'm going to do it on the 15th.
I'm going to knock off Mujib.

—Major Farook Rahman

Not one of the hundred or so guests at the Dhaka Golf Club on the evening of 12 August, 1975, is ever likely to forget the third wedding anniversary party given by the Acting Commandant of the Bengal Lancers, Major Farook Rahman, and his lovely young wife Farida.

Farook and Farida were a popular young couple, well-connected to the enduring upper crust of Bengali society, the polished old silver that gives the country its university chancellors, men of the Bar and senior civil servants. So their party was something of a social event. Even the heavens seemed to have taken note of it. Sunshine and a clear sky made a welcome break in the monsoons which had been soaking the city for weeks.

The party was a typical military bash since Farook was second generation army. Dozens of coloured lights strung between the acacias made a colourful canopy for the guests with their glasses of sherbet gathered in amiable groups on the lawn. The music came from the Army Headquarters band which set the mood with hits from the latest Bengali films. Inside the club house the buffet was a generous spread of lamb biryani, kebabs, an assortment of curries and more than a dozen bowls of fruit salad. There was enough to feed an army— and the army was everywhere.

The Chief of the General Staff, Brigadier Khalid Musharraf, who was Farook's 'Mamu' (maternal uncle) was there. So too was Brigadier Mashoorul Huq, Military Secretary to President Sheikh Mujibur Rahman. Farook's men, who had chipped in for an anniversary present, brought a handsome bedroom carpet woven from jute fibres. Friends and relatives had come with table lamps, vases and boxes gift-wrapped in the yellow, green and red kite paper favoured by the shopkeepers of New Market. But Brigadier Huq, who came later, upstaged them all. He brought an enormous bouquet of monsoon flowers made up by the head mali of Gonobaban, Sheikh Mujib's official residence. And he made a big thing of presenting it to Farida.

Three days later, with the benefit of hindsight, all those present would squeeze their minds searching every detail of the party for some clue that might have betrayed the momentous events which were to follow. And Brigadier Huq would silently thank his stars for his gallantry. Farida's bouquet may have saved his life.

But on that anniversary night Farook gave not a hint of the dark secret he carried. He recalled that he was in an unusually expansive mood. 'I sold my

1

automatic slide projector for 3500 Takkas and blew it all on the party.' For him it had an awesome finality. What he had set his mind on doing would either put him before a firing squad or indelibly carve his name in the history of Bangladeshis.

'I decided to enjoy myself. That party could have been my last.'

When the guests had left, a small family group gathered on the lawn for a snack and coffee. The hosts had been too busy to eat. With the couple were Farook's mother and father, Farida's mother who had come from Chittagong, and Farida's elder sister Zubeida, nicknamed 'Tinku' with her husband Major Khandaker Abdur Rashid who commanded the 2 Field Artillery based in Dhaka.

Farook took his brother-in-law aside.

'I'm going to do it on the 15th,' he told Rashid. 'I'm going to knock off Mujib on Friday morning.'

Rashid was startled. He looked round nervously to see if anyone had overheard Farook's bombshell. Suddenly the months of secret plotting had reached a conclusion. But Rashid was not ready. After a long moment of silence he hissed: 'Are you mad? It's too short notice. We don't have officers. We don't have equipment. How can we do it?'

Farook stared at Rashid, a glint of steel shining through the tinted glasses he wore. 'It's my decision,' he told the other major. 'I have the tactical plan ready. I'm going ahead even if I have to do it alone. You can keep away if you want. But remember, if I fail they will surely hang you also.'

Another long silence from Rashid. He appeared to be visibly digesting Farook's words. When their harsh meaning finally seeped through, the lanky artillery officer straightened out. 'All right,' he told Farook. 'If it's got to be done let's do it. But we must talk. I need to bring in some more officers.'

In another part of the city Sheikh Mujibur Rahman was relaxing with a small family group in his modest bungalow on Road No. 32, Dhanmandi, the landmark which was till then the centre of the world of the Bangladeshis. The clan had gathered two days earlier for the wedding of Mujib's niece, the daughter of his younger sister, and many of them had stayed on to pay their respects and to get the great man's blessings. Once the obeisances were made Begum Mujib gently ushered them out till her tired husband was left with a selected few. One of those present was Abdur Rab Serniabat, Mujib's brother-in-law, and husband of his favourite sister. He was a minister with a string of portfolios—Flood Control, Water Development, Power, Forests, Fisheries, and Livestock. Another was Serniabat's son, Abu Hasnat, who three days later would have a miraculous escape when disaster obliterated the rest of the family.

It was not unusual that the conversation that night should have as much to do with official matters as those concerning the family. Mujib's style made the two inseparable. In his world of suspicion and intrigue reliance was understandably placed on those nearest and dearest to him. And when he became absorbed with anything concerning his beloved Bangladesh, the family was inevitably drawn in. Tonight it was flood control.

Abu Hasnat recalled: 'Uncle was worried about the possibility of floods in the autumn months which could severely damage the rice crop. He told my father he should quickly press into service the dredger he was arranging to buy from India.' Mujib had a farmer's gift for anecdotes. Soon, in the manner of a village elder, he was framing the problem of the moment against a background of a personal experience deeply rooted in the soil of the delta country. The room filled with the aroma from his pipe. 'When I was a boy,' he told his listeners, 'I used to play football on the banks of the river with the Britishers from the dredger company. Then the war came and the dredgers were taken away to make barges for the Burma campaign. They never came back. Now there is no river where I used to play, only silt; and we have great floods every year.'

As he rambled on Mujib warmed to the idea of what he was going to do to solve the problem. 'I have no money for flood control, but I am getting my dredger,' he told the family. 'You will see how I comb the rivers. My BKSAL* will do it.'

Then his mood changed, enthusiasm deflating like a man suddenly overcome by futility. Hasnat remembers the last words he would hear his uncle speak: 'Nobody understands what I do for my country.'

That remark is Sheikh Mujibur Rahman's epitaph.

He was then nearing the end of a life-long love affair with the Bengalis. It was a tempestuous love-hate relationship which only intensely emotional and excitable people are capable of. They idolised him, calling him Bangabandhu, the 'Bengalis' friend', and they invested him with an unsustainable magic. And Mujib, the man and the idol, would relate to his people with a matching intensity—to their hopes, their joys, anguish and intrigues; to the proffered sycophancy and the demanding greed. 'My strength,' he used to say, 'is that I love my people. My weakness is that I love them too much.'

Since the birth of Bangladesh three and a half years earlier, Mujib had ruled them like a village headman, the guru who had suddenly—and a little awkwardly—been called upon to make good. He worked with unfailing zeal even if it was misplaced; and he had a secretariat full of good intentions. But then he also confused platitudes with policies; he would grasp at simplistic solutions such as the solitary dredger on which he pinned such high hope; and he would intrigue. Inevitably the magic faded and the adulation turned sour.

Despite all these shortcomings even the cynics sipping pink gin in the Saqi bar of Hotel Dhaka Intercontinental grudingly conceded that Mujib would somehow muddle through. To them, and to the others in Bangladesh, it was inconceivable that he would not. But on that August night the impossible was happening. The tumbrels had begun to roll. The majors were coming.

---

* BKSAL pronounced Bakshal, was the acronym for the Bangladesh Krishak Sramik Awami League, a one-party system of government announced by Mujib on 26 March 1975.

II

A False Start

*If he had asked us to eat grass or to dig the
earth with our bare hands we would have done
it for him. But look how he behaved!*

—Major Farook Rahman

A hotel room in central London, albeit a plush suite in Claridges, is an unlikely setting for the installation of the first president of the world's newest and eighth most populous state. Nevertheless on this grey winter's morning Razaul Karim, the acting head of the London Mission, was quietly informing Sheikh Mujibur Rahman of the new role that destiny had designed for him.

It was a little after 9 am on 8 January, 1972, a Saturday, exactly 23 days after the formal birth of Bangladesh was achieved by the surrender of 93,000 Pakistani troops to the Indian army in Dhaka. President Zulfiquar Ali Bhutto, who only a few days earlier had replaced General Yahya Khan as the new Pakistani head of state, had unexpectedly put Mujib and his former constitutional adviser, Dr Kamal Hussain, on a PIA Boeing for a secret flight to London. Why London? No one now remains to tell the full truth about this incident. But when the plane touched down at Heathrow airport at 6.30 that morning it brought to a happy ending the months of agonising uncertainty about Mujib's fate.

Although he looked travel worn, Mujib felt gloriously alive as he waited for the jubilant crowds to descend upon him. He ambled compulsively from room to room, the deferential Karim trailing behind. He admired the flowers. Now and then he flopped onto a deep-cushioned sofa as though testing its comfort. But what attracted him most were the big glass windows. He peered through them at the traffic on the road outside like a fascinated child. Mujib was savouring his first full day of freedom after nine months of solitary confinement within the shadow of the gallows in a Pakistani prison.

I had been tipped off about Mujib's arrival by Nicholas Carroll, deputy foreign editor of The Sunday Times, who had heard it as a BBC news flash. Mujib was an old friend and, professional interest apart, I was delighted to meet him again after the trauma each of us had suffered in the preceding year in the struggle for Bangladesh. We had first met in 1956 in the Karachi residence of his political mentor, Husseyn Shaheed Suhrawardy, who later became prime minister of Pakistan. The friendship developed in the summer of 1958 when for almost a month we shared hotel rooms in Washington, Flagstaff (Arizona), San Francisco and Los Angeles during a tour at the invitation of the American government. I still have a photograph of us taken in Paramount Studios, Hollywood, with our host the great movie moghul Cecil B. De Mille, Mickey Rooney and Ava Gardner.

It was a happy time. Mujib was then very much a junior politician without the inhibition of having to maintain a political image. It was summer. He was a million miles from home and let his hair down. In later years I used to tease Mujib that I knew him better than his wife. And once when things got rough in Bangladesh in 1973, I told my exasperated friend, 'Why don't you give it all up. You can make a better living at cards.' Indeed he could. If I could locate them now I'm sure three Indonesian journalists would confirm this.

We were on the night train from the Grand Canyon to Los Angeles and after dinner got together with the Indonesians for a game of 'Flush', the three-card poker popular in the East. The opening rounds were even. Then we began to lose steadily. Soon it became obvious from the way the cards were running that we were being sharked. I suggested to Mujib that we stop and cut our losses. Mujib silenced me. He asked the Pullman attendant for a new pack, shuffled the cards and began to deal. Abruptly the 'luck' changed. Try as they might all through the long night the Indonesians were never able to make it again. When we pulled into Los Angeles next morning Mujib and I were richer by $386, a wrist watch, a Parker 51 with a gold cap, and a thin gold ring in the shape of a snake.

I asked Mujib how he did it. His answer is seared in my memory. 'When you play with gentlemen, you play like a gentleman. But when you play with bastards, make sure you play like a bigger bastard. Otherwise you will lose.' Then he added with a laugh, 'Don't forget I have had good teachers.' It was a startling glimpse of this earthy, gut-fighting politician and the intrigue and the violence to which he was bred. Later, when his star soared and he began to make headlines, I would recall these words and have no difficulty predicting the response he would make to the crisis of the moment.

Now we were together again, friends/professionals, in London, with Mujib about to start the most momentous game of his life. We talked, and I sat and listened while he talked to the others. And when I finally left to write my story it was with the unsettling impression that Sheikh Mujibur Rahman, Bangabandhu, President and Bangladesh's man on a white charger, at the moment of taking up his stewardship had only the foggiest notion of what it was all about.

What's more, he was secretly nursing a tentative deal with Zulfiquar Ali Bhutto which would have maintained a 'link' between Pakistan and its breakaway province, Bangladesh.

I got a glimpse of this unsavoury deal, which was totally at variance with the Bangladeshi mood, when Mujib confided to me: 'I have a big scoop for you. We are going to keep some link with Pakistan but I can't say anything more till I have talked it over with the others. And for God's sake don't you write anything till I tell you.'

Apparently Bhutto, during the course of some lengthy private conversations with Mujib in a government rest house on the outskirts of Rawalpindi just before he sent him out to London, had talked him into an understanding for a 'link' with Pakistan. Thus the astute Bhutto hoped to inveigle Mujib into a concession that would have had the effect of turning the clock back and negating the Bangladeshi freedom struggle. What exactly the formula was, Mujib did not tell me. But my own instant reaction to the disclosure was one of horror. 'Are you mad?' I told him. 'Don't you know what's happened in Bangladesh? After what the people have gone through they will lynch you on the streets of Dhaka, Bangabandhu or no Bangabandhu, if you so much as utter one word about a link.'

Mujib did not have time to answer me. We were interrupted by the Indian High Commissioner, B. K. Nehru, who wanted a private word with him. Mujib's re-education had begun.

Mujib's isolation in prison had been total during the nine months Bangladesh was being fashioned in the crucible of genocide and war. He received no letters, read no newspapers, had no radio to listen to. He was not allowed to converse even with his jailors. He did not know how his country had been devastated by the Pakistan army or how two million people had died. And just as the world was uncertain about his fate, Mujib did not know the fate of his own wife and children.

Mujib had gone to jail the leader of the biggest party in the newly elected Pakistan National Assembly, valiantly striving for a wide-ranging autonomy for his province. Since then East Pakistan's autonomy demand had made way for the reality of Bangladesh's independence. Even the map had changed for Pakistan. It was not surprising, therefore, that when Mujib emerged once more into the sunshine, it was like a latter-day Rip Van Winkle, out of touch and out of tune with the times. And, it would seem from the circumstances, he had got up from the wrong side of the bed.

Time had stood still for Mujib the man, but not for Mujib the martyr. One of his party men, an Awami League adviser in Dhaka, was quoted as saying 'It's astonishing that this man can sit out the war for nine months and come back stronger than he ever was before.' Mujib's enshrinement was far advanced. 'You have been confined, but your spirit could not be imprisoned,' the Indian prime minister Mrs Indira Gandhi, said of him. 'You have become a symbol of the voice of the oppressed . . .'[1]

It was not the first time that imprisonment had made a demi-god of a national hero. But in Mujib's case the embellishing of the legend was a Bengali phenomenon, an exaggerated emotionalism which would become all the more unseemly when its application was abruptly reversed the day Mujib was killed. Now, however, the headlines roared 'Mujib is a magic word. Mujib is a miracle name.'[2]

Setting the scene at that time in Dhaka, Martin Woollacott said in a cable to the Guardian: 'Bengalis are awaiting the return of Sheikh Mujibur Rahman in reverential, near religious mood. The legend is about to be made flesh . . . (Ordinary Bengalis have mentally invested the Sheikh with extraordinary powers. Little credit goes to the Bangladesh government or to the Indian government for the successful liberation of the country: All belongs to the Sheikh, who controlled events even from a prison cell thousands of miles away.')[3]

Man had been made mountain and now the mountain was being asked to move. Mujib, however, on that winter's day in London was not in a mood for miracles. The strain of 'the long journey from darkness to light'[4] had begun to tell. 'I need some rest,' he told me. 'I want to relax in London for a few days. Then I will go back to my people. I will not do anything till I have visited every district and seen every face.' These were Mujib's plans—until the telephones began to ring.

The first call came through at 10.30. It was the Bangladesh Mission in Calcutta. Answering the squawks from the other end of the line, Mujib said 'Don't worry. I am safe. I am alive and in good health. Please tell them all—telephone to Dhaka—I endorse what has happened. Bangladesh has come to stay. No one on earth can change that fact.' There were three other telephones in the suite and they all began ringing together. Razaul Karim picked one up. 'Sir,' he called out, 'Dhaka on the line. The Prime Minister (Tajuddin Ahmad) would like to talk to you.' Another phone rang. 'Sir, you are wanted by Calcutta.' Then more calls from Dhaka and Calcutta, one from Mrs Gandhi in New Delhi and another from Edward Heath, Britain's Prime Minister at No. 10 Downing Street. By 11 o'clock Suite 112 in Claridges had become the temporary capital of Bangladesh. By that time also it was painfully clear to Mujib that if he did not get to Dhaka very quickly there was grave danger of the new government falling apart and the risk of civil strife. The war was over. The in-fighting, the jostling for power in the Awami League had begun.

Peter Hazelhurst in a despatch from Dhaka to the Times, London, painted a gloomy picture of the situation in the city. 'As the euphoria of victory begins wearing thin, the sense of jubilation is rapidly being replaced by a national mood of suspicion and resentment against the outsider ... There are also signs that the liberation movement is becoming disillusioned with the Awami League government ... (It is clear that the only cementing force capable of holding the country together is the charisma surrounding the one and only man who counts in the country today, Sheikh Mujibur Rahman.') [5]

The Awami League government, headed by prime minister Tajuddin Ahmad, ensconced in Dhaka was little more than a government in name. Its legitimacy was not questioned, but, paradoxically, its right to lead was. During the Bengali upsurge against the Pakistan army's campaign of genocide in East Pakistan in 1971, the Mujibnagar Government, as the government in exile in India was known, served as an umbrella for resistance. But Mujibnagar, true to its name (there is no such place) was an unsubstantial thing, the Bengali equivalent of 'God's Little Acre', moved about as convenience dictated. Mujibnagar was neither the command console nor the cutting edge of the resistance. Things were done in its name by fighting men in the field. They accepted only the most formal patronage and they gave only a ritual allegiance. Peter Hazelhurst, who is quoted earlier, with great perception underscored the distinction between 'the liberation movement' and the 'Awami League government'.

The most expositive commentary on the role of the Mujibnagar government is the fact that at the end of the liberation war it had no place whatsoever in the formal surrender of the Pakistani troops in Dhaka on 16 December, 1971. Nevertheless, shortly after that date the Awami Leaguers were installed as the government in Dhaka with no challenge to its legality. Welcoming the ministers when they flew in from Calcutta were members of all political parties, including Professor Muzaffar Ahmad, chairman of the left-wing National Awami Party (NAP), and the legendary Moni Singh of the Communist Party. [6]

The first and perhaps only real decision the 'government' took was to reject off-hand Professor Muzaffar Ahmad's proposal to have an interim national government of all parties. But before that the first government of Bangladesh had begun to show unmistakable signs of coming unstuck.

It was a mishmash of political entities, divided not so much by ideological considerations as by the extra-territorial labels that, rightly or wrongly, its members were supposed to wear. Thus ministers were commonly classified as pro-America, pro-Russia or pro-India. In this context Tajuddin Ahmad was labelled pro-India, Khandaker Moshtaque Ahmed as pro-America and Abdus Samad Azad pro-Russia. (Major Farook was to complain later: 'I couldn't find anyone who was supposed to be pro-Bangladesh!'). Tajuddin Ahmad, the prime minister and most able administrator among the lot, was the first among equals and no more. The system was a collegiate one. The throne was still vacant. [7]

These internal dissensions gravely handicapped the government in facing up to its many problems—and they were monstrous and pressing. The depredations of the Pakistan army during the eight months of Bengali resistance and the attrition during the 14-day war had devastated the country. There was no food or medicines in the shops. The jute and tea industries, in normal times the principal foreign exchange earners, had collapsed. At the same time ten million refugees who had gone to India and twenty million people displaced within the country needed shelter in addition to food and clothing. It was a mad race against time for the monsoons would shut down the country in summer. Topping it all was the destruction of the transport and communications systems which made the movement of relief supplies a daily miracle. There was extensive damage to the railway track, signalling equipment and rolling stock. In a delta area where cross-country movement is dependent on bridges and river ferries, every major bridge (at least 280 of varying sizes) and more than half the river transport were destroyed. The remaining river craft could only be used at great risk because in most cases navigation lights and buoys marking the narrow channels had been blown up along with the command stations of the delta navigation system. Chittagong, one of the country's two ports and the principal entry point for food imports, was rendered unservicable by 29 wrecks blocking the Karnafulli River channel. Fewer than 1000 of the country's 8000 truck fleet were servicable. There was no gasoline. Bangladesh desperately needed 2.5 million tons of food to avoid famine. And when this was forthcoming from the international community it required an additional miracle to get it to the country's 60,000 villages.

I have not been able to confirm it, but there was an hilarious story making the rounds in Dhaka in January, 1972, when the jostling among the Awami League ministers was at its height. Every move on the macabre chessboard was being carefully scrutinised for advantage and in these circumstances there was, apparently, no agreement about who should preside over the 'historic' first meeting of the cabinet. Should it be Vice President Syed Nazrul Islam or should it be Prime Minister Tajuddin Ahmad? The issue was resolved with Eastern ingenuity. It took the form of a tea party with Mujib's uncle representing the absent Bangabandhu, as chief guest. The cakes and the ministers were placed on two long tables joined at one end by a smaller one. In the middle of this head table sat Mujib's uncle flanked by Tajuddin Ahmad and Syed Nazrul Islam. Tea was served. The photographers were called in. The cabinet had its first meeting. Thus history was inscribed without loss of face!

No such delicacy was shown in another matter. Khandaker Moshtaque Ahmed, who was 'foreign minister' in the Mujibnagar government based in Calcutta, turned up at his office in Dhaka to find his chair occupied by a junior colleague, Abdus Samad Azad. It transpired that Prime Minister Tajuddin Ahmad had removed Moshtaque from the job because he had been secretly conspiring with the Americans for a political compromise intended to avoid the break-up of Pakistan. Henry Kissinger, the US Secretary of State, was anxious to help Pakistan because he was using it as a secret channel of communication to arrange President Nixon's historic visit to China. To this end the Americans began to secretly negotiate with Moshtaque. His colleagues never forgive Moshtaque this treachery. Thus, as part of the treatment, no one bothered to inform him that Tajuddin, on moving to Dhaka, had overnight changed his job.

Khandaker Moshtaque swallowed the insult. But he did not forget. Later, when he got the opportunity, he extracted a terrible vengeance on those who had insulted him.

The war had also left an estimated 350,000 guns with vast quantities of ammunition in private hands. Since the people were desperate short of their daily necessities, the underground armouries inevitably helped to create 'a dangerous law and order situation' as the official jargon described it. Topping this were numerous bands of heavily armed 'guerillas' such as those led by

Sheikh Moni, Nurul Alam Siddiqui, Tofail and Siraj whose attitude to the government was both militant and recalcitrant. They swore they would obey only Sheikh Mujib's orders.[8]

In these circumstances it is understandable that the Awami League ministers and politicians should burn up the telephone line to London demanding Sheikh Mujibur Rahman's immediate return to Bangladesh. He had no alternative.

The panoply of a state welcome is an impressive spectacle. The flags, massed bands, the cadence of the slow march of a Sovereign's guard of honour, the 21-gun salute: they are all carefully designed to impress. India, with its timeless pageantry and instant crowds gives the show a majestic dimension. When New Delhi rolled out the red carpet for Sheikh Mujibur Rahman it was with a fervour that those present will always remember. While flying from London to Dhaka, Mujib had made a brief stop-over in New Delhi to thank India for the assistance it had given his people ('The people of India are the best friends of my people.'). On hand to greet him at Palam Airport on the morning of 10 January 1972, were the President, Dr. V. V. Giri, Prime Minister Indira Gandhi, the Chiefs of the three Indian Defence Services whose prowess had underwritten the creation of Bangladesh, the Cabinet ministers and members of the Diplomatic Corps. Even more memorable than this glittering receiving line, I was told by one of those present, was the vibrant intrusion of uncounted millions of faceless Indians—the people who had supported the Bangladesh struggle for independence—who joined the welcoming through All India Radio's broadcast.

The heart of India was in New Delhi that morning. My friend, Narayan Swami, who is normally very cynical, recalled with awe: 'It was as if the radio had not only taken the ceremony to the people but by some strange mystique had also brought them to the spectator stands. You could feel them there!'

Mujib was deeply moved by it all. Until then a flag car was the most he had rated by way of official protocol, and that too very briefly during two short spells as a provincial minister in East Pakistan. Now, he was to tell his family: 'India itself turned out to do me honour.'

The transformation to demi-god was completed a few hours later when Mujib returning to Dhaka was overwhelmed by the reception he got. Thousands of people crammed every vantage point in the airport terminal building. Many hundreds of thousands more linked the roads all the way to the airport. And when Mujib reached Suhrawardy Udyan, the sprawling old race course where he had last spoken to the people at the height of the civil disobedience on 7 March of the previous year, it was as if a human sea had been packed into the three square mile arena. Nothing like this had happened ever before in Dhaka. There's been nothing like it since then. The frenzied cheering, the extravagant praise, the public worship and obeisance were beyond the wildest dreams of any man.

The day's events would leave a lasting impression on Mujib because, if anything, he was an impressionable man and very vain. In his mind's eye there would henceforth always be cheering crowds and flags. But the trouble was that even before the last echoes of the cheering had faded, Mujib the demi-god, was bought face-to-face with an overwhelming reality.

'My heart sang to be home again and among my people' he told me at our first meeting in Dhaka after London. 'But then I was brought face-to-face with the greatest man-made disaster in history. I could never imagine the magnitude of the catastrophe. They have killed more than three million of my people. They have raped our mothers and our sisters and have butchered our children. More than 30 per cent of all houses have been destroyed. Bangladesh has been flattened. There is danger of famine. We need help.'

My friend spelled out his nightmare problem with a series of questions he threw at me: 'What do you do about currency? Where do you get food? Industries are dead. Commerce is dead. How do you start them again? What do you do about defence? I have no administration. Where do I get one? Tell me, how do you start a country?' 9

Mujib's outburst was only temporary. There was another quick shift in mood, confidence returning with every sweep of his hands as though plucking it from the air. He was the demi-god again. 'I tell you I can do it; I will do it with these hands.'

Mujib's return to Dhaka had averted the threat of civil war in Bangladesh and given the government the substance and authority it had hitherto lacked. But this did not mean an end to the intrigue and in-fighting within the cabinet nor the extinction of the armed bands operating as a law unto themselves in the countryside. Only now Mujib's presence had temporarily put a lid on them. But exist they did in various shadowy forms which were for the moment tolerated by Mujib so long as the combatants made both public and private obeisance to him. But the internal pressures did influence his style. He conducted himself not as the 'father of the nation' nor as its all-serving President, but rather as the President of the Awami League. He played politics with his henchmen. He got embroiled in their intrigues. The savage in-fighting only whetted his natural instinct to retain all power for himself. That's why he chose to be Bangladesh's first Prime Minister, not its first President.

As mentioned earlier, the President's throne had been kept vacant for Mujib. Indeed he had been hailed as President of Bangladesh on reaching London and it was universally assumed that he would continue in that role. But being Head of State in a Westminster-style government meant Mujib should allow executive authority to vest in the Prime Minister, in this case Tajuddin Ahmad. Here came the rub. Mujib's perceptions were too narrow. He had a one-track mind in the matter of power. If the system required the Prime Minister to hold the reins of authority, then Mujib would be Prime Minister. But if instead supreme executive authority was vested in the President, then Mujib would be the President. His family and his shallow, sycophantic advisers would urge him on for the elementary reason that the more executive power he wielded the closer they would be to the fountain of patronage and wealth.

A minor reason for Mujib's decision—which was privately made much of at that time—were the anomalies there were about Tajuddin's position as Prime Minister. No one questioned Tajuddin's ability to run the administration. His authority, however, was never fully accepted by his senior colleagues. Even during the 'Mujibnagar' days they had resented his elevation with Indian help to the top job. In their eyes Tajuddin, despite his ability, remained almost an upstart. He had been general secretary of the 'provincial' Awami League, a relatively junior position, when the independence struggle began in March 1971, and there were several others holding 'national' office who considered themselves higher in the party's pecking order. Moreover, rightly or wrongly, Tajuddin had been lumbered with the pro-Indian label. In the circumstances this was a major impediment since it was generally recognised at that time that Bangladesh's entanglement with India should be speedily ended in favour of a 'regularised relationship' which would eliminate international objections to the recognition of the new state.10

Mujib kicked Tajuddin sideways and became Prime Minister. But at the same time he made sure that the Head of State would in fact be a sinecure and never a danger to him. For that role he chose a non-political person, the meekest, most inoffensive man he could find, Justice Abu Sayed Chowdhury, who had shot to prominence as the international spokesman for the Mujib-nagar government. President Chowdhury was admirably docile. And so that there should be no misunderstanding about his role he sported a large Mujib badge on his coat.

The scene in Gonobaban in the early days of Mujib's rule was a 20th century parody of a Moghul court. Mujib had an office in the secretariat but he spent only a minimum amount of time there, preferring to function from his official residence which he used as a private office. Its relaxed atmosphere was more to his taste. There he would hold court for his cronies, for party men and petitioners who like bees to a honeypot gravitated to Dhaka with outstretched hands. They would descend on him in big groups and small. When ushered into the presence they would garland Bangabandhu, touch his feet, weep loudly. Some would burst into song—some well-known Bengali folksong—and Mujib, eyes opaque with emotion, would join in. In between he would have a quiet word with one of his ministers, instruct a civil servant about some urgent matter of state, and receive visiting reporters and VIPs who came to see the uncrowned king of the world's newest state.

Everyone went away with a promise of action. Mujib would grab the paper from the outstretched hands of a petitioner, pat him on the cheek, then wave him on. 'Go. I will see to it.' That was the last the petitioner, or Mujib, would hear about it. Later, when commenting on Mujib's assassination, my friend, Abu Musa, a perceptive but disillusioned journalist, would tell me: 'He promised everything and he betrayed everyone.'

Soon the dual roles he had undertaken began to show up the folly of the arrangement. As prime minister, Mujib was required to inject harsh discipline into the government, to recreate a country from scratch along orderly lines. Most of all he had to sustain and guide into channels of reconstruction the tremendous patriotic fervour that galvanised the people in 1971. Mujib could do none of these things. As Bangabandhu, the friend and father-figure, Mujib had to be magnanimous, forgiving and helpful. This role was more suited to his nature, for Mujib was large-hearted, a kindly man, generous to a fault and one who never forgot a face or a friendship. Mujib did not have the capacity to compartment his hats. Every moment of the day he was simultaneously Prime Minister and Bangabandhu. The contradictions inherent in this situation inevitably led to chaos.

I was given a vivid example of the shape of things to come shortly after Mujib had been sworn in as Prime Minister. Just before the Muslim festival of Eid-ul-Azha, Bangabandhu, it transpired, had ordered that the workers of the Adamjee Jute Mills near Narayanganj be given one month's wages immediately in settlement of arrears. This was heartening news for the starving workers of the world's biggest jute mill. Like the rest of industry, the mill had come to a grinding halt with the outbreak of the India-Pakistan war the previous month, leaving thousands of workers not only unemployed but also unpaid for the work they had done. The owners had abandoned the mills with the advent of Bangladesh. There was not enough money to meet the payroll. Now the great festival, the first since independence, was approaching. Bangabandhu's intervention was therefore joyfully received.

When I called at the mill at 9.30 the next morning, I found at least 3000 people queued up outside the gates in a buoyant mood. Inside the mill the paymaster was well organised. A dozen tables had been placed in the compound. Each had a tally clerk, a ledger, tin moneybox, pen and inkpot. The only thing missing was the money. 'They money is coming from Dhaka' he told me. 'We are waiting for it.'

They waited and waited and waited. By 2 pm there was still no sign of the money. But that time angry cries and stones were coming over the wall from the seething crowd outside. The workers were demanding to be paid . . . 'as Bangabandhu ordered'. The paymaster, who had become a nervous wreck, had sent an SOS to the Deputy Commissioner, who in turn had arranged for an army contingent to reinforce the police guard to prevent the gates being battered down.

Before things got worse, someone had the bright idea of rushing a message to Bangabandhu 'to appraise him of the situation'. Accordingly a young officer was drafted for this purpose. Since he planned to sneak out by way of the river, I decided it would be the better part of valour not to stay behind. Two hours later we were in Gonobaban, Mujib's official residence, and the young officer was explaining the problem. Mujib was furious. He couldn't believe his orders had not been carried out after he had made a public commitment. 'Why have they not been paid?' he bellowed. 'I gave orders it should be done this morning. Who is responsible?'

His temper sparked a flurry of activity. Assistant Secretaries and PAs rushed up and down the crowded corridors looking for someone. When the offending officer from the Finance Ministry was finally brought before Mujib he explained that under the new regulations the mills could not draw more than 100,000 Takkas from the bank without special sanction and he had been patiently waiting in an ante-room for Bangabandhu's 'Daskat' (authorisation) for it. Mujib had all day been receiving a flood of visitors: party workers, old friends, relatives, senior civil servants with files and ministers wanting a quiet word in his ear. The officious guardians of the Prime Minister's door had apparently thought the matter of paying 3000 workers not important enough to 'disturb' him and the officer requiring authorisation for money had been kept out. Mujib scolded them. He ordered a senior Awami Leaguer to 'proceed to Narayanganj immediately and promise the workers that Inshah Allah, they definitely will be paid tomorrow'.

The young officer from the mill was shattered by the experience. When I took him out for a belated lunch, he told me: 'Bangabandhu commands there shall be rain and he cannot understand why the rain does not fall. God help us!'

The Prime Minister's house was a long way from Tungipara, the tiny village in Faridpur district where Mujib was born on 17 March, 1920, one of six children in a middle class family of modest means. His father, Lutfur Rahman, was an official of the local district court. When Mujib went to the mission school in Gopalganj his studies were interrupted for a while by an attack of beriberi which permanently affected his eye-sight. He finished high school when he was 22.

At an early age he displayed the qualities which would one day make him the central figure in the politics of the India sub-continent. One was a hyper-active social conscience; another an over-riding passion for politics. When ten years old he was caught distributing rice from the family supplies to tenant farmers who worked the property. Mujib told his father: 'They were hungry, and we have all these things.' Nineteen years later while a law student in Dhaka University, Mujib received a two and a half year jail sentence for championing another underdog, this time the university's menial workers. He grandly explained: 'I did not come to the university to bow my head to injustice.' But before that, when he was 17, he was caught in the front line of an anti-British demonstration and spent six days in jail. The experience only whetted his appetite for politics.

The tumultuous events of the early 1940s when the demand for Pakistan as a separate state for the Muslims of the sub-continent was pressed by the Muslim League, came as food and drink to the young Mujib. He was then a student of history and political science in the Islamia College, Calcutta. Mujib flung himself into the Pakistan movement. Within months his great talent for political organising began to be noticed and he moved up rapidly in the hierarchy of the Muslim League. When graduation coincided with the creation of Pakistan in 1947, Mujib moved to Dhaka the capital of East Pakistan province, and enrolled as a student of law in Dhaka University.

One day in March, 1948, he joined thousands of other Bengalis in the Paltan Maidan to hear Mohammad Ali Jinnah, the founding father of Pakistan, speak on his one and only visit to the eastern province. They had gone to cheer the Quaid-i-Azam or 'great Leader', but Mr. Jinnah stunned his audience when he bluntly told them 'Urdu is going to be the lingua franca of this country . . . Anyone who says anything else is an enemy of Pakistan.'

Bengalis are nothing without their culture and the language is its greatest manifestation. The support of the Bengali Muslims for the Pakistan cause had been fundamental to its success. Even at that time they constituted more than half the new state's population. Yet here was the Pakistan Head of State asking them to forswear the Bengali language in favour of Urdu which he arrogantly equated with Islam, the established religion of Pakistan. Mr. Jinnah's remarks therefore came as a slap in the face of the Bengalis. It was doubly galling to the students in the vanguard of the language movement. Apart from language and culture, it was an economic proposition which would put the young Bengali at serious disadvantage with his counterpart in West Pakistan who would automatically have command over Urdu since it was widely spoken there. The Bengali student would have to learn an additional language, Urdu, along with the burden of his regular studies in order to qualify for a decent job in the government or outside.[11]

The angry students at the meeting, Mujib among them, immediately rose in protest. They carried the agitation to the streets. From there it quickly spread to the rest of the province to become the first step in the Bengali disenchantment with Pakistan. Meanwhile Mujib, as one of the ring leaders, was clapped into jail for seven days. It was his first taste of solitary confinement.

The language agitation marked the turning point in Mujib's life. Henceforth he would turn his back on sectarian politics, which he condemned as divisive, giving himself fully to a relentless crusade against the economic and political exploitation of the Bengalis by their compatriots in West Pakistan.

Mujib's great strength—and success—lay in an elemental ability to fathom the full measure of his people's emotions and to arouse and articulate them with a resounding eloquence. He had a fantastic ability to relate to crowds. Because of this his opponents would deride him as a rabble rouser. However that may be, time and circumstance put a high premium on his talent and at a crucial moment he became the symbol and supreme spokesman of a gigantic human upsurge against discrimination and tyranny. For his pains Mujib was cruelly hounded, spending $11\frac{1}{2}$ years of the next 20 in Pakistani prisons. Martyrdom, however, only served to enhance his image. 'He was a great man before,' someone once said, 'But those bastards made him even greater.'

Mujib only briefly savoured the fruits of ministerial office. He had neither the taste nor the talent for it. In his second short spell as a provincial minister (in 1956 when he held the portfolios of Commerce, Labour and Industries, and Anti-Corruption in Ataur Rahman Khan's Awami League cabinet), Mujib couldn't stomach the routine. So he requested permission to bow out and devote his restless energy to reorganising the Awami League. Field work, his first love, remained his forte and took him to the top. But this apostle of agitation was never able to overcome the fundamental flaws in his make-up. Mujib saw everything in simplistic terms. He had a tendency to over-simplify even the most complex economic and agricultural problems. And to an over-riding obsession for power was added an immensely suspicious nature. He would unscrupulously intrigue to eliminate the slightest threat to his supremacy, however imagined it might be. This was the dark side of the beguiling moon. When Mujib became Prime Minister of Bangladesh it was these traits, more than anything else in his complex character, that came to the fore.

Two weeks after he had installed himself in Dhaka I asked him if he still had a mind to undertake the meet-the-people tours he had planned in London. Mujib was affronted by my question. 'How can I do it?' he said very crossly. 'Don't you see I have to erect an administration?' He was doing this in the free-wheeling Mujib style. Available bureaucrats were posted under his direction. Even office assistants and clerks were not too small for his attention. Offices in the secretariat began filling with an odd assortment of people, many of them quite evidently not at all suitable. Sinecurists were found everywhere.

Many appointments were made on the basis of a nodding acquaintance with Mujib or on the recommendation of his close friends. The Awami League leaders had been installed in key positions and they brought in their relatives and friends. Some even took commission for a chit. You had to have a god-father to get a job. If you had one, all disqualifications were overlooked, even the cardinal sin of collaboration with the defeated Pakistan military regime.

A prime example was Mahboobul Alam, the Dhaka correspondent of DAWN. Published in Karachi, DAWN was the leading English-language newspaper of West Pakistan and those connected with it were held in esteem by the authorities. After the Pakistan army had launched its campaign of genocide in East Pakistan, West Pakistanis in Dhaka used to jokingly refer to Mahboobul Alam as a 'sarkari' (i.e. pro-government) Bengali to differentiate from the other Bengali journalists who were either openly hostile or sullenly uncooperative. True to this reputation, Mahboobul Alam later that year wrote scripts for Radio Pakistan's PLAIN TRUTH programme—a highly-coloured propaganda or disinformation effort aimed at the Bangladeshi freedom struggle. For this he was paid between Rs 30 and Rs 50 per piece, about £4 at the prevailing rate of exchange. After the liberation of Bangladesh Mahboobul Alam found himself both without a job and covered with the odium of having betrayed the freedom movement by backing the wrong side. But instead of being locked up in jail on charges of collaboration, as another journalist writing for PLAIN TRUTH was, Mahboobul Alam wangled a job, of all things, as Prime Minister Mujibur Rahman's press officer. But because of the stink it created even Mujib had to get rid of him. It must make the Bangladeshi martyrs turn in their graves to know that this posturing turn-coat, as some others like him, went on to become a Bangladeshi ambassador.

Before long the carnival atmosphere of Gonobaban began to assume a most sinister aspect. Mujib, it was evident, had not erected a new administration of Bangladeshi nationalists filled with patriotic zeal. What he had done between the rounds of musical chairs, was to retain and refurbish the old discredited bureaucracy of the erstwhile East Pakistan. Unlike the large mass of Bengali military officers and men who had actively fought against the Pakistanis or had suffered the agony of being disarmed, isolated and marooned in West Pakistan, many of the civilian officers of East Pakistan administration—with some notable exceptions—had for the most part remained in their jobs and ostensibly loyal to Pakistan during the Liberation War. A variety of reasons were advanced for not joining the resistance. A few had ideological reservations about the Bangladesh movement because of the support it was receiving from India. Others found excuses to play it safe and not to risk jobs and property. Some—and a lot of policemen fall into this category—even distinguished themselves as instruments for the repression of their own people. When Bangladesh became independent on 16th December, 1971, they quickly jumped on the bandwagon, proclaiming their new-found nationalism as loudly as they had denied it the week before. For this these turncoats were derisively dubbed the '16th Division'.

M. R. Akthar ('Mukul') in his book 'Mujibur Rakta Lal', trenchantly observed: 'There is no parallel in the history of any country where after a protracted and bloody liberation war the defeated bureaucracy and the military officers were not only given continuity of service but were also accepted in the new regime with great respect while the patriots were excluded.'

I am not one of those who advocated a witch hunt of collaborators. Far from it. As we will see later, there were obvious pitfalls in that direction since in the circumstances the charge of collaboration could be—and was—used by knaves to pay off old scores or to demolish political opponents. The objection was to place in the most sensitive and influential positions men who had no intrinsic dedication and only an accidental loyalty to the new state. During the crucial days of 1971 some of these provincial civil servants had shown themselves to be utterly selfish, opportunistic and alienated from the mainstream of the national upsurge. It could hardly be expected that they suddenly, overnight, become selflessly dedicated to the uplift of Bangladesh or, in the circumstances, be immune to the immense opportunities for aggrandizement their pivotal positions offered in a state starting from scratch.

A Yugoslav delegation, conveying greetings from President Tito in January, 1972, exhorted Sheikh Mujib at that time to give those involved in the freedom struggle the central place in the Bangladesh administration. 'They may be inexperienced and make mistakes,' the Yugoslavs told Mujib, 'But their hearts are in the right place. They will learn quickly and they will push the country forwards.'

Mujib, however, did not see it that way. He was persuaded that the former East Pakistan bureaucrats, by their training and experience, were indispensible in the context of the overall shortage of qualified civil service alternatives. Another suggestion—and this appealed to Mujib's vanity as Bangabandhu— was to 'forgive and forget'. After all, it was argued, the government had to accommodate this sizeable group somewhere. So why not in the empty Bangladesh secretariat?

This was a woefully hollow argument. If, indeed, training and experience were the criteria for the appointment of Bangladesh's new senior bureaucrats, then the obvious place to look for them was the pool of talent made up of several hundred Bengali members of the elitist Civil Service of Pakistan. In talent, training and experience they were head and shoulders above most of the provincial officers. But in most cases their sin was to be in the wrong place—i.e. West Pakistan—when Bangladesh came into being in December 1971. The Bangabandhu charitable concept of 'forgive and forget', if at all necessary since most of them had not collaborated, should have applied to them also. But it never did. The East Pakistan bureaucrats were in the right place at the right time and with the help of their relatives and Godfathers in the Awami League, grabbed all the best positions.

If the clock was turned back, it would not be Mujib alone who was guilty. Later Khandaker Moshtaque Ahmed, who was put in power after Mujib's assassination, and General Ziaur Rahman who followed him, put the seal on it all. All this—resulting in corrupt, unresponsive and effete administration—had had the most disastrous consequences for Bangladesh.

Another blunder closely connected with Sheikh Mujib's misguided efforts in creating a civil service, was his public policy towards the freedom fighters. On the one hand he virtually excluded from the new Bangladesh secretariat all those FFs who were not already civil servants. On the other, he took pains to identify the FFs as a separate group—even more, a separate class—actively fanning, as the political gain required, their demands, hopes, ambitions and ultimately their frustrations.

A senior functionary of the Mujibnagar Government and a staunch supporter of Sheikh Mujib, estimated that there were approximately 300,000 Mukhti Bahini guerillas actively engaged against the Pakistani forces in 1971, both inside and outside Bangladesh. Nevertheless, in 1972, Sheikh Mujibur Rahman's government, as a sop to public demand, issued as many as 1,100,000 certificates designating their holders as 'Freedom Fighters in the War of Liberation'. With each certificate went the implied entitlement to a host of privileges ranging from two years seniority in government service to preferential treatment in the matter of jobs, university admissions, cash grants and the hopes of a pension. The tragedy is that, like everything else, the FF certificates became instruments of political patronage and corruption. And not all the real Mukhti Bahini got them. Those who did, quickly discovered that the FF certificate served only a decorative purpose unless it was backed up by access to the patronage being funnelled through the Awami League old-boy network. Thus a whole new embittered and emotionally-hungry class was created, both in civilian life and the armed services. Over the years it became a key element in the continuing violence in the country.

This is particularly true of the armed services.

In December, 1971, on the attainment of independence all Bengali army, navy and air force personnel and members of the East Pakistan Rifles (now East Bengal Rifles) serving with the Mukhti Bahini were designated 'Freedom Fighters' and given two years seniority in service. For the first 18 months they served as the nucleus of the new Bangladesh defence forces until their less fortunate compatriots began to arrive. These were the 35,000 Bengali officers and troops, all professional soldiers, who had been posted in West Pakistan in 1969 and 1970 and had been stranded there when the Liberation War started in March, 1971. A handful of officers, among them Major Mohammad Abul Manzoor (later Major General Manzoor, the man behind the coup that resulted in President Ziaur Rahman's assassination in 1981) managed to escape across the Kashmir border into India to join up with the Mukhti Bahini. All the other officers and men stranded in West Pakistan were subjected to the humiliation of being disarmed by the Pakistanis and kept secluded and secure in well-guarded camps. Though never formally designated as such by the Pakistanis, they were in effect prisoners of war suffering all the attendant adversity, tension and trauma. Undoubtedly they suffered for the independence of Bangladesh.

Major Rafiq-ul-Islam, the distinguished freedom fighter who led the Bengali troops of the East Pakistan Rifles in a courageous stand against the Pakistan army in Chittagong in March, 1971, underscores their trauma in his book, A Tale of Millions. 'The situation for the Bengali army personnel stranded in Pakistan was worse,' he said. 'They were driven out of their homes with their families, herded into concentration camps, mistreated, humiliated, abused and insulted, and some were even tortured beyond imagination. Medical facilities were withheld, other amenities virtually cut off. They were forced to sell their valuables, specially gold ornaments at throw-away prices, only to buy essential items at exorbitant prices. They were left with no option. It was almost impossible for them to escape. Yet they tried. Some succeeded; others were caught, taken prisoner, isolated and tortured. The attempts of the few symbolised the spirit of all of them. Their passage through the seemingly unending days of humiliation and agony was silent and memorable. Their sacrifice is equally great . . .'

All this was forgotten when the 35,000 Bengali officers and men were returned to Bangladesh in 1973 in an extended repatriation programme. Where the appellation 'FF' was considered a badge of valour, the word 'repatriate' became a term of derision for these unfortunate men. This was an unworthy slander of men whose only sin—if sin it can be called—was the accident of geography which found them against their volition on the wrong side of the sub-continent when Bangladesh was born.

Not only were the 'repatriates' superseded or passed over for promotion, but they were kept hanging around on the 'attached list' of the army. All their appointments were 'ad hoc'. As such for over two years and in some cases three, none of them could get their promotions, seniority and the regularisation of their service. Thus uncertainty about jobs, promotions and appointments undermined military morale terribly.

The differentiation between the FFs and 'repatriates' also politicised the defence forces and riddled them with factionalism and indiscipline. Ultimately it would lead to the killing of Sheikh Mujib, the Jail Four and President Ziaur Rahman. They were all 'FFs' and, ironically, it was the 'FFs' who were responsible for their slaying.

Towards the end of March, 1972, according to a hot rumour making the rounds in Dhaka, Mujib was grossly overworked and 'in the interests of health and administrative efficiency' was about to reappoint Tajuddin Ahmad as Prime Minister. Mujib, it was said, would step down to reorganise the Awami League and act the Father figure. When I asked Tajuddin about it, his answer was precise and telling: 'Someone is trying to cut my throat!' Mujib's own reaction to my inquiries was equally severe. 'Nonsense,' he told me, 'do they think I am not capable of running the government?' The rumour, which was obviously inspired by interested quarters, had the desired effect. Henceforth Mujib was all the more suspicious of Tajuddin and had him carefully watched.

Mujib was to soldier on in the hot seat and obviously he was not as happy as he pretended to be. All his life had been spent in the field, face-to-face with the people. Now he was isolated from them. The official restraints that were imposed on him, the demands on his time made by matters of state, and the high fence that surrounded him at all times were indeed galling. He would sometimes complain about them. But then this complex personality would also gloriously bask in the spotlight at the centre stage, savouring every nuance of the protocol and all the perks that went with it—his personal standard, the honour guard, the foreign dignataries coming to court, the long black limousines. Once I rashly asked him why he didn't drive a smaller car, setting an example of the austerity to which he exhorted his people. Before answering Mujib gave me a long, dirty look. When he saw no malice was intended, he smiled and told me: 'Surely the Prime Minister of Bangladesh can afford to drive in a Mercedes!'

Mujib never fully awakened to the realities of the new dispensation over which he presided. The dramatic events of the nine months preceding the birth of Bangladesh—and all the trauma and patriotic fervour that it generated—would remain a blank spot in his consciousness. He would never fully know it because his vibrant personality had not experienced it. Mujib, after all, was essentially a projectionist, a prism translating light to rainbow. Total isolation in prison had been an obliterating experience. Time stood still for him while the people moved on to a new life and new hope. So when he emerged from the 'darkness to the light and the sunshine of a million victorious smiles', Mujib, true to form, continued exactly from where he had left off. He did not have the capacity to catch up. Nor did he try. His record in office underscores this dismal fact. He blundered terribly. Thus the formative days of Bangladesh were distorted. Within six months disenchantment set in.

Recalling these events, Major Farook told me: 'If he had asked us to eat grass or to dig the earth with our bare hands we would have done it for him. But look how he behaved!'

Rip Van Winkle had not only risen from the wrong side of the bed but had also got off to a false start.

Notes
1. Message to Mujib in London, 8.1.72.
2. Yatindra Bhatnagar (quoted by S. S. Sethi, The Decisive War, New Delhi, p 155).
3. The Guardian, London, 10.1.1972.
4. Press Conference in London, 10.1.1972.
5. The Times, London, 10.1.72.
6. Sethi, The Decisive War, p 109.
7. The Guardian, London, 10.1.79.
8. D. R. Mankekar, Pakistan Cut to Size, New Delhi, pp 139/140.
9. The Sunday Times, London, 16.1.1972.
10. ibid.
11. Mohammad Ayub Khan and K. Subramaniam, The Liberation War, New Delhi, pp 51/52.

III

The Decline of the Demi-God

The army will not fire on the people; but if
you press it, it might take action against you
and the ruling clique!

—Abdur Rab

The scene: Paltan Maidan, Dhaka. The date: 17 September, 1972. The occasion: The first public protest against Sheikh Mujibur Rahman's rule.

Eight months after he had taken over as prime minister, the tide of popularity had begun to run out for Mujib. The great agitator, the champion of the people's grievance, the beloved Bangabandhu on whom the most fulsome praise had been lavished, had now become the target of criticism from an outraged public.

More than 100,000 people had gathered to hear another powerful rabble rouser bitterly denounce the prime minister for betraying the Bengalis and failing to fulfil pledges made before independence. He was Abdur Rab, the student leader and former Mukhti Bahini freedom fighter who was once one of Mujib's staunchest supporters. Now Rab was telling the crowd: 'Mujib said no one would be allowed to die of starvation after independence. Now people are dying for want of food.' Egged on by the irate gathering Rab ticked off a long string of grievances—soaring prices which put food and other necessities beyond reach of the people, shortages, market manipulation, official corruption, nepotism, mounting unemployment, mass arrests and beatings by the police, an irresponsive government, a muzzled press. 'The Awami Leaguers are more corrupt and much worse than the Pakistanis ever were,' Rab declared, in a punchy summation of public sentiment that brought the crowd screaming to its feet. 'You have been arresting us and using all sorts of violence against us. In your speeches you have used the metaphor of weapons. But have you ever used a gun? We know how to use real weapons.' Then calling for the dismissal of corrupt cabinet ministers and officials and the formation of a national government, Rab prophetically warned Mujib: 'The army will not fire on the people; but if you press it, it might take action against you and the ruling clique!'

The wheel had turned full circle for the Bengalis. Once more there was an outcry against exploitation and repression. Only this time, ironically, Rab was echoing the charges Mujib had hurled against the Pakistan government eighteen months earlier.

For Mujib it was an especially bitter pill. Three days earlier he had returned from an extended visit to London where he had undergone a painful operation for the removal of gall stones. He was still a sick man and very exhausted. A ten day convalescence in Geneva, away from the crowds of importuning Bengalis who had descended on him in London, had failed to improve his disposition. During his enforced absence the government was formally headed by Syed Nazrul Islam, the deputy prime minister. But he had neither the intelligence nor the political muscle to assert himself. The savage in-fighting among

19

the Awami League leaders had re-surfaced. Cabinet ministers, like so many defiant war lords, went their separate ways. In London and in Geneva Mujib had once more been overwhelmed by panic calls from Dhaka. For seven weeks Bangladesh was at the mercy of God and the telephone.[1] Now Mujib was back and after an orchestrated welcoming, was publicly pilloried on the Paltan Maidan.

It all came as a nasty jolt to his ego; but for Mujib there was no contrition, only a shifting of blame from the master to his dogs. 'I'm with the people,' he declared on his return as though disassociating himself from the party. He turned on his party men, dismissing 19 members of Parliament for 'smuggling, nepotism and corruption'.

This unprecedented purge of the ruling party was well received. When Mujib wrathfully announced 'Nobody will be spared; I will take action against anyone who is guilty', many saw this as an indication that the old dynamism of the hustings had returned and they ardently believed that given the opportunity Mujib would yet vindicate the public trust. A Bengali journalist told me: 'Leader will straighten things out. Now you will see the fun.' That would be another promise belied. The events, however, did mark a new phase in Mujib's decline. Henceforth he increasingly temporised with all sorts of political stunts, deluding himself that bravado and showmanship would substitute for his deficiencies as the executive head of government. In the process he discarded everything Bangladesh was supposed to represent: constitutionalism, the rule of law, freedom of speech, the right to dissent, equal opportunity. Gradually tragedy in Bangladesh settled into permanence.

If the new state did not collapse within the first eight months of its founding it was only due to the efforts of the international community. UNROD, the United Nations Relief Operation in Dhaka, was an unprecedented rescue mission both in magnitude and effectiveness, one of UN's unsung success stories. Even the name signified a practical effort to cut through formalities, legalities and red tape, to come to terms with the explosive reality of 75 million people in the gravest distress. Since the area, hitherto East Pakistan, was still formally recognised as part of Pakistan, a member state, the UN operation could not be designated as aid to Bangladesh. To give it the East Pakistan label would similarly have been offensive to the sensitive Bengalis and their international friends. So the UN Relief Operation to Dhaka was launched and with it the greatest single international outpouring of money, food, equipment and technical assistance known to date. At least twenty countries were represented in Dhaka with men and material. Money, men and supplies also came in from the ICRC (The International Committee for the Red Cross in Geneva) and its affiliates, particularly the Norwegian and Swedish Red Cross Societies, and from a number of German and British charities such as Caritas, War on Want, Save the Children Fund and Christian Aid.

UNROD coordinated this gigantic operation. It had some difficult moments. Sometimes there were some hilarious boners, even heated debates about the type of operation it should be—and there was some corruption of course. But its ultimate success is judged by the fact that not only did it save Bangladesh from collapse, but UNROD was also generally free from contention and recrimination by the local government and the people it sought to help. Although food was scarce and available on the open market only at a mounting premium, UNROD ensured that the statutory ration of rice was maintained. Bengalis did not die of starvation while UNROD organised the supply and distribution of food.

I remember an enormous chart hanging on the wall of the Dhanmandi office of Dr. Viktor Umbricht, UNROD's director. Popularly called 'the bed sheet' (it could easily cover a fair-sized bed), it served as a ready reckoner for the war damage, the money/supplies available for rehabilitation from donor countries and the various task forces in the field. UNROD estimated there were ten million people destitute in the rural areas and another two million in towns. At least 1.5 million houses had to be rebuilt. But the immediate requirement in the spring of 1972 was $78 million for housing and food; $80 million for additional food imports; $200 million for industrial and agricultrual inputs and equipment; $45 million for housing materials; $15 million for railway repairs; $13 million for inland water transport and $6 million for schools.

UNROD had its own wireless network and transport system with the blue United Nations flag flown on minibulkers, trucks, helicopters, aircraft and barges. Russian and Indian navy salvage teams cleared the wrecks blocking Chittagong and Khulna ports and the Chalna anchorage. British army engineers repaired the big bridges in the North. Indian technicians helped to restart the railways. Scandinavian doctors and nurses worked round the clock to control epidemics of smallpox, cholera and typhoid. There were hundreds of East European engineering specialists repairing war damage. An American specialist working entirely with local dock labour and the most primitive equipment set a record for clearing food ships in Khulna. French and Japanese technicians helped to restart the mills.

Correspondents wanting a quick run-down on the way things were shaping would make a bee line for UNROD headquarters where the amiable Director of Information, Fernando Jaques da Silva, would provide instant answers. This remarkable Brazilian, who after-hours would regale us with refreshment and his guitar, did much to keep the massive rehabilitation effort in perspective. While spelling out what the UN specialists were doing, he would quietly promote the idea of close cooperation between UNROD and the Bangladesh government and in no way discount the latter's overall responsibility. Thus, to the government's satisfaction, press reports invariably gave the impression of Bangladesh achievement whereas UNROD in fact was doing all the pushing and most of the running.

One evening during an informal conversation over dinner, Dr. Umbricht appeared to be concerned about a meeting he had earlier in the day in the Bangladesh Foreign Office. 'I can't understand why,' he told me with evident exasperation, 'if the government is so anxious to join the United Nations and receive international recognition, it is refusing to attend a UN-sponsored conference.' It transpired that Bangladesh, though still far from being admitted to membership of the world body, had been extended an official invitation to participate in the conference on the environment in Stockholm. The invitation was unconditional and would have marked Bangladesh's first appearance on an international forum. Nevertheless Dr. Umbricht, as the UN representative in Dhaka, had been called to the Foreign Office that morning and given a letter expressing the government's inability to attend. The formal excuse was that it was not fully geared to participate. But Dr. Umbricht had been privately informed about the real reason. Apparently, the German Democratic Republic, which had rushed in to open the first diplomatic office in Dhaka and like Bangladesh was not a member of the United Nations, had also received an invitation to Stockholm but only as an Observer. Because of this qualification, the GDR refused to attend. So it had been suggested to Bangladesh by its East European friends that as a gesture of solidarity with the countries which had given ardent support to the struggle for independence, it should also refrain from attending. The Foreign Office at that time was presided over by Abdus

Samad Azad, the man with the 'pro-Russian' label who had summarily replaced Khandaker Moshtaque Ahmed. Azad decided to make the gesture to the East Europeans and after issuing the required directive to the permanent head of the Foreign Office, S. A. Karim, flew off on an official visit to Nepal.

Next morning, which was a Sunday, I walked over to Bangababan for a quiet chat with Mujib and casually brought up the question of the rejected invitation without mentioning my source. Mujib was in an upstairs bedroom chatting with Law Minister Kamal Hussain while his servant vigorously massaged his legs. That was Mujib's way of relaxing. My question seemed to disturb him. Abruptly sitting up on the bed Mujib told me with unconcealed irritation: 'What nonsense are you talking? Have you also started picking up bazaar rumours? We have not received any UN invitation so how can we reject it?' Properly chastened and smarting from the outburst, I wondered why Dr. Umbricht was trying to sell me a line. In that mood I looked him up on my return to Hotel International. He was both annoyed and puzzled by the imputation of Mujib's denial. To prove the point he had made earlier, he showed me a copy of the politely worded Foreign Office refusal.

I went back to Mujib that evening and told him that far from being bazaar gossip I could prove that the great prime minister was not aware of what was going on under his very nose in the Foreign Office. The upshot was that Mujib sent for the Foreign Secretary and after establishing the truth of the matter, reversed the decision. Dr. Umbricht was warmly received by the Prime Minister and told that the Bangladesh Ambassador to Stockholm had been instructed to attend. Two days later when Mujib confronted the Foreign Minister on his return from Nepal, Abdus Samad Azad hotly denied having issued the order. Mujib knew this to be a barefaced lie. Nevertheless he accepted Azad's contention that Foreign Secretary S. A. Karim had acted without his knowledge. The latter, in disgust, asked to be relieved of his post and went to New York as the Resident Observer at UN headquarters.

By the summer of 1972 everything was going wrong for Sheikh Mujibur Rahman. Rice is the staple food of the Bengalis and its price is always the definitive indicator of the public mood in Bangladesh. When the price is low the administration, however unpopular it may be in other ways, can hope to muddle through. When the price is high all the danger signals start flashing and it is generally assumed that the government is on its way out. By June, 1972, the price of paddy, the unhusked rice, had soared to 120 Takkas per maund (80 lbs) in the 'hats' or country markets. That was almost double what it had been under Pakistani rule and well above the crisis level for Bangladesh. Mujib was gravely embarrassed and tried to explain it away as the consequences of the war. But hungry villagers would not be fobbed off with such an excuse when other essentials such as paraffin, cooking oil, salt and soap were also difficult to come by because of the outrageous market manipulation. The country was in the grip of a severe money famine since unemployment, which had risen spectacularly during the liberation war, showed no signs of declining during the peace. In the public mind the Awami League government was not merely corrupt. It was considered to be totally degenerate. And, adding to the overall distress there was a pervasive lawlessness and violence.

Armed gangs openly plundered and killed. It was a common sight in the districts to see groups of bare-footed young men in lungis and 'gangis' or undershirts, sporting military caps and rifles, ambling through the market place. They had their will—be it eggs, fish, vegetables, cash or jewellery. Even Dhaka, the capital, was not immune to their depredations. Longhaired boys with green

22

or black berets, dark glasses and Castro beards would tear through the streets in stolen jeeps and cars. The number plates were only casually plastered with mud. Sometimes they carried rifles and sten guns. Sometimes not. But if they didn't get their way when demands were made in shops or houses the intended victims knew they would return after dark with the guns.

Mujib had dismally failed to retrieve the vast quantities of arms and ammunition which had remained in private hands in the aftermath of the war. His efforts in this direction had been inept from the start.

A little more than a week after taking over as Prime Minister and obviously acting on the advice of his non-combatant Awami League Cabinet ministers and the bureaucrats of the '16th Division', who both feared the freedom fighters, Mujib suddenly issued a public directive that all unauthorised arms should be surrendered within ten days. It was another case of the demi-god commanding 'let there be rain'. The folly of the order was immediately evident. Apart from the fact that the government was then incapable of enforcing its writ, the ending of the amnesty period coincided with the festival of Eid-ul-Azha when the country is shut down for at least three days. In this case it was the first Eid after independence and there was an immense pressure on everyone to return to their village homes for the festivities. Consequently the skeletal administration had begun to slow down. Even if it had wanted to, the government was not able to get the message effectively circulated in the countryside or for that matter arrange for the collection of arms had they been forthcoming. The timing was all wrong. Mujib was compelled to extend the deadline to the end of the month.

But there was a deeper reason for the directive being ignored. The proud, patriotic young freedom fighters of the Mukhti Bahini were willing to fall behind Mujib's leadership if they could be assured of responsible positions in the new state they had helped to create. But their willingness and goodwill were undermined by Mujib's own actions. First, he had imposed his Awami League cadres, who had little or no part in the fighting, as the eyes, ears and channels of government authority in the areas which the freedom fighters had controlled for several months. Guerrilla leaders, operating under cover, had 'governed' sizeable chunks of territory during the liberation war. They advised the population on resistance tactics, collected 'taxes' to sustain the struggle, even presided over 'courts' where justice may have been rough and ready but invariably evenhanded. Now they found themselves supplanted by Awami Leaguers whose role in the freedom struggle had been minimal, if not suspect, and who now flaunted themselves as the local barons.

Secondly, by adopting en masse the old East Pakistan bureaucracy—the notorious '16th Division'—as the administration of Bangladesh, Mujib did not only shut the door on the freedom fighters. He also laid them open to victimisation by the turncoat police and district officers who had only recently been the targets of the guerrillas. Mujib, of course, did offer to absorb the Mukhti Bahini in the armed forces, the national militia and police or to provide grants to those who wished to return to their studies. Some did take up the offer. About 8000 of them were absorbed in the national militia. But by and large the freedom fighters found these options, which were never clearly spelled out, distinctly uninviting. At best they seemed to imply subsistence level jobs for them, the true blues, while the plums went to others less deserving. So they clung to their guns. If nothing else they were the best form of reassurance in uncertain times.

Before the deadline ran out Mujib's political advisers after a great deal of negotiation, persuaded some guerrilla groups to ceremonially had over their weapons to the Prime Minister. Two TV spectaculars were organised for this purpose. The most impressive of these was in Tangail, and involved Kader Siddiqui, the 26-year-old guerrilla leader nicknamed 'Tiger'. He had won great distinction during the liberation war. It was a day to remember. Ten miles into Tangail the road on either side of Mujib's motorcade was lined at regular intervals with elements of the 'Kader Bahini'. They were Tiger's men, each in a khaki uniform, armed with a rifle and standing stiffly to attention. Inside the town and in the vast grounds where the ceremony was held the force and the discipline were equally impressive. This was the Tiger's territory and he was making sure Mujib got the point.

Wearing khaki uniform, his long, bushy hair standing out on either side of his cap. Kader Siddiqui ceremonially escorted Mujib past a long display of rifles, sten guns, and at least a dozen mortars. He picked up an automatic rifle and laid it at the Prime Minister's feet in a gesture of disarmament. Then taking rice from an aide, Tiger knelt before Mujib, a feudal lord pledging allegiance to his king. He swore he would be loyal to Mujib as long as he lived. Many others had taken the pledge before him; many since then. Only Tiger Siddiqui has kept the faith. He is now an outlaw.

Mujib, who was overcome with emotion, and the officials who accompanied him would remember that day for another reason. The massive display of fighting strength, discipline and dedication to a man other than Bangabandu would haunt them in the days to come. The sycophants would pour poison in Mujib's ears and he, more fearful than jealous, would try to crush the 'Bahini'. But this would only push them underground. The surrender ceremonies had more propaganda effect than practical value. About 30,000 guns were handed in, 70,000 less than the government expected. Neither Mujib nor Khandaker Moshtaque Ahmed and General Ziaur Rahman who followed him were able to mop up the rest.

Another reason for the chaos in the country was the manner in which the Collaborators' Order was implemented. Promulgated on 24 January, 1972, the Order was intended to bring to book those who had actively collaborated with the Pakistan army and government during the nine months of 1971 following the army crackdown. In the circumstances obtaining at that time it was almost a merciful alternative to uncontrolled blood-letting in the aftermath of the liberation war. No one can fault the Bengalis for seeking to punish those who assisted the savagery perpetrated on their people. The Israelis are still doing it 40 years after Hitler. What is inexcusable is the way in which an understand-able, even justifiable, emotion was allowed to deteriorate into a capricious witch-hunt and the paying off of old scores.

The main thrust of the Order was directed against Bengali politicians who had cooperated with the Pakistan authorities (such as the former Governor of East Pakistan, Dr. A. M. Malik, and his law minister Jasimuddin Ahmad) and the pro-Pakistan armed gangs such as the Razakars and the notorious Al Badar. The latter had been involved in acts of murder, rape, arson and looting and as such the guilty ones deserved to be brought to justice. But it was invidious to single out the collaborating politicans for punishment when the entire civilian admininstration of East Pakistan had not only been immunized from retribution but had also been installed as the new administration of Bangladesh. When all is said and done these government functionaries and policemen were in a natural position to collaborate—and collaborate many of them did. Yet the Collaborators' Order, with minor exceptions, was not directed against them.

At the same time the Awami Leaguers found the Order a convenient instrument to pay off old scores against political opponents and to silence the opposition. At the end of November, 1972, the Chief Whip of the Awami League, Shah Moazzam Hussain, complained that those who were trying to oppose the party in the forthcoming general elections were the same collaborators who had sided with the Pakistan army junta.[2] Even some '16th Division' officers seized the opportunity to hit back at unfortunate individuals who had crossed them at some time or other. All they had to do to ensure an opponent's ruin was to denounce him as a collaborator. The government did the rest. He was clamped in jail. His property was seized—all before the charge was investigated. Understandably some tried to defend themselves against this misdirected zeal. And since guns were readily available the violence spread. Soon the jails began to fill. On 3 October, 1972, the Home Minister publicly stated that 41,800 people had been arrested under the Collaborators' Order.

The first collaborators trials were held in Jessore. M. R. Akhtar ('Mukul') relates an interesting incident in his book 'Mujibur Rakta Lal'. The man in the dock, who had been accused of being a Razakar, stood silent when the magistrate repeatedly asked him, 'Are you guilty or not guilty?' In exasperation some lawyers in the court shouted at him, 'Why don't you plead?' The man finally answered: 'Sir, I'm thinking what to say.'

Magistrate: 'What are you thinking?'

Accused: (pointing to magistrate) 'I'm thinking that the person who occupies that chair is the one who recruited me as a Razakar. Now he has become a magistrate. It's a cruel twist of fate that I am in the dock and he is conducting my trial.'

Another interesting comment comes from Robert MacLennan the British MP who was an observer at the trials. 'In the dock the defendants are scarcely more pitiable than the succession of confused prosecution witnesses driven (by the 88-year-old defence counsel) to admit that they, too, served the Pakistan government but are now ready to swear blind that their real loyalty was to the government of Bangladesh in exile.'

The whole thing was a mockery of justice. The government finally put an end to it but not before the disorder intensified.

As the violence continued to escalate in the summer of 1972, at least 36 people were officially reported killed and another 80 injured in a riot in the port of Khulna. (Unofficial estimates, which were closer to the truth, put the death toll over 2000.) The incident is noteworthy because it involved the first of Mujib's experiments with private armies. This was the Lal Bahini, a paramilitary group raised by one of the Prime Minister's henchmen to 'control' the industrial areas. They became too officious in their task and the riot was a result of the confrontation with the police.

Not long after that Mujib, again in typical Bangabandhu fashion, issued another two-week ultimatum. This time it was to hoarders and smugglers in Dhaka to surrender illegally-held food stocks and arms. After the ultimatum ran out without noticeable result, checkpoints were established at cross roads. Police and militia searched motor vehicles and pedal rickshaws. Others raided shops and warehouses for hidden food stocks and stolen goods. The results were disappointing. A lot of small fry was netted but the big fish got away. They always do. They were of course part and parcel of the government and the ruling Awami League.

Corruption is not only a Bangladesh phenomenon. But few countries in the world have been so riddled with corruption as the new state was from the moment of its founding. It was as if a plague of locusts had descended on the country and set about devouring anything that offered the slightest margin of profit. And since Bangladesh was starting anew, there were endless opportunities for aggrandizement.

Instances of corruption could fill several volumes. They range from petty cupidity to outrageous criminality. It's a matter of record that a certain head of a Bangladesh diplomatic mission, who had made a great display of his piety, solemnly swore an affidavit that his grandson was his son in order to claim an additional family allowance of about £50 a month. Another diplomat charged a flat 5% on all government purchases made through his Mission. One of Mujib's senior officers was so adept at manipulating the food market that he arranged, first a shortage of salt, and then a famine of chillies before flooding the market with imports of these items brought in by his own cargo vessels. Others manipulated the rice trade, the edible oils market. Still others organised the smuggling of jute and rice to India, and through agents in London and Singapore controlled the fantastic Bangladesh black market in foreign exchange. Corruption was not the preserve of the Awami Leaguers and bureaucrats, but these two groups were ideally placed to make immense fortunes because they were the government. Some operated through relatives; some flagrantly in their own names. Others saw no harm in getting the Public Works Department to convert their modest village homes into well-equipped mansions.

Mujib, who had a proprietory attitude to the country, had no need for money. His preoccupation was power. No one has produced evidence to substantiate rumours that he had amassed a vast fortune abroad. But it is known that some members of his family, particularly his son Kamal, were not immune to helping themselves to the substantial gifts that came their way or to get investment-free partnerships in trading ventures which seemed to attract lucrative import business. After Mujib's assassination Brigadier Manzoor, the Chief of the General Staff under General Zia, citing examples of corruption, told me Mujib's brother had rapidly built up an immense fortune by cornering large numbers of barges and other river craft. But let it be said that in this respect Mujib's family did not distinguish itself any more than the scores of prominent Awami Leaguers, Cabinet Ministers and senior civil servants. Corrupt, money-grabbing people were to be found everywhere—even among some of the retired majors involved in Mujib's killing. Those who took less pointed a finger at those who took more. In such a convoluted society wrongdoing was not in question; guilt was a matter of degree.

The fault lay as much in the system as in the quality of men who had come to prominence in Bangladesh. Since the country had to be re-started from a collapsed position after the war, the government had perforce to control almost every aspect of life in Bangladesh. It soon developed into a system of licences based on an economy of want. Those who at the various stages controlled the issue of licences were therefore in a pre-eminent position to make their demands. Graft soon became a way of life. As my Bengali friends still say 'If you want to succeed you must pay.' Things got out of hand when those who controlled the system used the licences themselves to multiply their profits many times over.

In the matter of personnel, the Awami League did not have a creditable record. In fact some ministers in Prime Minister Suhrawardy's cabinet which ruled Pakistan in 1957 had shown themselves to be more corrupt than anything known in Pakistan till that time. When the party was installed in power in Bangladesh it was inevitable that old habits should be given full play. The doors to corruption were opened wide when Mujib installed Awami Leaguers as his eyes and ears in every district, sub-division and 'thana' (group of villages). The intention obviously was to keep a tight grip on the country. But the party men had to be paid off in patronage. When this took the form of distribution outlets for food, consumer goods and industrial raw materials, everyone took a cut.

Then again, Mujib, rather curiously, reinstated several senior officers with established reputations for corruption who had been dismissed from the Pakistan civil service. Some of them were placed in positions of influence near the throne. It would, however, be unfair to single out these men for blame. As pointed out earlier, many other officers had little or no commitment to Bangladesh. As they say in London pubs: they were only 'here for the beer'— and made no bones about it.

Closely entwined with the official corruption was the colossal smuggling of food and jute out of the country into India. The practice existed long before the birth of Bangladesh. With more than 1000 miles of border cutting through swampland, dense jungles and winding rivers of the delta country, smugglers operated with impunity from the early days of Pakistan. Merchants in the rice and jute growing areas of East Pakistan, where prices were low, were attracted by the Indian high-profit markets in metropolitan Calcutta and its industrial suburbs. Major Abdur Rashid, one of the two ring leaders of the coup against Mujib, had evidence of this when, as a Pakistan army captain, he was temporarily posted to border patrol duties with the East Pakistan Rifles in 1959. Rashid found his fellow officers deeply involved with the smugglers and when he took action against one of them he was summarily returned to his old regiment in West Pakistan. When Bangladesh came into being the smuggling operation greatly expanded, one reason being that border vigilance had become very relaxed because of the cordiality between the two countries.

Toni Hagen, at one time head of UNROD, reported early in 1972, that 'Bangladesh is like a sieve suspended in India.' Many merchants found it more advantageous to export the rice across the border where they got almost half as much again for their crops.[3] Not long after that Dr. K. U. Ahmad, a Bengali lecturer in Brunel University in England, after making a detailed study of the problem came to the conclusion: 'Food prices are soaring in Bangladesh chiefly because supplies sent in from abroad to relieve widespread hunger are being smuggled out to the Indian market by Bangladeshi traders aided by corrupt government officials.'[4] After Mujib's assassination the Bangladesh government itself said that 'smuggling of goods across the border during the three and a half years of independence cost approximately 60,000 million Takkas' (£2000 million). The goods smuggled out of the country were mostly jute, food-grains and materials imported from abroad.[5]

To the government's own estimates of smuggling (£2000 million sterling) must be added the vast sums funnelled out of the country through the black market in foreign exchange and the 'side money' (commissions) skimmed off the large purchases of rice, sugar, cement and other commodities made on government account. Corruption in Bangladesh was therefore of a magnitude exceeding anything known anywhere.

It was fashionable and politically expedient for Bangladeshis to blame India for its economic ills. Anyone who had access to the inner workings of Bangababan would know that while Mujib and his ministers publicly extolled the close ties with India, they also privately made it the scapegoat for their own inadequacies. The Indians cannot be absolved of blame for some of the incidents that have vexed relations between the two countries, and it is a fact that Indian merchants benefited enormously from the clandestine trade with

Bangladesh. But it is also a fact that the Bangladeshis themselves did the actual smuggling and had a proportionate share of the loot. The point was underscored at a cocktail party given by a Western diplomat in Dhaka in February, 1974. There were some local editors and journalists present and one of the latter was waxing hot about how the Indians were 'bleeding the country'. Finally our host had had enough. 'Tell me,' he asked this man, 'do the Indians come all the way into Bangladesh and carry off the rice and jute or do the Bangladeshis carry it out to them?' That was the end of the argument.

From the start the governments of Bangladesh and India had tried to prevent the business houses of Calcutta from dominating the economy of Bangladesh. To this end they signed an agreement in January 1972, putting all trade and economic exchanges on a state-to-state basis. Thus any unacceptable entanglement could have been pinched off at the start had it been found necessary. But there were some drawbacks and curiously as pointed out earlier, it was the cordiality making for easy movement across the border which ultimately undermined efforts to control the flow of commodities from Bangladesh to India. Clearly the flood of goods smuggled could not have developed if it was not supported, in the first instance, by corrupt politicians, officials and traders in Bangladesh, and secondly, by corrupt politicians, officials and merchants in India.

Sheikh Mujibur Rahman, in a moment of introspection, publicly put the finger on the malady: 'Who takes bribes? Who indulges in smuggling? Who becomes a foreign agent? Who transfers money abroad? Who resorts to hoarding? It's being done by us—the five percent of the people who are educated. We are the bribe takers, the corrupt elements . . . It seems that society is worm infested.'[6]

Nevertheless Mujib adopted a cavalier attitude to all this corruption. Once when a leader of another political party drew his attention to a particularly seamy scandal involving one of his ministers, Mujib shrugged it off with the remark, 'Yes, I know he is a greedy bastard.' This makes clear that it was not the lack of accountability that allowed corruption to spread, but the fact that Mujib did not enforce this accountability. It's the price he paid to retain a hold on anyone he thought to be dangerous to his own position. Mujib knew which minister and which officer took bribes, who manipulated the markets and who were the king-pins behind the smuggler gangs and currency racketeers. His intelligence services kept tabs on everyone. To their reports was added the gossip and tattling that poured down like monsoon rain on Gonobaban. Mujib carefully noted it all and used it when necessary to silence the guilty ones. Once a man became vulnerable he ceased to be a threat and he was tolerated as long as he kept in line. This tactic is as old as politics itself and no different from what is practised in varying degrees in other countries, and in Bangladesh itself, after Mujib's death. But while it did give Mujib a hold on people it did not guarantee their loyalty. Those who made money resented the idea that others were allowed to make a lot more. Thus no one was entirely satisfied and they all eventually turned on Mujib.

The haemorrhage of national resources almost killed off the new state at its founding. By the end of 1973 Bangladesh was bankrupt, though more than two billion dollars in international aid had been pumped into it. The tragedy is that the haemorrhage was not staunched after Mujib's death. Some corrupt politicians were removed from positions of influence but were replaced by influence-peddlers of another kind. Corrupt civil servants to a large extent remained untouched; so also did the well-heeled business sharks operating on the periphery of the palace. Like the rivers, they seemed to go on forever. And if smuggling was halted temporarily it was only because the new tensions between Bangladesh and India made for extreme vigilance on both sides of the border. Mujib's successors were hardly in a position to point the finger at him. Their attempts at cleaning up have at best been cosmetic.

Bangladesh would never have been brought to such straits in so short a period had it not been for the unbelievable sycophancy which filled Gonobaban and Bangababan like the clouds of intoxicating vapours in an opium den. Sycophancy is on a par with maladministration, corruption and smuggling as the prime cause for the decline of both Mujib and Bangladesh.

The Greeks and Romans used to say a god is nothing without worshippers. Mujib, the demi-god, had these in abundance. They clung to him like scabious leeches, greedily sucking all available patronage while at the same time isolating him from reality and the people. There were all kinds of 'durbaris'. Some were inoffensively obsequious, their only purpose being to demonstrate they were on the right side of the fence. Others were outrageously servile and grasping. They flattered Mujib, indulged his every mood and instantly echoed each utterance from the lips of the Leader. They aped the way he dressed. Mujib-style jackets over white cotton pyjamas became the uniform of the 'in' group. Mujib's picture blossomed on postage stamps and on currency notes, calendars, desk ornaments and daily on the front pages of almost every newspaper.

A bust of the Bangabandhu would also have adorned a cell in the Dhaka jail had not the 'durbaris' intervened. During his long career in the opposition, Mujib had spent more than ten years in solitary confinement, most of them in a condemned cell in the Dhaka central jail. He proudly called it his second home. In 1974 a senior officer of the Jails Department came up with the idea that it would be a fitting tribute to the Bangabandhu to place a bust of him in the cell. Accordingly one of Bangladesh's well-known sculptresses, Shamin, was commissioned to do the bust of Mujib for a fee of 20,000 Takkas (about £750). She came up with a large, very presentable work in bronze. The jail authorities spent another large sum building an appropriate pedestal and preparing the cell for the great occasion. Then they invited Mujib to the formal commemoration. When the invitation reached Gonobaban, Mujib was greatly touched by the gesture. The sycophants, however, were indignant. It would be 'insulting and inauspicious', they advised Mujib, to 'have Bangabandhu put in jail'. Mujib began to waver. When his family joined in opposing the idea, the bust was quietly removed from the cell and placed in storage.

The worst sycophants were among Mujib's advisers and ministers. Among the former were Tufail and Sheikh Fazlul Huq Moni, Mujib's nephew who would also die with him. Most prominent among the latter was Tahiruddin Thakur, the Minister of State for Information. Thakur was once a journalist, and would later play a shadowy role in Mujib's assassination. He geared the entire government information machinery, TV, radio and press to extolling the virtues of Mujib. He also distinguished himself by extreme public obeisance to his master.

Thakur's attitude so revolted some of his officers that one of them, an executive of Bangladesh TV, on one occasion hit on the idea of the camera focusing on Thakur as he bent down to touch Mujib's feet in a gesture of fealty at Dhaka airport. That night TV viewers in Dhaka were regaled with this spectacle of ministerial obeisance. But it is a measure of the national degradation at that time that instead of showing up this nauseous personal debasement as it was intended to, the touching of feet henceforth became the form for the durbaris. It inflated Mujib's ego—to the point where he took severe note of those who dared not to touch his feet.

Only one minister, Tajuddin Ahmad who was in charge of Finance, had the courage to stand up to Mujib publicly. In November 1974, on his return from an international conference, Tajuddin publicly criticised the government for incompetence and mismanagement. In the circumstances it was akin to political suicide and probably reflected the desperation he felt. On being summarily dismissed, Tajuddin immediately announced his retirement from politics. One other minister, General M. A. G. Osmani, who successively held the portfolios of Defence, Civil Aviation and Shipping, was never comfortable in Mujib's Cabinet, and in July, 1974, asked to be relieved of his portfolios. The other ministers, whatever may have been their private opinions, did not show hesitation in falling into line behind Sheikh Mujib whatever he did. The same is true of some senior civil servants and military officers. They had no reason to take sides, but take sides they did for rapid promotions. The numerous turncoats in evidence after Mujib's assassination underscores this sad story.

In their own way each of his principal political advisers made notable contributions to the Mujib legend. Tufail was the first to give him the grandiose title of Bangabandhu, the Friend of the Bengalis. That was during the Bengali upsurge against Pakistan and Tufail's influence with the emotional leader was carried over when Bangladesh became a reality and Mujib the Prime Minister. He was appointed Mujib's political secretary and in that capacity was one of the most powerful shadows behind the throne. The other adviser, Sheikh Fazlul Huq Moni, was the author of 'The Four Pillars of Mujibism—Nationalism, Socialism, Democracy and Secularism.' These were bombastically enshrined in the constitution as the 'Fundamental Principles of State Policy.' But in actual terms of guiding concepts they remained illusory, if not grotesquely debased by contrary practices. For propaganda purposes the Four Pillars of Mujibism were eminently suitable as banners for the long march to 'Sonar Bangla' or the Golden Bengal. But Bangladesh in fact was going nowhere and thus they assumed merely a decorative purpose. In his time Mujib would shoot down every one of the 'pillars' and Moni and Tufail would cheer him on. But this did not deter the durbaris from taking up the chant.

The 'principles' were developed into the cult of 'Mujibism', complete with badges, books, essays and newspaper articles proclaiming and explaining the 'new philosophy'. Even Mujib was embarrassed by what was done in his name. When the author of a voluminous treatise on 'Mujibism' ceremonially presented him with a copy, Mujib self-consciously accepted the book with the remark, 'Yes, I'm sure I'll find it very interesting.'

Some people got hopelessly tangled in their enthusiasm. On 25 September, 1974, Shahidul Haq, the Editor of Bangladesh Times cabled this despatch to his newspaper from New York:

'It seemed all so incredible yet so convincing. The moment of triumph for Bengali nation and more particularly for Bangabandhu came at 3.30 pm today when UN General Assembly reverberated to an impatient appeal for universal peace by him.

'It was the first time that someone spoke in Bengali in the 29-year history of UN. And it was only in the fitness of things that the speaker was Bangabandhu. As a leader of a delegation put it, the parliament of man was "totally captivated by the sound melody, serenity, onrush and aural majesty of language and delivery" of which most members did not know a word of . . .'[7]

Mujib's isolation was completed by his own Awami League party. When he took over as Prime Minister in January, 1972, Mujib installed his party men everywhere, making them his eyes and ears and hoping they would open up a two-way channel of communication. But in their outright scramble for perks and patronage and by their excessive sycophancy, the channels got clogged and the system broke down. Mujib was only made aware of the people's distress when trouble broke out somewhere. And then the sycophants quickly denounced it as the work of 'trouble-makers' and 'anti-state elements'. Thus, like the Greek gods of old, they made him mad and destroyed him.

Bangladesh's showing in the first year of independence was aptly summed up when on that anniversary day a 31-gun salute intended to grandly mark the occasion petered out after five rounds and had to be replaced by rifle and automatic fire.

Notes
1. Reported in The Sunday Times, London, 10.9.1972.
2. The Guardian, London, 1.12.1972.
3. Reported in The Sunday Times, London, 19.3.1972.
4. The Observer, London, 15.10.1972.
5. Bangladesh Today, 1.4.1976.
6. Speech in Dhaka, 26.3.1975.
7. Quoted in Bangladesh Today, London, 1.10.1974.

IV

Mujib's Military Nightmare

*I don't want to create a monster like the one
we had in Pakistan.*

Sheikh Mujibur Rahman

The year 1973 started inauspiciously for Sheikh Mujibur Rahman. His first year in office had been one of frenetic effort and gloom relieved only by a single golden success. That was Bangladesh's first Constitution. An imposing document enshrining the noblest values to which an emotional people could aspire, the Constitution had been master-minded by Mujib and piloted by him through the National Assembly. The task was completed on 4 November, 1972, clearly a record for newly-emerged Third World states. After it was handwritten by a master calligraphist, the Constitution was signed and sealed by the middle of December. Bangladesh may have been ruled by a lame-duck administration, but it had a Constitution which any country could be proud of.

Mujib was certainly proud of his handiwork. He had thereafter taken the next logical step on the road to orderly government. Elections had been set for 7 March, 1973. It should have been a happy time for Bangabandhu and Bangladesh, but suddenly on New Year's Day there was unbelievable violence on the streets of Dhaka. Chittagong and Khulna were also shut down by rampaging students. Crowds were stomping the streets of the three main cities hurling abuse on Sheikh Mujib.

It had started as a students' demonstration in Dhaka protesting the US bombing of Hanoi during the bloody days of the Vietnam war. A large crowd gathered outside the US Information Centre and Library in down-town Dhaka. They were agitated but no one anticipated a breach of the peace. It was generally assumed that the students would move on after they had shouted their protest. Suddenly, however, someone provoked them to attack the building, and within minutes the crowd was involved in a fierce battle with police reinforcements who were hastily called in. The police opened fire, killing two students and injuring at least six others.

In the circumstances it was a disaster for Mujib.

There is a special sanctity attached to students in Bangladesh beause they have in the past been in the vanguard of the struggle for the people's rights. Mujib was one such student who had risen to leadership on the shoulders of the young men and women who had championed Bengali causes over the years—language, political rights, economic justice and, finally, total emancipation from Pakistan. It was therefore inconceivable that barely a year after the founding of Bangladesh students should be killed in Dhaka by Mujib's police.

The event was doubly significant in that it also marked the first outbreak of mass violence in Dhaka since independence. There had, of course, been a public airing of grievances in the capital four months earlier when Abdur Rab, the left-wing students leader, denounced Mujib for betraying the country.

32

Mujib had dismissed it as a political stunt. The violence and shooting in the streets now was something more ominous. Mujib's instincts warned him that it was an attempt to undermine his position and he became convinced of a plot when the trouble rapidly spread to Chittagong and Khulna, and left-wing student leaders, in an obvious attempt at a showdown, called for a general strike.

Mujib decided to take up the challenge. He may have been hesitant and unsure of himself in the secretariat, but the streets were home ground to him. Accordingly he took the fight to the students. First he shut the door on criticism by ordering a judicial inquiry and making plain that he would not shirk his responsibility to protect foreign Missions. Then, in a clear reference to the Soviet Union, he ordered his people to crush 'the agents of a foreign power who are trying to push this country into a certain bloc'. The results were stunning. Within hours at least 100,000 villagers armed with sickles and bamboo staves crossed the river to join up with members of the Awami League's student wing in Dhaka. Together they routed the left-wing mobs first from the students' hostels where they were entrenched, and then from the streets of the city. The defeat was so complete that Maulana Bashani, the ageing Chief of the (Marxist) National Awami Party hurriedly called off his own protest meeting and fled to the seclusion of his village.[1]

The left-wing leaders had badly miscalculated in attempting a head-on clash with Mujib. They had not realised that however much the people suffered, there would remain in the Bangladesh peasantry a reservoir of affection for the Bangabandhu. In a delta country subject to floods, cyclones, famine and pestilence people have learned to live with disaster. They take a lot of punishment so long as it does not intrude against their simple values such as ownership of land, the sanctity of the family, Islam their religion, and their pride in being Bengalis. The Pakistanis did not understand this in 1970 and 1971. When the Pakistanis denigrated the piety and the pride of the Bengalis and hunted down their youth, they provoked the heart of Bengali nationalism and were thrown out. In all this Mujib had become the symbol of Bengali hope and pride, albeit in abstract terms, and would remain so for a long time even though his policies were shattering the state. Mujib used this feeling with characteristic agility on this occasion to turn disaster into a resounding victory.

The day's events had two significant results.

First, it drummed into the heads of Mujib's opponents that they could never hope to topple him in a straight fight. Ultimately such an assessment would be fatal for Mujib. Major Rashid, when asked why Mujib was killed and not deposed, replied: 'There was no other way. He had the capacity for mischief and given the chance he would have turned the tables on us.'

The second had happier consequences for Mujib. Having demonstrated his strength by demolishing the opposition, he sailed through the elections three months later to a landslide victory. His Awami League won 307 of the 315 seats in the National Assembly. The other parties could not muster enough strength between them to be formally recognised as the Opposition in the House. There were, of course, allegations made by some defeated candidates that the election had been rigged against them. Professor Muzaffar Ahmad said his faction of the National Awami Party would have won 25 seats but for intimidation, false votes and other malpractices. Apart from one well-recorded incident where one of Mujib's ministers, Mr. Mannan, unaccountably had an upsurge of votes at the close when the count had been going against him all day, these charges were not taken seriously by independent observers in Dhaka.

Maulana Bashani, an astute political weather vane who had earlier come out against Mujib, after the election quietly fell into line behind the government with the remark that the election result 'was the signal for the arrival of undiluted socialism in Bangladesh'.[2]

Sheikh Mujib understandably took the election result as a personal triumph and a vindication of his policies. 'The result shows that my people love me as I love them', he told reporters. Thus not only were the pressures for reform brushed aside but Mujib and the Awami League also saw their election victory as a licence to press on as they had done in the past. The tempo of the Mad Hatter's dance in Bangladesh picked up perceptibly.

One significant facet of the elections not made public at that time but which Sheikh Mujibur Rahman and his advisers took careful note of, was the pattern of voting by the troops. The government was disturbed to find that the votes recorded in the military cantonments had gone overwhelmingly against Mujib's Awami League candidates. I had heard a rumour to this effect during a visit to Dhaka in February, 1974, but it was not till December of the following year, after Mujib had been killed, that I was able to pin it down. General Zia and Brigadier M. A. Manzoor told me that a little more than 80% of the troops had voted against the Awami League.

Among the troops was a sizeable proportion of men who had been in the forefront of the independence struggle when Mujib was both flag and father to his people. Now 15 months later they constituted the biggest single bloc against him. The reasons for this disenchantment have been advanced by Majors Farook and Rashid, by Brigadier Manzoor, some other officers and jawans and by Major General Ziaur Rahman, the Chief of Army Staff, himself. In an interview on 11 December, 1975 in Dhaka after Mujib was killed, General Zia told me: 'We were really not an army and did not exist on paper. There was no legal basis for the army. There was no T.O.E. (Table of Organisation and Establishment). Everything was ad hoc. The army was paid because Mujib said it should be paid. Our existence depended on Mujib's word. Our chaps went through hell and they suffered but did not complain because they were involved in serving the country and were willing to make whatever sacrifices that were necessary.'

On the same day Brigadier Manzoor, Zia's Chief of General Staff (CGS), said: 'This is a volunteer's army. The officers and men are all volunteers because they chose the army as a career. What were they given in return? They were ill-fed, ill-equipped and ill-administered. I tell you they had no jerseys, no coats, no boots. They stood on guard duty in the cold at nights in their slippers with blankets wrapped around them. Many of our troops still are in their lungis and without uniform. Then there was the humiliation.' Explaining this Manzoor said: 'Our men were beaten up by the police. The bureaucrats, as they had been in Pakistan, hated the army and they carried over their hatred when they came to Bangladesh. Once some of our boys were killed . . . two jawans (privates) . . . and we went to Mujib and asked that the people who did it should be punished. He promised to look into the matter. Then he informed us that the jawans were killed because they had been collaborators!'

According to Manzoor, Mujib had done his best to destroy the army. He had also adopted the policy of divide and rule, getting rid of anyone who seemed to be a threat to him. 'It was he who divided the army into so many groups', Manzoor said. 'He called them separately, giving one a promotion, another a perk. Things were done without reference to the Chief of Staff'.

General Zia and Manzoor and some other officers I talked to suspected that Sheikh Mujib had been grooming his second son, Jamal, for a senior position in the army. According to Manzoor, after putting Jamal in the army, Mujib immediately sent him off for training at the Yugoslav Military Academy. Jamal, it seems, couldn't cope with the studies there and to Mujib's great disappointment returned to Dhaka. Thereafter Mujib wanted him sent to Sandhurst. He, in fact, peremptorily telephoned General Shafiullah (who was then the Chief of Army Staff) insisting that Jamal be appointed a cadet at Sandhurst. This created a difficult situation all round.

In the first place, cadets for Sandhurst are chosen by an exhaustive selection process and there were many other candidates brighter and more suitable than Jamal. And it was thought that Jamal would not be able to meet the standards required by Britain's premier military academy. Secondly, Sandhurst did not cater for ad hoc appointments. But since Mujib insisted that he be admitted, they agreed to accept Jamal as a special case on payment of a £6000 training fee. This was immediately agreed to and, according to Manzoor, the money was remitted secretly through army channels without the knowledge of the Finance Minister.

Jamal was a likeable lad, and unlike his abrasive older brother, Kamal, was well-behaved and respectful. Not long after returning from Sandhurst—and within a month of his wedding—Jamal was gunned down with the rest of the family when Mujib was assassinated by the Majors.

Mujib had an understandable hatred for all things military. He had suffered grievously at the hands of Pakistan's two military dictators, Field Marshal Ayub Khan and General Yahya Khan. Ayub had arrested Mujib on 7 October, 1958, the day he seized power. During the next $10\frac{1}{2}$ years of Ayub's dictatorship Mujib had been jailed for long periods in solitary confinement. Then in 1968, while once more in detention for political activity, he was made the principal accused in the notorious Agartala Conspiracy trial in Dhaka. The charge: conspiring with India for the secession of East Pakistan. It was a capital offence and Mujib only escaped the gallows because a countryside upsurge against Ayub in 1968 forced him to drop the charges and bring Mujib to the conference table.

While a prisoner of General Yahya Khan in 1971 during the Bangladesh independence struggle, Mujib had had an even closer brush with death. The story he told me was splashed on the front page of The Sunday Times. According to Mujib, he had been tried by a military court and found guilty of treason and sedition. On 15 December, 1971, the day before the Pakistan army surrendered to the Indian troops in Dhaka, General Yahya Khan had ordered Mujib's execution. A military team went from Rawalpindi to Mianwali where Sheikh Mujibur Rahman was being held in jail. The team went about its task in a methodical manner. A shallow grave was dug in the cement floor of the room adjoining the Bangladesh leader's cell. He was told that this was being done 'as an air raid precaution'. But Mujib knew what it was for and prepared himself for the worst. Fortunately for him the ceasefire was ordered that night. The jailor, taking pity on Mujib and knowing that Yahya Khan was about to abdicate, smuggled him to his personal quarters where he kept him for two days. The operation was helped by the confusion that attended the surrender of the Pakistan army. When Zulfiquar Ali Bhutto replaced General Yahya Khan as President, he refused to revalidate the execution order when asked to do so. Two weeks later Mujib was a free man and on his way to Bangladesh via London. He never forgot the jailor who saved his life. In June, 1974, when President Bhutto visited Dhaka, Mujib invited this man along as his personal guest.

Mujib carried his hatred of the army with him to the grave. This attitude was shared by his ministers and other senior Awami Leaguers who had also escaped death at the hands of the Pakistan army in 1971. To their basic hostility of things military was added, after independence, the fear that the Bangladesh army might try to supplant them. This anxiety was grounded in the fact that the Bengali military men had been in the thick of the fighting during the independence movement while the Awami Leagues stayed safely in Calcutta out of the line of fire. As such it would have been understandable if the army men with the other freedom fighters had insisted on positions of influence in the new state. The army as an institution at least did not make this demand. It was content to let Mujib rule and in the first two years of independence gave him loyalty and support.

Mujib and his ministers, however, from the very start deliberately emasculated the role of the Defence Forces. Before he was one month in office Mujib took the first step in this direction by signing a 25 year Treaty of Friendship and Mutual Assistance with India. The Indian army had helped to create Bangladesh and it was to India that Mujib now looked to protect it from external aggression. The treaty thus obviated the need for an effective fighting force and the country's defence establishment was reduced to a police-keeping and largely ceremonial role.

Sheikh Mujib himself told me in February, 1974, that he was against a powerful military force. 'I don't want to create another monster like the one we had in Pakistan'.

Mujib wanted the army to wither on the vine—but almost by accident it didn't happen that way.

During the Arab–Israeli war in October, 1973, the Bangladesh government, anxious to make a show of support for the Arab cause, decided to make a gift of a plane-load of the finest domestic tea to Egypt. In the absence of more tangible support with money and arms, the tea was at best a token gesture. But it did have the esoteric virtue of providing the hard-pressed Arab troops with refreshing rounds of the cup that cheers. The government was delighted when Egypt gratefully accepted the offer. Accordingly, a Bangladesh Biman 707 with the fragrant cargo took off from Dhaka on 27 October, and after attempting a landing at Cairo airport, which was closed, was diverted to Benghazi in Libya where it off-loaded the tea.

Coincidentally the discharge of the cargo was watched with considerable interest by two of my colleagues from The Sunday Times who were stranded at Benghazi airport. Tea was the last thing on their minds. What they wanted was a lift to London and they had heard that the plane would soon be headed in that direction. Captain Bill Mackintosh, after checking with Libyan authorities, was happy to oblige.

No one, least of all Sheikh Mujib, could have guessed at that time that the gift would rebound with the most tragic consequences for him and Bangladesh.

As it happened President Anwar Sadat after the war remembered Bangladesh's unusual gesture and decided to make a handsome gesture in return. He knew Bangladesh had no armaments worthy of the name and there were any number of T-54 tanks parked in the desert sands outside Cairo. President Sadat decided to make a gift of thirty of them to Bangladesh. The offer was conveyed to Mujib in the spring of 1974. It dismayed him. He was alarmed at the prospect of having such military equipment in Bangladesh. He did not want tanks. They did not fit in with his ideas about the army. The Foreign Office and his ministers, however, persuaded Mujib that he could on no account refuse Sadat's gift.

The thirty T-54s with 400 rounds of tank ammunition arrived in Bangladesh in July, 1974, making a very welcome addition to the army's strength which was then built around all of three vintage ex-Pakistan army tanks left over from the 1971 war. When they were ceremonially handed over to the 1st Bengal Lancers, Bangladesh's only 'armoured' regiment, one of the officers taking delivery of the tanks was Major Farook Rahman. Though officially second in command of the regiment, he was the most experienced armoured corps officer and the tanks came effectively under his control. Thus man and weapons were brought together—all because of a gift of tea. One year later Farook led the tanks to Mujib's house and changed the course of Bangladesh. But before that Mujib tried to build an alternative to the army.

The Jhatiyo Rakhi Bahini, which roughly translated means National Security Force, was an elite para-military force whose members had to take oaths of personal loyalty to Mujib. Despite its high-sounding name, it was a sort of a private army of bully boys not far removed from the Nazi Brown Shirts. It was formed originally as an auxiliary force—a group of 8000 hand-picked men from the old Mukhti Bahini—to assist the police in the main-tenance of law and order. As opposition to Mujib increased, he found it a convenient alternative to the army, which he mistrusted, to be brought in wherever necessary to aid the civil administration. The Rakhi Bahini was raised to 25,000 men who were given basic military training, army-style un-iforms, steel helmets and modern automatic weapons. Its officers were mainly political cadres and it was freely used to crush opponents and critics of Mujib and the Awami League. In time it completely terrorised the people.

There are several documented cases of murder and torture committed by the Rakhi Bahini. In May, 1974, after a 17-year-old boy was found to have 'disappeared' after four days of torture, the Supreme Court severely castigated the Rakhi Bahini for 'operating outside the law'. The Court found that Mujib's storm troops had no code of conduct, no rules of procedure and no register of arrests and interrogation. Mujib's answer to the Court's censure was to strip it of its powers to intervene in such cases.

A feature of 1973, the second year of independence, was the expanding violence in Bangladesh. The upsurge of violence was in direct proportion to the increase in corruption, market-manipulation, smuggling and political repression by the cohorts of the Awami League who were savouring their election victory. The people fought back with guns carried over from the liberation war. Gangs of dacoits roamed the countryside at nights, looting granaries and village shops for food and everyday necessities. Mujib countered with the Rakhi Bahini and by liberally arming his party men, many of whom were allowed to carry prohibited bore rifles and automatics. According to Brigadier Manzoor, who was Brigade Commander Jessore at that time, the profusion of arms was caused as much by illegal arms cached after the war as by the Awami Leaguers' free access to the government armouries. He said he was able to recover 33,000 weapons and 3.8 million rounds of ammunition from the six districts under his command. By the end of 1973 the total of politically motivated murders in Bangladesh had crossed the 2000 mark. The victims included some members of Parliament and many of the murders were the result of intra-party conflicts within the Awami League.

Most of the MPs and senior Awami Leaguers had their personal body-guards. One of them, according to Dhaka journalists, was so insecure that when he went to his village he not only ringed the house with armed followers, but also stationed others in every room. 'The bloody fellow even has a bodyguard in his bedroom' I was told.

Dhaka, the capital, was not immune to the violence. An unofficial curfew was enforced after midnight when rickshaws, taxis and private cars were checked and searched by the Rakhi Bahini and police. One such incident, which vividly describes the scene in Dhaka in those days, nearly resulted in the death of Mujib's eldest son, Kamal.

Kamal was a hot-headed, very abrasive young man who, like his father, had a proprietory attitude to Bangladesh. Criticism and opposition, in Kamal's book, meant 'anti-national activity' and Kamal was not above using a heavy hand to crush it. Sheikh Mujib perhaps did not like some of the things Kamal did—but nevertheless allowed the young man a free hand. A particular target of Kamal's venom was Siraj Shikdar, the leader of the Maoist Sharbohara (proletarian) party, who had fought the Pakistan army during the liberation war in 1971, and had then come out against Mujib. Shikdar and his men used to observe 16 December, the anniversary of Bangladesh's liberation, as a 'Black Day' because they resented what they felt was a gift of independence by India. In 1972 Siraj Shikdar and his men had plastered the capital with anti-Mujib posters and graffiti and had set off bombs in police stations to mark the occasion. This year when intelligence reports indicated they would repeat the performance, Kamal decided to prevent it. On the night of 15 December he and his cronies, armed with sten guns and rifles, went out in a microbus 'hunting' Siraj Shikdar.

They were not aware that the 'Special Branch' of the Dhaka police, under Superintendent Mahboob, had received similar orders from their Chief. Their paths crossed during the course of the hunt. The police squad under Sergeant Kibria in an unmarked Toyota car noticed the armed group in the microbus and decided to follow it. Kibria thought he had come upon the Shikdar gang. Kamal, in the microbus, for his part thought Shikdar's men were in the Toyota.

The showdown came opposite the Bangladesh Bank headquarters in the Motijeel area of the city. In the exchange of fire Kamal was hit in the neck, the bullet narrowly missing his wind-pipe and jugular vein. With blood spurting from his wound he jumped from the microbus shouting 'Don't shoot. I'm Kamal. I'm Kamal.' When they realised their mistake, some of the policemen rushed him to the Postgraduate Medical College Hospital. The panic-stricken Sergeant Kibria meanwhile fled to the bungalow of the Deputy Commissioner of Dhaka, Mr. Abdul Hayat, where he told him 'we have made a terrible blunder and brought heaven down upon our heads'.

Hayat was an experienced officer and realised that heads would roll because of this blunder. After making sure that Kamal was still alive, he lost no time driving to Bangababan for an immediate audience with Bangabandhu 'on a matter of the greatest importance'. Mujib's reaction on hearing the new surprised the Deputy Commissioner. 'Let him die', he said, clearly furious that Kamal had once again taken the law into his own hands. When Abdul Hayat asked what he should do about the policemen, Mujib told him to return them to duty. 'They have nothing to fear' he said. It is a matter of record that on that occasion at least Mujib kept his word.

My friend Zackaria Chowdhury ('Zack') who recounted this story saying he had got it firsthand from the Deputy Commissioner, told me Mujib refused to visit his son in hospital for two days. When on the day after the incident 'Zack' called at the hospital, Begum Mujib was very distressed and told him in Bengali: 'Bhai, he has come to have such a big head that he doesn't come to visit his own son who is dying'. The fact is that Mujib was becoming increasingly embarrassed by Kamal's behaviour. I know of several occasions when he remonstrated with him about his free-wheeling ways. Then paradoxically he also indulged Kamal and sent him on political errands or to work among the various student groups. As such Kamal was never far from the throne. On this occasion, father and son were soon reconciled. When Kamal left hospital and had fully recovered he was temporarily taken out of political work and given the task of organising a series of football tournaments. It was hoped that this would keep him out of mischief while at the same time giving the people something to take their minds off their problems.

Among the angry young men in the Bangladesh army were two young Majors who took immense pride in their professional competence and who now found their careers on the rocks because of Sheikh Mujib's studied neglect of the armed forces. One was Farook Rahman, second in command of the 1st Bengal Lancers, the country's only tank regiment which till the middle of 1974 had only three obsolete tanks in its armoury. The other was Khandaker Abdur Rashid, the Commanding Officer of the 2 Field Artillery, also based on Dhaka.

Farook and Rashid, both born within a month of each other in 1946, were good friends and brothers-in-law since they had married the daughters of Mr. S. H. Khan who belonged to Chittagong's leading industrial family. (Mr Khan's older brother was A. K. Khan, a former Industries Minister in the Pakistan government). A single wall separated their bungalows in Dhaka cantonment and in the evenings the sisters and their husbands would often get together, as they put it, 'to pass the time'. It was these family ties that allowed them to confide in each other about their disenchantment with the way things were going in Bangladesh. The two Majors were otherwise poles apart in terms of personality and came from very different backgrounds.

Farook—his full name is Dowan Esheratullah Syed Farook Rahman—comes from the upper crust of Bengali society and claimed that on commissioning he was the first second-generation Bengali officer in the Pakistan army. His father's family are known as the 'Pirs' (religious leaders) of Rajshahi, claiming direct descent from Arab Syeds who had settled on a modest estate in Nauga. His mother belongs to a land-owning zamindar family of the Jamalpur/Islampur area of Mymensingh who claim descent from Turkish soldiers of fortune under the Moghul emperors. Between them Farook was closely related to Dr. A. R. Mullick (former Finance Minister and University Vice Chancellor), Syed Nazrul Islam (Acting President of Bangladesh while Mujib was in jail), Syed Ataur Rahman Khan (former Chief Minister of East Pakistan and Prime Minister of Bangladesh) and Major General Khalid Musharraf who was very briefly Chief of Staff of the Bangladesh army in November 1975, before being killed in the sepoy mutiny.

Farook's father, Major Syed Ataur Rahman, was an Army doctor and Farook's education reflects the pattern of his postings. He criss-crossed the sub-continent six times in thirteen years starting off in the Fatima Jinnah girls school, Comilla (Farook jokes about his 'one and only time in a convent'). He went to Abbottabad (Burnhall), Dhaka (St. Joseph's), Quetta (St. Francis' Grammar School), Rawalpindi (Station Road school where Field Marshall Ayub Khan's daughter Naseem was also a student), Dhaka (Adamjee College), ending up in a college in Kohat for a crash course in maths.

Farook was the eldest of the three children—he has two sisters—and it was not intended that he should go into the army. His love of flying got him a solo licence at the age of 17 and he had unsuccessfully tried to join the Pakistan Air Force. So the family got him admitted to Bristol University for a course in aeronautical engineering and he would have gone to the UK in 1966 but for the intervention of hostilities with India in the spring of 1965 over the Rann of Kutch.

Caught up in the prevailing patriotic fervour Farook, on his way to college, stopped off at the Inter-services Selection Board office in Kohat and volunteered for a commission. A week later when the call came there was initial disapproval from his mother who didn't want to lose her only son to the army. But Farook, with his father's consent, finally made it to the Pakistan Military Academy at Risalpur where he quickly distinguished himself by becoming battalion sergeant major. When he graduated fourth of three hundred officer cadets, he was given his choice of service. Farook chose the armoured corps. 'I don't want to do foot-slogging in the army' he said politely turning down suggestions by Majors Ziaur Rahman and Khalid Musharraf, then instructors in the P.M.A., that he should join the Bengal Regiment. Instead, Farook was appointed to the 13th Lancers.

Later Farook transferred to the 31st Cavalry, then based at Sialkot, and in 1970 at the age of 24, he found himself a captain, acting squadron commander, of 'Charlie Squadron' and 'in the command chain of the armoured corps'. This significant career opening was made possible by his success in the tactical armour course which he topped with $B+$.

In October, 1970, Captain Farook Rahman received a note from his CO informing him that he had been selected for secondment to the oil-rich Sheikhdom of Abu Dhabi where Pakistan was involved in training and servicing the Sultan's armed forces. Farook has no idea why he was chosen for secondment, but the fact remains that at the beginning of 1971 when the political upsurge was getting under way in East Bengal, Farook found himself a squadron commander in the Abu Dhabi armoured regiment based near the oil port of Jabaldhana.

It was a happy time for the young tank commander. Military duties, in which he exulted, took up only a portion of his time. He had lots of it left for his other loves—reading volumes of military history and tactics, driving fast cars, and music. Farook bought himself the best stereo system he could find and an Opel Commodore GS in which he would tear along the desert roads at 100 mph. He was billeted in the British Officers mess and it was there that in the middle of June, 1971, he found a bundle of British newspapers, among them the Sunday Times featuring my massive exposé of the Pakistan army's campaign of genocide in Bangladesh. It marked the turning point in his life.

As Farook put it, 'What actually convinced me about your writing was your technique and reporting.' 'The way you wrote about those Pakistani officers straightaway struck me that this man is not a fraud. Only a chap who has been in close touch with the Pakistan army knows exactly how they behave. I know. And I also know that no one can simulate it. That's why I was solidly convinced that this chap knew exactly what he was writing and couldn't be wrong. This forced me to decide to go'.

I asked Farook 'Would you have gone if you had not read the article?'

He answered: 'As I said, I was not interested in politics because I was rising very fast professionally with the little service that I had. I was only interested in seeing how fast I could go. I was only interested professionally in being a general officer. Then suddenly this thing came to me and disrupted my whole damn career'.

Confirmation of the disaster that had staggered the Bengalis came in a letter from his uncle, Nurul Quader, a Bengali civilian officer who had fled to Calcutta to join the Mujibnagar government. Farook is an ardent nationalist. He is also single-minded, with decisiveness grounded on careful planning. After carefully weighing the situation, Farook decided he could no longer serve in the Pakistan army.

On 12 November, 1971, he packed a bag and drove to Dubai airport where he abandoned his car. Then he caught the first flight to Beirut and London for the long journey to Bangladesh.

Farook saw Farida for the first time when picnicking with Major Rashid and his wife, Tinku, on the Kaptai Lake near Chittagong. Farook was instantly smitten by the younger sister's beauty, refinement and quiet charm. 'I want to marry her' he told Rashid in the matter-of-fact manner they converse with each other. 'You must arrange it'. Rashid did the needful. Farook and Farida were married on 12 August 1972. After the marriage Farook and Rashid became inseparable.

The Majors first met in the Pakistan Military Academy at Risalpur. Farook belonged to a senior batch, but it did not matter. The Bengali officer cadets, who were heavily outnumbered in the Academy by Punjabis and Pathans, sat together in the cafeteria 'to chit-chat' as Rashid tells it. Rashid was very talkative; Farook a good listener.

Like Farook, Khandaker Abdur Rashid's own presence in the military academy was the result of the effusion of patriotism during the Pakistan-India war in 1965. Rashid came from the tiny village of Chaypharia on the road between Comilla and Daudkhandi where his father was a primary school teacher of modest means. He is not connected to the great or the learned, and is the first to deny Bangladesh gossip that he is a nephew of Khandaker Moshtaque Ahmed, the Awami League minister the two majors installed as President after knocking off Sheikh Mujibur Rahman. Rashid insists that the only connection with Khandaker Moshtaque is an accident of geography. They come from the same sub-district.

Rashid was studying soil science, geography and geology at Dhaka University when the war broke out in 1965, and he thought it was a patriotic duty to seek a commission in the Pakistan army. He was selected and after a run-of-the-mill showing in the PMA, graduated 92nd in his class. Rashid requested posting to the Bengal Regiment but instead was given his second choice and commissioned in the 2 Field Artillery then based in Bannu in the North-west Frontier Province.

In 1968 when promoted to captain, Rashid went to Dhaka on a short holiday and lived with an uncle. He was an eligible bachelor and his uncle's friend had a very eligible niece, Zobeida ('Tinku') the elder daughter of S. H. Khan of the Chittagong industrial family. The match was arranged and Rashid took his bride back with him to Bannu where the first of their two daughters was born.

For a brief period in 1970 he was posted to the East Pakistan Rifles and stationed at Khulna where he was employed in policing the border with India. One day he caught an NCO with Rs 100,000 in his pocket. The man had evidently obtained a big bribe from the smugglers operating in the area. Rashid promptly arrested him. His action was not appreciated by his commanding officer. Rashid says this man, a Punjabi, 'was also involved in making money from the smugglers'. Later when he caught some gold smugglers red-handed, Rashid suddenly found himself back to his Artillery unit. The excuse, he was to learn later, was a secret report by his CO that he had 'developed parochial tendencies'. In the military jargon of that time this meant that he was a Bengali nationalist. It was a bad certificate for any Pakistani army officer.

When the Pakistan army cracked down on the Bengalis in March 1971, Rashid's unit was stationed in Hajira on the Pakistan side of the ceasefire line in Kashmir. It was a trying period for the young Bengali officer. The radio reports he was picking up from different parts of the world gave horrifying stories of the trauma in East Pakistan. Rashid decided to defect from the Pakistan army.

Explaining his reasoning he said: 'I thought that once the movement had started, whatever the cause may be, and right or wrong, it had to be seen through to the end. If we failed to liberate our country then we would have been tremendously subjugated by the Pakistanis. They would never have treated us like human beings again. We therefore had no choice. It became a duty of every Bengali to fight for his country's liberation so that we could live independently with honour and respect'.

Like millions of other Bengali women at that time, Tinku rallied bravely behind her husband. 'The country comes first', Rashid recalls her saying 'other things are not important. We must go'. To break out of their isolation in Hajira, Rashid applied for a 10-day furlough on the excuse that his parents were ill and he had to see them. After an agony of waiting his request was granted and on 2 October, 1971, he took Tinku and their baby daughter to Dhaka. Rashid sent his wife and child to her parents in Chittagong and himself tried to cross the border into India at Agartala. Twice he was nearly caught in the cross-fire. The third time, on 29 October, he slipped through.

He re-entered East Pakistan through Sylhet at the beginning of December with a Mukhti Bahini howitzer battery attached to Ziaur Rahman's 'Z' Force. After independence this battery was raised to a regiment, the 2 Field Artillery, and Major Khandaker Abdur Rashid became its Commanding Officer.

Farook and Rashid, like the other Bengali officers and men involved in the liberation movement—the Bangladesh army itself—had high hopes for Bangladesh after its creation. They were proud of their country, extremely nationalist and the fact that they were willing to take a back seat in the first years of independence clearly shows that they had no political ambitions. Sheikh Mujibur Rahman, however, did not see it that way. His bitter experiences in Pakistani jails made him suspicious and hostile to all things military. In his anxiety not to re-create the 'monster' he had known in Pakistan he ended up doing that very thing—and it destroyed him.

Notes
1. Abu Moosa in The Sunday Times, London, 7.1.1973.
2. The Guardian, London, 9.9.1973.

V

A Summer of Tigers

There was crisis everywhere.

—Sheikh Mujibur Rahman

The summer and autumn of 1974 to many people in Bangladesh were the worst in living memory. The orgy of killing by the Pakistani army in 1971 had been traumatic; but in retrospect it was accepted as the price of independence, and in the darkest days of the freedom struggle the hope of a new life burned fiercely in the hearts of the Bengalis. Now in the third year of independence hope was extinguished.

The food supply had progressively deteriorated due to smuggling, market manipulation and corruption at all stages of the import and distribution network. Rice prices were soaring beyond the 300 Takka crisis mark. Then the floods came, engulfing 21,000 square miles or two-fifths of the total land area of the delta country during July, August and part of September. Famine and crisis stalked the land like the big jungle cats. People in the countryside began to die like flies.

Sheikh Mujibur Rahman himself publicly admitted later that 27,000 people died of starvation. In the circumstances this was a very conservative estimate. Bodies take a long time to get run down, and for every human being who ultimately falls victim to starvation, many others are killed off by diseases arising from malnutrition and low resistance. Since at least 3,000,000 people were living below the starvation line, by that reckoning the death toll as a result of the famine was well into six figures.

Indeed confirmation of this assessment came from the Prime Minister himself. Before emplaning for New York to address the General Assembly after Bangladesh had been admitted to the United Nations, Mujib ordered his ministers to open gruel kitchens in all the 4300 'unions' (i.e. groups of villages) in the country. Ultimately 5700 gruel kitchens were opened to give three to four million people a meagre life-sustaining meal each day.[1]

Millions of people in the countryside surged to the towns in search of food. Thousands of them gravitated to Dhaka, the capital, in the hope that Bangabandhu would give them something to eat. But the Prime Minister was hard-put to maintain even the weekly ration for the population which was multiplying at the rate of three million a year. It was calculated that the Bangladesh population of 75 million would double itself in 26 years.

The influx of people to the city brought new tensions to Dhaka where the government was embarrassed by the large swarms of beggars and destitutes everywhere. On 3 January, 1975, a massive cosmetic operation was launched forcing 200,000 destitutes and slum dwellers either to return to their villages or to be moved to three 'camps' that had been hastily laid out several miles from the city. The worst of these was at Demra, 14 miles from Dhaka, which the Guardian (dated 18.2.1975) described as 'Mujib's man-made disaster area'. Conditions in the camp were appalling.

More than 50,000 people were crowded into the camp which was ringed with barbed wire and guarded by the Rakhi Bahini. The authorities had provided a few latrines and water pumps. Each family was also given a 19′ × 9′ plot of land for a hut but no building materials. There were also no medical supplies, no means of income for the people and only a meagre food ration. The four-bed 'hospital' was used as a dormitory for the camp officials. An old man told visiting journalists, 'Either give us food or shoot us'. According to Grace Samson, a Dutch Salvation Army volunteer, the tragedy was 'not an act of God, but an act of government; a man-made disaster'. It is not known how many perished in these camps. But it marked another turning point, for the people now not only cursed the government but also Sheikh Mujib himself.

He had till then generally managed to escape the public odium for the mess in Bangladesh. People blamed Mujib's ministers and the officials around him, rather than him personally. This may have been for emotional reasons because many still had lingering hope that Bangabandhu would ultimately live up to public expectation. Mujib for his part did not miss any opportunity to blunt criticism by diverting it on to his ministers.

M. R. Akhtar ('Mukul'), who was close to Mujib, tells an interesting story of how on one occasion this was done. According to him, at the beginning of March, 1975, Sheikh Mujib was secretly in touch with some leaders of the opposition Jashod party who were supposed to be underground at that time. The Jashod, which rightly or wrongly had the reputation of being a pro-Indian party, wanted to refurbish its image with a big demonstration against the government, including an assault on Bangababan. According to Mukul, Mujib persuaded them to march instead on the house of the Home Minister, Mansoor Ali. A deal was done. So on 17 March after a big protest meeting at the Paltan Maidan the mob was led to Mansoor Ali's house, which it savaged. The minister, rather conveniently, had gone out of town with his family for a few days. The affair ended when the Rakhi Bahini opened fire on the mob killing eleven people. Thus according to Mukul, the Jashod's image improved without any real damage to Mujib's. Mujib had another cause for celebration that day. It was his 53rd birthday.

The violence continued to mount. Mujib himself at the end of 1974 claimed that almost 4000 Awami League party workers, including five Members of Parliament, had been killed 'under cover of darkness' by opposition groups. Brigadier Manzoor said that much of this killing was the result of intra-party squabbles. Khandaker Moshtaque Ahmed, who succeeded Mujib as President, told me that sometimes in his house in the old quarter of Dhaka the nights were made hideous by the wailing of women whose husbands and sons had been dragged away by the Rakhi Bahini on Home Minister Mansoor Ali's orders. Moshtaque claims these unfortunate people 'just vanished'.

Sheikh Mujib's reaction to the mounting crises caused by mismanagement and corruption was to launch a series of cosmetic operations. To him it was inconceivable that he had failed the people. He dismissed nine ministers blaming them for the mess. He prosecuted some minor officials and party men and in a grand gesture ordered the army to clean up the smugglers and hoarders. This last act was one of a series of colossal blunders that year which hastened his end.

Till then the soldiers, isolated in their barracks, had been only distant ob-servers of the fading Bangladesh dream. Now they were brought face to face with all the gruesome details of the terrible rot afflicting the country. They did not like it. Inevitably some of them began to think it was a patriotic duty to save Bangladesh from the waywardness of the politicians. Thus the army was drawn into politics and it destroyed Mujib.

When dramatic gestures failed to stem the rot, Mujib persuaded himself that it was not his policies that were wrong but the system of government. Apparently the parliamentary system with a Cabinet of ministers collectively responsible to the National Assembly hampered his style. He began to complain that the parliamentary system was not suited to the requirements of Bangladesh. There was a curious redundancy in Mujib's desire for more power. His towering position as Bangabandhu, and the tight grip he had on all but eight seats in the National Assembly since the elections in the previous year had reduced Parliament to the position of a rubber stamp. No one dared deny him anything; yet Mujib hungered for more power. He decided to switch to a presidential system loosely devised on the French/American pattern. He did this in an outrageous manner.

First on 28th December 1974, he proclaimed a 'State of Emergency,' suspending fundamental rights and completely stripping the courts of their power to intervene in any of his actions. Then he rammed through the Assembly a series of far-reaching amendments to the Constitution which reduced the National Parliament to an advisory status and 'legitimised' his own grip on absolute power.

In less than a month the National Assembly rubber-stamped the changes, 294 members voting in favour and none against. The captive press chorused its approval. The sycophants cheered. Sheikh Mujib described this action as the 'Second Revolution' aimed at 'emancipating the toiling people from exploitation and injustice'.[2] He was sworn in as President on 25 January, 1975. In the short span of three years the great parliamentarian had become the great dictator!

The farcical nature of the 'Second Revolution' was exposed by the composition of his new Cabinet. There were the same docile faces, operating in the old servile manner. Syed Nazrul Islam, who moved up to Vice President, was put in charge of the Ministry of Planning. Mansoor Ali, designated Prime Minister, continued in the Ministry of Home Affairs with a string of other portfolios. Khandaker Moshtaque Ahmed became Commerce Minister. The government, as a whole, continued its rapid journey downhill. Apparently all that had happened was that the Mad Hatter's dance had briefly halted for a game of musical chairs and Mujib, the puppet master, had got himself a new whip. Otherwise nothing had changed. But Mujib had irrevocably harmed himself. By concentrating all state authority in himself he had also concentrated public criticism and hostility against his own person. No longer could he pass the blame on to his ministers, officials and party men. This was a curious blunder for so astute a politician.

Towards the end of January, 1974, some young army officers were involved in an incident which would have a direct bearing on Sheikh Mujibur Rahman's assassination. The occasion was a wedding reception in the Ladies Club, Dhaka. Among the guests were Major Sharful Huq 'Dalim' and his attractive wife. She is the daughter of Mr. and Begum R. I. Chowdhury. The Chowdhurys were close friends of Sheikh Mujib and his family. Begum Chowdhury, a senior member of the Awami League, had accompanied Begum Mujibur Rahman when she came to London for medical attention in 1973. R. I. Chowdhury, who was First Secretary (Consular) in the London High Commission, had also been favoured by Mujib with more than the normal extensions of service after reaching retirement age. Thus Dalim and his wife were considered part of the 'in' set, but perhaps not so well in with Mujib as the brother of another guest at that wedding, Ghazi Gholam Mustafa. Apart from holding a very lucrative position as Chairman of the Bangladesh Red Cross, Ghazi was also the Awami League's hard hitting city boss in Dhaka. In the later capacity he was Mujib's right-hand man, very tough, powerful and free-wheeling.

According to those present that day, during the party Ghazi Gholam Mustafa's brother made some insulting remarks about Mrs. Dalim. In the altercation that followed, Ghazi's bully-boys are said to have joined in and roughed up the army couple. Some say the thugs attempted to kidnap them, but there is no confirmation of this. In any case Dalim's army colleagues decided to take immediate action. Accompanied by their troops they piled into two trucks, went hunting for the offending gang and ended up wrecking Ghazi Gholam Mustafa's bungalow.

Both parties appealed to Sheikh Mujib for redress, and he managed to temporarily soothe their ruffled tempers. Later, after another incident of 'indiscipline' was reported from Comilla cantonment, Mujib instituted a military inquiry into the young officers' misconduct. As a result 22 young officers were dismissed or prematurely retired from service. Among them were Majors Dalim, Noor and Huda. As a gesture to the family Mujib tried to make it up to Dalim by assisting him in setting up a business venture. The hurt, however, rankled. A year later the three ex-army officers would figure prominently in Mujib's assassination. Meanwhile the Dalim incident caused widespread resentment among the younger officers. They felt betrayed not only by Sheikh Mujib but also by their seniors in the army. Many of them began to carry side arms for personal protection whenever they went out with their families and they talked openly about their dissatisfaction. Military messes became centres of plotting. The intelligence services kept close tabs on all this and when their reports reached Mujib he made no secret of his intention to supplant the army with the Rakhi Bahini. The more he moved in that direction, the more he alienated the army.

But at that time the immediate threat to Mujib's life was not from the army but from a totally unexpected quarter.

It so happened that Siraj Shikdar, leader of the Maoist Sharbohara (proletarian) party and the man Mujib's son Kamal had once tried to hunt down, was finally caught by the police near Chittagong towards the end of December, 1974. According to his brother-in-law, Zackaria Chowdhury ('Zack'), Siraj Shikdar was escorted to Dhaka and taken to Gonobaban to meet Sheikh Mujib. Mujib tried to win him over. When Shikdar refused to compromise Mujib ordered the police to 'deal' with him.

Zack said Siraj was driven handcuffed and blindfolded to the police control room on the disused Dhaka racecourse and then taken out at night on a lonely road and shot. The official explanation given at that time was that Siraj Shikdar was shot dead 'while trying to escape'. His sister, Shamim, who is Zack's wife, however, maintains that the bullet wounds on Siraj's body clearly showed he had been shot from the front six times in the chest, probably with a sten gun.

Whatever the reason, it was openly talked about in Dhaka that Siraj Shikdar had been liquidated on Mujib's instructions. Shamim herself was convinced that her brother had died by Mujib's hand. So this 19-year old girl decided to take revenge. 'I got a revolver from the (Sharbohara) party and looked for an opportunity to kill this murderer' she told me. Shamim was banking on the fact that, as she was one of Bangladesh's best known sculptresses who had won the President's award for achievement the year before, she could get close enough to Mujib to shoot him.

She made several requests for an appointment with Mujib. Each time she was put off. Then she invited him to an exhibition at the Dhaka University's school of art. Mujib accepted the invitation but failed to turn up. 'I was getting desperate' she recalls. 'However much I tried I just couldn't get within shooting distance of him'. She never did. Fate intervened to save Mujib. Shamim fell in love, got married to Zack and left the country with her husband.

Bravo Squadron of the First Bengal Lancers under the command of Major Farook Rahman in July 1974 moved from its base in Dhaka to Demra, just south of the capital. The move was part of a dramatic 'Operation Clean-up' ordered by Sheikh Mujibur Rahman in a grand gesture of public appeasement. Farook's command at first extended to the whole of the Narayanganj industrial complex. Later he was moved further south to Munshiganj. He took up his new assignment in an ebullient mood. 'Ah, very good' he told his troops, 'the Prime Minister has at last found out what his chaps have been doing and since he wants the army to fix them, let's do a good job.'

Farook went about his task in characteristic no-nonsense manner. Within days he had cleared up a particularly black spot near the roundabout on the Narayanganj Road which was infested with dacoits. The leading bandit in the area was a 20-year old man professing to be an Awami Leaguer. After being arrested by Farook he freely confessed to having killed 21 people. 'I asked him why he had done it' Farook told me later, 'and the bloody fellow answered "I did it on my ustad's (chief) orders". The 'ustad' was Mujib. What the hell was I supposed to do?' The incident gravely disturbed the young officer. He was even more upset by the increasing political interference whenever action was taken against Awami Leaguers.

Elsewhere other army officers were having similar experiences in the course of their police-keeping operation. Hundreds of people were arrested by them for smuggling, hoarding and intimidation and murder. Invariably, after a telephone call from Dhaka to the local police, charges were quietly dropped against the most prominent of these men and they were allowed to go free. 'It was a damned awkward situation' Farook recalled. 'Every time we caught a chap he turned out to be either an Awami Leaguer or a very staunch Awami League supporter. They were getting protection from the top and we were getting a shelling for doing our job.'

Farook said he received a general order in writing informing him that should he arrest anyone he would be acting on his own responsibility and that his regimental commanding officer and the brigade commander would not be answerable if anything went wrong. 'None of the senior commanders would accept responsibility because the Prime Minister had said 'If you take any funny action you will be hanged for it",' Farook said. 'It meant that we were supposed to root out corruption and malpractices, but we were supposed to stop short of the Awami League. The whole thing was a damn farce.'

At the same time Farook and the officers were being told to have no mercy on the opposition, particularly Naxalites (Maoists) and other leftists who got caught in the army's net. 'I was given orders to beat them up, get information from them and then throw them in the river' Farook told me. 'Colonel Shafat Jamil (then Brigade Commander Dhaka) said they were vermin and must be destroyed'. Farook said Shafat Jamil was reflecting orders from the top. 'As far as Sheikh Mujib was concerned' he said 'the indirect orders to us were for leftists like Siraj Shikdar and Col. Ziauddin and such groups, if we catch them to kill them.' Farook refused to comply with these orders. 'I was not deeply interested in Marxists,' he said 'but what impressed me was that these chaps did care for the country. They may have gone the wrong way ideologically but they had not so far done wrong to the country.' So whenever he caught one of these men Farook quietly let him go.

One day during a combing operation in the Tongi area north of Dhaka, Major Nasser who was commanding another squadron of the Bengal Lancers, arrested three small-time thugs. In the course of interrogation one of the men broke down and told the army officers a story about a particularly gruesome triple murder which had rocked Tongi the previous winter. It transpired that a newly married couple travelling to their home in a taxi had been waylaid on the outskirts of the town. The bridegroom and the taxi driver were hacked to death and their bodies thrown in the river. The bride, who was carried off to an isolated cottage, was repeatedly raped by her abductors. Three days later her mutilated body was found on the road near a bridge.

Confessing to his part in the crime, the thug told the army men the police investigation was called off when they found that the ring-leader of the gang was his boss, Muzamil, chairman of the Tongi Awami League. According to Farook the confession so infuriated the interrogating officer, a boyish lieutenant named Ishtiaq who has since resigned and left the country, that 'he started kicking the chap so hard that he died of internal injuries.'

Muzamil himself was taken by Major Nasser to Dhaka for prosecution after he had confirmed from police records that the thug had been telling the truth. According to Farook, Muzamil offered Nasser 300,000 Takkas for his release. 'Don't make it a public affair,' the Awami Leaguer advised him. 'You will anyway have to let me go, either today or tomorrow. So why not take the money and forget about it?' Nasser, who was affronted by this blatant attempt to bribe him, swore he would bring Muzamil to trial and make him hang for his crime. He handed him over to the civil authorities. Farook said they were all astonished a few days later to find that Muzamil had been released on Sheikh Mujib's direct intervention. 'I told you to take the money,' Muzamil crowed. 'You would have been the gainers. Now I have been released anyway and you get nothing.'

The incident shattered Farook and his colleagues. Tongi marked the turning point for them. 'It seemed as if we were living in a society headed by a criminal organisation. It was as if the Mafia had taken over Bangladesh. We were totally disillusioned. Here was the head of government abetting murder and other extreme things from which he was supposed to protect us. This was not acceptable. We decided he must go.'

Major Farook wanted to kill Sheikh Mujib that very day. He recalled: 'I lost my temper. I told Capt. Sharful Hussain "Sharful Hussain. This is absolutely useless. Let's go and knock off this chap." He said "Yes Sir. But think about it a bit more." I said, "All right, I'll think about it."'

'That's all I could do, think about Sheikh Mujib and how to kill him. I had my troops with me, the solid hard core who I had myself trained in detail, how to handle weapons, how to shoot, how to ambush, to surprise. Mujib was being guarded by our troops (Lancers) at that time. I thought I should just drive the trucks in and tell the guards, Okay. Relax. Then go inside and shoot him up.'

'Then I realised that that was a very stupid thing. I was not thinking. I was working on emotion. I had not developed that far. That's why I trusted my troops so much. They knew my feelings. They did not betray me.'

Explaining his metamorphosis, Farook continued: 'Do you remember how we wept when we heard that Sheikh Mujib had returned? Remember the whole country, people mad all over! The man was almost made a god! In 1972 if he told us, "Alright you all round up the Awami Leaguers or the Brigade Commanders, tie them up and throw them in the river' we would have done it. Why? Because Sheikh Mujib had said it. What for? Nobody would have asked. I would not have asked. We felt we have got a country, we have got a leader. We were prepared to do anything. We did not mind any problem. Soldiers, men, rank, nothing mattered. It was such an extreme emotion and it was not just one person, but hundreds of thousands of people. All differences had died. That's why it turned so bitter. I say this chap (Mujib) has created the crime of the century by destroying the feeling of such a large number of people.'

Farook said the Tongi incident made him a rebel. 'After that I was just not interested in promotion, courses, career or anything. I only thought about one thing—how this government should go.'

In Bangladesh at that time there were many others with the same fixation. There was a lot of quiet plotting going on all over, including those such as Mujib's political advisers and ministers who daily fawned at his feet. Politicians used to meet with exaggerated casualness at weddings, funerals and at the mosques after 'namaz' (prayer) on Friday. They were extremely careful in their intrigue. Talk could be dangerous since sycophants among them had the habit of running off to denounce each other. And there were swarms of Mujib's intelligence men. But there was less restraint in the army. The Dalim incident followed by the retirement/dismissal of 22 young officers had not only created resentment against Mujib but had also thoroughly exposed the ineffectiveness of the senior army commanders. Thus with their careers in a mess and no one in the army to stand up to the politicians, the young officers and men could not have cared less about who heard them sounding off.

Farook recalls: 'Everyone was fed up. They were all talking about ideologies, coups, counter-coups, Marxism, communism, and the formation of cells. Everywhere there was talk about plots and counter-plots.' Mujib's intelligence services faithfully monitored everything. But the Bangabandhu, supremely confident of his ability to deal with the youngsters, dismissed it all as bravado. His main concern was how the commanders behaved—and he had tamed them.

During this period Farook missed his brother-in-law and confidant, Major Khandaker Abdur Rashid, who had gone to India earlier on a 14-month gunnery staff course at Deolali near Bombay. He began to discuss politics with his troops, carefully sounding out their own ideas and, where necessary, motivating them with his own. In Rashid's absence Farook also talked to other officers, individually and in small groups. There were several young majors, a colonel from army headquarters and an air force officer who used to get together. Farook identified them as Col. Amin Ahmed, GI-OPs in army headquarters, Major Hafiz (Brigade Major, 46 Dhaka Brigade), Major Salim of the Artillery, Major Nasir, Major Ghaffar and Sq. Leader Liaquat. They met occasionally and not all were present on every occasion. 'We used to meet by pre-arrangement at somebody's house at odd times' he said 'but I soon found these chaps had long-term thinking and I wanted to act quickly'. The secret meetings, however, were productive in that they compelled Farook to undertake a self-taught, crash course in politics. His strictly army background had left him sorely lacking in this department. 'We were thinking in national terms and suddenly I felt I had to read a lot because I found that I was blank'.

In the autumn of 1974 Farook read several dozen books, among them Che Guevera's Diaries, some writings of Chairman Mao and a thesis on the political problems of South-East Asia. He was not impressed by the Marxist patterns. 'The only conclusion I came to was that they had their own problems and had tackled them in their own way. But this was not a solution for Bangladesh. There was nothing I could find in any textbook or anywhere which fitted our situation'.

During the course of these researches Farook read about the Indonesian experiment and the overthrow of Sukarno whose political experiences bore some resemblance to Mujib's. It led him to a crucial decision.

He recalls: 'I asked myself should Sheikh Mujib be deposed like Sukarno and retired to a palace? I debated the idea for a long time. If we had the whole army or the whole population behind us things would have been different. But there were very few of us. If we took him prisoner, counter-forces would come out in his name and over-run us. I also knew he was depending strongly on India. There was always the possibility that someone would call in the Indians on behalf of Sheikh Mujib or that the Indians would object to Mujib being deposed and send in their armies to support him. Even if he were killed at that stage it would have made no difference because by then Bangladesh would have come under India. This would have defeated my whole purpose. Bangladesh would have been in a bigger soup'.

Farook continued: 'I realised that if he was killed nothing would happen in the country, at least there would be no cause for India to wave the flag and come in. In a way Sheikh Mujib signed his own death warrant because of his love affair with India. We could not put him away like Sukarno. I was convinced there was no alternative. Sheikh Mujib had to die'.

Major Rashid concurred with this assessment. 'Mujib had to die,' Rashid said, 'because he was more experienced politically and if he lived we would not have been able to control the situation. He would have brought in outside powers, even if it meant a civil war. And he would have turned the tables on us'.

In December 1974 Major Farook Rahman told his fellow plotters of a plan to kill Sheikh Mujib. It was the Prime Minister's habit to travel by one of the Bangladesh Air Force's Russian-built helicopters whenever he went any distance out of Dhaka. Not only did it save time, but for security reasons his family and personal staff thought helicopter travel an ideal arrangement. Farook proposed to knock off Mujib in the air when he was most vulnerable.

One of the plotters was Sq. Leader Liaquat who was flight control officer at Dhaka. Farook suggested that Liaquat arrange to fly Mujib the next time he went out and to take along with him an automatic pistol. At the point of the radio cross-over from Dhaka control to the next control zone, when radio contact with the ground would normally be suspended for a brief period, Liaquat was to switch off the radio, shoot Mujib and toss his body into a convenient river. He was then to proceed to his destination as though nothing had happened. Meanwhile Farook and the others would 'take necessary action on the ground'.

Farrok is an amateur pilot and he thought the plot had much to recommend itself. It would have been the easiest thing to kill Mujib when he was isolated from his bodyguards. The Prime Minister's travel plans were however unpredictable. The plot, like several other schemes discussed by the group, was never tried out.

As the days passed Farook began to get restive. The young officers were having endless discussions about ideological matters and planned to establish cells throughout the army. In practical terms, however, they were getting nowhere. Coup by conversation did not appeal to the practical armoured corps officer particularly as Sheikh Mujib was showing signs of strengthening his own position. Mujib's promulgation of the State of Emergency was yet to come.

But meanwhile Dhaka was humming with rumours about his plans to change the Constitution and instal himself as President with absolute power, presiding over a one-party state. Without telling the others, Farook quietly began to work on an elaborate operational plan of his own. It was the middle of December 1974, a few days after they had discarded the idea of hijacking Mujib's helicopter.

Farook proceeded in a military manner. First the targets were identified. Mujib, of course, was the primary target. But on the list was also every single person or unit capable of reacting against Farook at the decisive moment. Among the civilians Farook listed some of Mujib's senior ministers and Awami Leaguers. Among these were Farook's own uncle, Syed Nazrul Islam, Tajuddin Ahmed and Mansoor Ali. The major considered them dangerous because he felt they were capable of getting help from India. On the army side Farook listed Major General Shafiullah, the Chief of Staff, his deputy Major General Ziaur (Zia) Rahman and Brigadier Khalid Musharraf, the CGS who was also his own uncle and friend. Then there was the Rakhi Bahini, Mujib's storm troopers, to be taken care of.

Each of these targets had to be covered—i.e. neutralised as far as possible, eliminated if necessary. When he worked out the numbers of troops required for each task Farook found he needed a small army. 'It was more than brigade strength and I asked myself where the hell am I going to get all these troops?'

He then briefly toyed with a commando-style operation deploying 50 men for a strike on Mujib's house. Probably all 50 would have died because no blocking operation was planned and the Rakhi Bahini and other army units would have retaliated smartly. Farook discarded this plan as impractical and went back to reducing his operational plan to more manageable proportions.

At the same time he took extreme precautions against discovery. He would spend the night drawing charts, making detailed calculations, writing in target assessments and troop requirements. These he would fix in his mind. When morning came every scrap of paper would be scrupulously burnt. 'I had my wife, children, father and mother with me in the cantonment. All our lives were at stake. There was no point in taking any chances'.

Farook was similarly careful in rearranging his target list. 'Each man had to be studied carefully,' he told me. 'I used to ask myself what is his capability? Will he react or will he not react? When I found people not relevant to the problem I would cut, cut, cut.'

He made a searching study of the army commanders, particularly Brig. Khalid Musharraf, the CGS. 'I knew he was an intelligent person capable of reacting, so I decided he should be neutralised even though I had discussed things with him. Only in the final stages was I finally convinced that Khalid Musharraf would not react against me, at least, and for that matter neither would Zia or anybody else'. The assessment would prove to be amazingly accurate. After Mujib's assassination, the army commanders, like frightened sheep, fell quickly into line.

Farook finally narrowed down his list to three persons: Sheikh Mujib, his nephew Sheikh Fazlul Huq Moni, and his brother-in-law, Abdur Rab Serniabat. These were the men closest to Mujib. Moni was an extremely shrewd, capable and ruthless politician with a powerful influence in labour and student groups. He was also Editor-in-Chief of the semi-official Bangladesh Times. Serniabat was acquisitive and ambitious. Like Mujib, both hated the army and had strong vested interests in Sheikh Mujib's mantle. They were also part of Bangabandhu's family.

Major Farook decided that these three men should die.

*

At around 10 o'clock every night that winter when the social set in the fashionable Dhanmandi area of Dhaka was settling down to the enjoyment of life, a dark figure would slip out of a cycle-rickshaw on the Mymensingh Road, Dhanmandi, and after a short walk past the lake would casually turn into Road No. 32. There was nothing about the grey-checked lungi, the dark cotton bush-shirt and the well-worn chappals (slippers) to place the sauntering figure apart from the many domestic servants relaxing in the cool air after a hard day's work. The only difference was that while the others were out for a life-sustaining breather, this dark figure was the Angel of Death. Major Farook Rahman was stalking Sheikh Mujib like the Hound of Hell.

'I could not trust anyone' he told me 'I had to check Mujib over personally for a period to see exactly what were his movements, his habits, what he did, where he went. I had to firmly establish the pattern of his life. In the final moment when my troops went into action there was no question of a single slip'.

Farook's diligence in piecing together his tactical plan was immeasurably helped by the fact that the 1st Bengal Lancers, his own troops, provided the night guard at Mujib's three-storey bungalow. A grateful nation had provided the Prime Minister with a palatial residence, Gonobaban, but Mujib used it as a private office outside the secretariat while continuing to live in his own house in Dhanmandi. All this flattered his vanity as a man of the people. But it also made him more vulnerable. Mujib however, in January, 1975, did not think of this because he was riding the crest of a new wave. He had grabbed absolute power by emasculating the Constitution and the National Assembly. With his private army, the Rakhi Bahini, rapidly multiplying, he felt he had nothing to fear from the military establishment, least of all from any army major. And he had never even heard of Farook!

'No. 32' as Mujib's bungalow in Dhanmandi was known, had a triple cordon security system. The outer ring consisted of a police post with armed police placed strategically on both sides of the house. Backing them up were the army sentries who manned the gates and patrolled the inner walls of the small compound. Mujib's handpicked personal bodyguard carrying side arms and sten guns sprawled in the ground-floor corridors of the house itself.

From their vantage point inside the compound and contacts with the domestic staff, the Bengal Lancer unit knew exactly who the visitors were and what went on in the big house. Invariably Farook would slip in for a chat with his men. Ostensibly this was to check on their vigilance, but in reality he was casually pumping them for information. He would then proceed on his nightly rounds reconnoitring the area, marking obstacles and the traffic patterns of the busy Mymensingh Road. He would repeat this at the residences of Abdur Rab Serniabat and Sheikh Fazlul Huq Moni. He had no Lancer sentries outside their homes to help him so he just squatted in the shadows observing everything he could.

Ranges and depths for the back-up artillery he planned to use posed a serious problem. The only area maps available were in the Operations Room of Army headquarters. To ask for even a quick glance at them would have aroused suspicion. So Farook did it the hard way. He obtained a small city map from a guide book put out by the Bangladesh Tourist Bureau. Using it as a reference, he foot-slogged his way around the city. Distances in each area were calculated with measured strides. Then he computed the angle of fire for each target and put down precisely where his blocking teams would be located.

The tension of the surveillance and the exhausting walks soon began to affect the health of the young Major, who had once turned down a position in a prestigious infantry regiment because he hated to march. Farook started taking Valium 5 tranquillisers three times a day. But by the middle of February, he had his tactical plan complete. Only the timing had to be pencilled in. On 15 February 1975 Farook noted in his diary 'OFFENSIVE PHASE'. He was ready to launch the coup.

Just before completing the Gunnery Staff Course in India, Farook's brother-in-law Major Khandaker Abdur Rashid applied for leave to make a trip to Singapore and Malaysia where he had been invited by other officers attending the course. The application was sent to Farook with the request that he push it through army headquarters. Farook, however, had plans of his own. He withheld the application and urgently summoned Rashid back to Dhaka. 'I need you,' he told him 'there are too many things happening here'. Rashid required no further urging. He had been greatly alarmed by the reports he had been getting from his family about the deteriorating situation in Bangladesh. His instincts warned him something was afoot and he didn't want to be left out. Once the course was completed he hurried back, reaching Dhaka in the middle of March.

Farook briefed Rashid about his plans and when he concurred, the two majors got down to the serious business of overthrowing Sheikh Mujib.

'Rashid and I agreed that removing Sheikh Mujib was not enough' Farook said 'There must be positive benefit. We had to have a positive goal so that at least the slide towards the hell we were heading for could be stopped. We wanted to put on the brakes. If that was done we could have achieved something'.

First, the obvious questions was how to divide responsibility when they seized power. Answering my question, Rashid said: 'If we had gone for power then probably Farook—who is a very good soldier, even better than I am—would have been Commander-in-Chief of the army as well as the Defence Ministry with total power over the armed forces. I would have looked after the civil administration', he added.

'Who would have been the top man, the boss?', I asked.

It was an awkward question and Rashid was embarrassed. 'Well you see . . .' he said hesitatingly. 'You see . . . we did not go for power because we couldn't do justice to it . . .'

'You mean you were not qualified to run the country?' I interrupted.

Rashid: 'Not that alone, but also because we didn't have the support required for it'.

So the two majors decided to put in power someone who they thought could do for Bangladesh what Sheikh Mujib had failed to do. To this end, both of them began looking for candidates to replace Mujib.

Farook recalled: 'The first and obvious choice was General Zia because at least till then he was not tarnished. Till then he was the only one in whom I had a little bit of faith. A lot of junior officers who were thinking of what should be done to stop the rot used to say: "Let's find out from General Zia what we should do". But nobody dared to approach him'. Farook decided to have a try.

He had known the General, who was ten years his senior, since the latter had been his instructor in the Pakistan Military Academy. Zia was a popular figure in the Bangladesh army, with an impressive reputation. He had been commissioned in the 2nd Punjab in 1965 before transferring to the 1st East Bengal Regiment. Later he spent five years with military intelligence. Reverting to the Bengal Regiment in 1966, Zia did a three-month stint with the British Army on the Rhine. In 1971 he gained considerable fame as the man who announced the independence of Bangladesh over Chittagong Radio after the Pakistan army cracked down on the Bengalis. Later, his war-time service as commander of 'Z Force' added to his reputation. After the liberation of Bangladesh, promotions came rapidly; Full colonel in February, 1972, Brigadier in mid-1973, Major General in October of the same year.

'At that time I had a strong respect and affection for General Zia' Farook said. 'I hoped to interest him in taking over the leadership of the country with the backing of the army.'

After much effort Farook managed to get an interview with General Zia on 20 March, 1975. It was a Thursday and when he reported to General Zia's bungalow at 7.30 pm he found Col. Moin, the Adjutant General, about to leave.

Farook said he broached the subject of his mission very cautiously. 'I was meeting the Deputy Chief of Army Staff and a Major General. If I bluntly told him that I wanted to overthrow the President of the country straightaway like that there was a very good chance that he would have arrested me with his own guards, there and then, and put me in jail. I had to go about it in a round-about way'.

Farook continued: 'Actually we came around to it by discussing the corruption and everything that was going wrong. I said the country required a change. Zia said "Yes, Yes. Let's go outside and talk" and then he took me on the lawn.'

'As we walked on the lawn I told him that we were professional soldiers who served the country and not an individual. The army and the civil government, everybody, was going down the drain. We have to have a change. We, the junior officers, have already worked it out. We want your support and your leadership'.

According to Farook, General Zia's answer was: 'I am sorry I would not like to get involved in anything like this. If you want to do something you junior officers should do it yourself. Leave me out of it'.

Curiously the Deputy Chief-of-Staff of the Bangladesh army, when informed about the impending mutiny, did not lift a little finger to protect the legally appointed President of the country. Though General Zia did not fall in with the plot he also did not arrest Farook. Instead he quietly turned a blind eye to the plotting while taking steps to secure himself. According to Farook Zia instructed his ADC that the major should on no account be allowed to see him again.

In July, 1976, while doing a TV programme in London on the killing of Sheikh Mujib I confronted Zia with what Farook had said. Zia did not deny it—nor did he confirm it. Instead he put off giving me an answer and when I persisted did his best to keep me out of the country for many years.

At the end of March 1975 Farook decided to make his move. There was no special reason for the timing; only a sudden end to patience brought on by his failure to recruit General Zia for the coup. 'I was getting frustrated and fed up with the waiting' Farook said, 'so I decided to get on with it'. Impulsively he abandoned his meticulous planning and went to see Sq. Leader Liaquat. 'What about taking off in some MiGs and doing a bit of strafing on his house,' Farook asked him. 'I'll surround the house and you can control the whole thing with your aircraft.' Liaquat's answer was an equally casual 'Let's go'. Farook then quickly outlined the operation scheduled for dawn next day the 30 March, and went off to brief the others. It was typical of Farook that he should assume they would fall in with his bravado. But he was due for a surprise. 'I got the greatest disillusionment of my life' he said. 'People like (Major) Hafiz, Colonel Amin and Ahmed Chowdhury and the others all backed out. All these chaps had been talking big, spending nights talking like hell about doing this and that, but when it came to doing it nobody was willing to come forward'.

Everything went black for Farook. The sleepless nights, the foot-slogging, the months of surveillance, all seemed to have been wasted. The great coup had failed to get off the ground because of an unsuspected human factor: when faced with the reality of killing Mujib the other plotters got cold feet!

Sheikh Mujib, however, would not escape heart-rending grief on the day set for the aborted plot. It was the day his father died.

The collapse of the plot only confirmed Major Farook Rahman's determination to kill Sheikh Mujib. Henceforth he would go it alone. But first he took pains to draw suspicion away from himself. 'I told everybody to forget it. I withdrew completely from all discussions so that they would think that I had cooled down. I believe in tactical surprise. The idea was to let the others believe that I had gone to sleep'. Farook did this by acting the part of a carefree army officer. He took Farida to parties, picnics and every possible social occasion. Bangladesh was in turmoil, but for the moment they were the happy couple without a care in the world. It all ended with the big bash on 12 August 1975. The wedding anniversary party was intended to disarm suspicion at the crucial moment. Meanwhile Farook continued to secretly weave his web around Mujib.

He estimated he required about 800 men for his tactical plan which would have allowed him to block the Rakhi Bahini and other army units and thus avoid unnecessary fighting. But with modifications a minimum of 300 men would be sufficient for a limited purpose. These were readily available from his own troops. The 1st Bengal Lancers had been raised by him in 1972. Later as second-in-command he had selected certain of the men for private specialised commando-style training in addition to their normal duties in the Armoured Corps. These he called his 'Hunter-Killer Teams'. They were all trustworthy, stable and quiet types—'not loud talkers'—and intensely loyal to him. Divided into groups of three, they had been motivated with Koranic injunctions about honesty, integrity, discipline, the love of Islam and their obligations to their fellow men. Farook had 150 Hunter-Killer teams at his disposal and he was certain he could depend on them at all times.

Farook tentatively decided that his next strike should coincide with the summer monsoons when torrential rains make the delta country a quagmire. His reasoning, again, was the fear that Mujib's death might provoke India to intervene in support of pro-Mujib elements. 'If India does anything and we are forced into a civil war then the monsoon is the one season they will be badly tied down' he said. 'If everything fails, at least we will have the protection of the monsoon'.

Meanwhile Rashid was bravely facing up to an embarrassing personal problem. Having completed the Gunnery Staff Course in India, he had automatically been posted to the Gunnery School at Jessore, near the western border with India. It was miles away from the projected action in Dhaka. Even worse, it deprived him of the command of troops. All this tended to make him a passenger in the plot. So Rashid was burning up his one month 'holiday' in Dhaka trying to drum up support for the plot within the army.

He joined in the political discussions going on in the cantonment. But he always played it safe. 'I didn't commit myself' he said. 'Rather I used to make them commit themselves so that if anything went wrong it could be said that they had approached me, not that I had approached them'.

On one occasion he cautiously broached the subject with the Dhaka Brigade Commander, Col. Shafat Jamil. He recalled that after they had traded words about how bad things were in Bangladesh, Shafat Jamil asked him: 'Ha, Ki, korun?' (What shall we do?). Rashid promptly backed out. 'No sir' he told the colonel. 'I won't do anything unless you order me. After all you are my brigade commander'. Rashid was quite shaken by the experience. He warned Farook not to trust anyone because he feared the other officers were playing a double game and would put them in trouble.

The meeting with Shafat Jamil did, however, have a very fortunate and totally unexpected result. During their conversation, Rashid said, Shafat Jamil had suggested that instead of going to the Gunnery School at Jessore, why not request a transfer to Dhaka 'so that we can keep in touch more conveniently'. This was, to say the least, a curious suggestion and raises question marks about the Dhaka Brigade Commander's intention. It staggered Rashid. A posting to Dhaka was then beyond his wildest dreams. He immediately suspected Shafat Jamil was trying to trap him. So rather cunningly Rashid told him that any transfer request he himself made may not go down well with army headquarters. Why not the brigade commander wangle it for him? Rashid did not expect anything to come of it. But the Brigade Commander *did* oblige. Once again, in April, 1975, Major Rashid found himself commanding 2 Field Artillery very conveniently based at Dhaka.

Farook was delighted with the turn of events. The brothers-in-law could now go ahead with their plot without depending on the assistance of other officers. The 2 Field Artillery had 6 Italian Howitzers, 12 Yugoslav 105mm Howitzers and 600 troops. Farook's Lancers had 30 T-54 tanks and 800 troops. With the backing of Rashid's artillery and troops Farook was confident that the Bengal Lancers could take on the Rakhi Bahini and any infantry units that might try to go to Sheikh Mujib's assistance. The problem was how to get them together without arousing suspicion. Here Rashid came up with the answer.

According to instructions from army headquarters, the Bengal Lancers twice a month went on night training exercises. The intention was to familiarise the troops with sorting their equipment in the dark. Accordingly the tanks used to be started up and the crews put through mock firing drill while the whole area was disturbed by the noise. After six months of night training exercises the roar of the tank engines and the clatter of tracks as they moved around their base had become a regular feature of cantonment life. So the movement of the Bengal Lancers at least would not arouse suspicion. Major Rashid now proposed to his superiors that the tank regiment's night training exercises would be more meaningful if they coordinated with his artillery unit. Both units would then learn to work together as they would be expected to do in battle. Rashid's proposal made sense and was accepted with alacrity by army headquarters. Thus to Farook's delight the tanks and the field guns were brought together.

About this time Farook decided to seek celestial sanction for his terrible purpose. He sought out in the crowded Hali Shaar quarter of Chittagong a Bihari holy man who would have a powerful influence on the killing of Sheikh Mujibur Rahman.

Andha Hafiz (blind holy man) as he is known, was born without sight. His piety and austere life, however, had brought him the blessing of a phenomenal extrasensory perception and the gift of prophesy. The accuracy of his predictions had won him a sizeable following, among them the Khans of Chittagong who were Major Farook's in-laws. Farook decided to consult him—and found an early opportunity to do so. The Bengal Lancers were scheduled to go to Hat Hazari near Chittagong for range firing between 7th and 11th April. When this exercise was put back by two days, Farook took time off for a quick trip to Chittagong on 2nd April to see Andha Hafiz.

Squatting on the floor of the hut Farook placed his hands in the hands of the holy man. Andha Hafiz held them gently for a long time. Clearly he was disturbed by the vibrations he was getting. Before Farook could confide the dark secret he carried, Andha Hafiz told him: 'I know you are going to do something very dangerous. Do whatever you have to do, but if you do not follow the principles I give you, you will be destroyed'. He then told Farook he must faithfully observe three things: '(1) Don't do anything for personal gain but only to serve the cause of Allah and Islam. (2) Have courage; and (3) Select the correct timing.' He also advised the major 'Wait three months. After that chances of success are good though there will be difficulties'.

Farook was deeply moved. Even the heavens were pointing to the direction in which he was moving. The three months Andha Hafiz told him to wait also coincided with his own evaluation of the best time for the coup. In his heart he knew that this time he would not fail.

On 7 June Sheikh Mujibur Rahman achieved what to him was the crowning glory of his administration—the formation of the Bangladesh Krishak Sramik Awami League (BKSAL pronounced Bakshal). It formally made Bangladesh a one-party state in which all political and administrative authority was personally vested in Mujib, the President. In no way was he now more powerful than when he started off as Prime Minister in January 1972, when his word was law and every wish a command to his adoring people. But as public affection waned during the 3½ years of prodigality, the declining demi-god found it necessary to assume increasingly more dictatorial powers. Now through the BKSAL Mujib sought to legalise his grip on the supreme power that public affection had ceased to offer.

With characteristic bombast Mujib described the change as 'The Second Revolution'. In fact it was nothing more than a palace coup which removed the last vestiges of democracy, justice and hope from a country whose founding was intended to epitomise these virtues.

Mujib had started the process in January of that year by ramming through the National Assembly the 4th Amendment to the Constitution. Apart from emasculating Parliament and conferring ill-concealed dictatorial powers on the President the Amendment authorised Mujib to create a one-party state. It also specified that 'when the National Party is formed a person shall:

(a) In case he is a member of Parliament on the date the National Party is formed, cease to be such member, and his seat in Parliament shall become vacant if he does not become a member of the National Party within the time fixed by the President

(b) Not be qualified for election as President or as a member of Parliament if he is not nominated as a candidate for such election by the National Party.

(c) Have no right of form, or to be a member or otherwise take part in the activities of any political party other than the National Party.'[3]

Thus Mujib's catch-all legislation completely shut out all opposition. No one could engage in any form of politics without being a member of BKSAL;

57

and BKSAL membership, according to the Party's constitution, could only be obtained with the consent of the Chairman, Sheikh Mujib. Only BKSAL, i.e. Mujib, would decide who would be candidates for election and voters would make their choice from among those empanelled by him. ('I shall nominate one, two or three persons for contesting a seat in Parliament. People will choose who is good or bad'). Nothing like this had been attempted during the worst days of West Pakistani repression.

The BKSAL system which was to have come into force on 1st September 1975 would have enabled Mujib to get his fingers deep into the soil of Bangladesh. It was an elaborate structure of tightly-controlled parallel pyramids embracing political affairs and administration. Sheikh Mujib, as President and Party Chairman, straddled both. On the political side the top tier was a 15-member Executive Committee of his closest colleagues. Among them was Syed Nazrul Islam, the Vice President; Prime Minister Mansoor Ali who was also Secretary General of the party; Khandaker Moshtaque Ahmed (ranking third in the party hierarchy after Mujib) and the leader's own nephew, Sheikh Fazlul Huq Moni who was designated one of the three influential party secretaries.

The next tier was a Central Committee of 115 members followed by five Committees of between 21 to 32 members dealing with labour, peasants, youth, students and women. Mujib's son Kamal was in the students committee.

Every member of each of these committees was nominated by Mujib. So also were the 61 powerful District Governors who formed the backbone of the administrative pyramid. According to Mujib they were 'to look after law and order, development works, ensure proper distribution of goods coming from abroad, allocate money for works programmes, formulate family planning schemes, do publicity and oversee production'. They would 'see whether the harvesting of paddy has been made or not, whether interest is taken by mothers and you are to stop corruption in the thanas'.[4]

The District Governors would also control the Bangladesh Rifles (the para military border security force), the Rakhi Bahini, police and army units stationed in their areas. They were to be the President's hands, feet and mouth and were expected to work closely with the 61 BKSAL District Secretaries who would be the Party Chairman's eyes and ears. These too would be nominated by him. In every case Sheikh Mujib's criterion for selecting people for these posts was, as he publicly admitted, 'because they are good to my eyes'.

Mujib gave a variety of reasons for creating this tight chain of command going down to each of the 65,000 villages in the country. When the 4th Amendment was passed by the National Assembly he said the one-party system was intended to implement the four State Principles—nationalism, democracy, socialist and secularism. Later, at a public meeting in Dhaka on 26 March, Mujib spoke about 'four plans' being the basis of BKSAL. 'Number one plan is to eliminate corrupt people. Number two is to increase production in fields and factories. Number three is population planning and number four is our national unity.' Then again on 21 July, while addressing the 61 District Governors designate in Dhaka Mujib said 'The change was necessary to bring about the welfare of the people, to remove oppression, injustices and suppression, so that easily and simply the constitutional structure can reach the people directly'.

Mujib's many reasons for BKSAL are not contradictory, and it could be argued that they were the facets of a radical reform of national life. But was reform what he really intended? If indeed that was his purpose then he had a curious way of going about it. In the first place he never lacked authority. Even as Prime Minister in a Westminster-style government his towering position as Bangabandhu would have allowed him to enforce any reform he desired. Had Mujib wanted he could have sent the whole Cabinet, Parliament and Civil Service packing and replaced them with persons of his choice.

Secondly, the personnel appointed to flesh out BKSAL were the same grasping Awami Leaguers and civil servants whose incompetence and corruption had helped to bring Bangladesh to the brink of collapse. There was nothing to indicate that they had changed their ways. Thirdly, Mujib himself had not changed his style. He still confused platitudes with policies as though they were enough to conjure away the crises. And when all is said and done, Mujib's talk about removing 'oppression, injustices and repression' begs the question: Whose? Since the State's founding the people had known no other government than Sheikh Mujib's. It could therefore be correctly assumed that he was responsible for all the terror and the rot which he now professed to reform by the 'Second Revolution'.

All this makes clear that BKSAL was another one of Mujib's political games and reform was not the objective. BKSAL was intended to shut out all opposition and give him a stranglehold on the country. He would have achieved this ambition on the 1st September 1975 had he lived.

Tragically this total extinction of democracy and the perpetration of one-man rule brought no significant public protest. As before, the press and politicians acclaimed the move; even the venerable old revolutionary, Maulana Bashani, who had from time to time come out against him, announced 'total support' for Mujib's 'Second Revolution' in a statement issued from his home in Kagmari Village, Tangail, on 8th March.[5]

Once it was made clear that exclusion from the new system meant virtual extinction, everyone started climbing on the bandwaggon. More than 500 journalists in Dhaka went in procession to Sheikh Mujib's house requesting membership of BKSAL. At the same time the editors of nine leading Dhaka newspapers similarly petitioned Mujib in the most sycophantic terms. Stating that 'after the war of liberation you have given a call to the nation to unitedly respond to the Second Revolution for the economic emancipation of the masses', the editors said they would 'feel glorified if they got the opportunity to work as BKSAL members under the leadership of Bangabandhu'[6] Mujib had reason to be pleased.

Rather curiously, in the midst of all this sycophany, the one sobering thought about the new system was expressed by no other than Sheikh Mujib himself. Addressing the District Governors designate in Dhaka on 21 July, he instinctively warned them: 'The cause for alarm by the (BKSAL) members nowadays is that the people of Bangladesh reacts much and you will be smashed. It is good to remember this. You will make devoted efforts throughout (your) whole life but you do one wrong, you will perish from Bangladesh. This is the rule of Bangladesh'.

Unfortunately Sheikh Mujib did not heed his own warning. By that time his mistakes were beyond recall.

Notes
1. High Commissioner Sultan at Commonwealth Parliamentary Association meeting in London, 19.11.74.
2. Bangladesh Today, 1.2.1975.
3. ibid., 15.2.1975.
4. ibid.
5. ibid., 1.4.1975.
6. ibid., 15.6.1975.

VI

Moshtaque is Willing

I asked (Moshtaque), Will there be any jus-
tification at this stage if somebody takes a deci-
sion to remove Sheikh by force? He said: 'Well,
probably for the country's interest it is a good
thing'.

—Major Rashid

In Farook's pocket diary, noted against the 3rd July, 1975 in large red letters, are the words START WORK. 'By that time', he told me, 'I had fixed Mujib was going to die. It didn't matter whether it was today, tomorrow or the day after. My tactical plan was ready. I had my troops'.

He continued: 'From that point, as the Americans say, all systems were Go. Whether I go myself, alone, or whatever happens, I was finally committed on 3rd July. I had completely written off everything about myself. Khalas.* The past, the present, for me everything was dead. Suddenly I had crystallised in my mind that I would not wait longer than the 15th of August.'

Farook's diary told him that the next convenient training night exercise for the Bengal Lancers and 2nd Field Artillery was in the early hours of 15th August, a Friday. The day had a resounding significance for him, for Farook was Friday's child. All the great events of his life had occurred on Fridays. He was born on a Friday ('at the time of Azan'—the Muslim call to prayer). He defected from the Pakistan army on a Friday. He was married on Friday. The day also had great religious significance because Friday is the Muslim sabbath. Farook thought Friday would be a propitious day for the act he intended as a service to Islam.

He didn't tell Rashid about the date he had fixed for the coup because he wanted to ensure there was no last minute slip. But in the course of their discussions they mutually agreed that the strike should be well before 1st September when the BKSAL system was due to become operative. Before that date the District Governors accompanied by units of the Rakhi Bahini and the army would have taken up positions in the 61 districts. 'In that case,' Rashid said, 'the situation would have become very difficult to control because instead of being centralised in Dhaka you will have 61 different places where your enemy is spread'.

Rashid was not involved in Farook's tactical planning. The latter had a distaste for politics and after General Zia had turned him down he gave Rashid the responsibility of finding a suitable replacement for Sheikh Mujib from among the available politicians. In this department the artillery major showed an unsuspected talent for politics.

Rashid was well aware that Mujib's killing could unleash a spontaneous storm of violent opposition which they would not be able to contain with the meagre forces available to them. He therefore saw Mujib's successor not only in terms of a fairly untarnished and competent political leader, but also one

* Urdu for finished.

whose presence would go a long way to containing any adverse reaction to the killing.

Explaining his reasoning, Rashid said he had to eliminate four potential sources of trouble. The first was the Awami League, the monolithic party spread throughout the country which had substantial numbers of armed cadres among the youth and students. The second was the Rakhi Bahini, Mujib's 25,000 well-armed storm troopers who were personally loyal to him. These groups would either react strongly—in which case it would be the end of the majors—or they would seek temporary asylum in India as they did in 1971, before returning with the assistance of Indian troops to rout Bangabandhu's killers. The third consideration, according to Rashid, was the possibility that once Mujib was killed the vengeful people might turn on the Awami Leaguers and kill them. This again could create an impossible law and order problem while at the same time provoking a flood of refugees to India with the attendant dangers of Indian intervention.

'We did not want to create a refugee problem' Rashid said, 'because it would have created another situation like that in 1971 and India would have come in. That would have been totally self-defeating.' So the fourth consideration, Rashid said, was to cut out any possible reason for Indian intervention.

'I wanted someone who would immediately make everyone sit back quietly and tell themselves, "Let's see what happens"' Rashid said. 'Once people decided to wait and see developments we would be safe'.

These considerations automatically excluded anyone from the Opposition because it would have stampeded the Awami League and Rakhi Bahini. Rashid decided he must look for Mujib's replacement from among suitable members of the Awami League's hierarchy. 'Such a person would reassure pro-Mujib groups and the Rakhi Bahini' he said. 'The public seeing another Awami Leaguer in charge would not dare to take revenge. There would be no refugees and India would have no reason to intervene.'

The coldly calculated stratagem to bring in the hated Awami League was not such a difficult decision for Rashid to swallow. He had privately decided that it would only be a temporary measure. 'We knew what they were, these men of the Sheikh Mujib group' he told me. 'We knew they will do all sorts of hypocrisy, bungling and other things. They can never get rid of it. But meanwhile if we can consolidate and get the army and the air force combined under the proper leadership structure then we can sort them out at any time'. For his part Farook had made it perfectly clear to Rashid 'If after removing Sheikh Mujib there is no positive benefit I will not tolerate anyone else'.

Despite the bold words, the two majors were showing themselves to be incredibly naive in the matter of choosing the man to succeed Sheikh Mujibur Rahman. The criteria that Rashid was working to were essentially security considerations, not the winning combination for a much-vaunted change. The most important requirements for the latter—statesmanship, integrity, a man who could deliver the goods where Sheikh Mujib could not—did not figure at all on Rashid's list. It was unbelievably arrogant for him, or still worse, unforgivably puerile, to assume that Khandaker Moshtaque, the man eventually chosen, would be merely a puppet who would allow himself to be used and discarded at their convenience. It was well known that Moshtaque was a 'survivor', the leading alumnus of the rough-and-tumble school of Pakistan/Awami League politics. With any intelligence Rashid should have realised, at least at their first meeting, that here was an old fox who could eat them for breakfast, which he did.

*

61

Thus in the spring of 1975—a season for flowers in Bangladesh which, lamentably, has also become a season of woe—Farook and Rashid were plotting what in effect would become an assassination, not a coup; it would be a savage blood-letting that made a mockery of their pretentions to perform cleansing, health-restoring surgery. Because they had neither the wit nor the maturity to tell the difference, the majors besmirched the proud name of the army they professed to love and set in train dark forces that have been more destructive to the dream of Sonar Bangla than Sheikh Mujib ever was.

But at that time they were too absorbed in their narrow purpose to look for its wider implications. Rashid, for one, received a nasty shock from a totally unexpected quarter.

Farook's sister dropped in to say that Dhaka University was buzzing with rumours of an imminent army coup and Rashid was being named as one of the ringleaders. He instantly realised that the plotting and exchange of revolutionary ideas by the young officers had somehow been leaked by loose talk. And if the rumours had reached the university, which was a sensitive listening post, then surely they must also have got to Sheikh Mujib whose intelligence services monitored everything.

Rashid was all the more alarmed the next day when he was summoned to the office of the Dhaka Brigade Commander, Col. Shafat Jamil, the man with whom he had discussed the political situation earlier. Col. Shafat Jamil told him that there was too much talk about a coup going on and as his name was being mentioned, something may have to be done about him.

In desperation Rashid decided to take the bull by the horns.

He recalls: 'I told Shafat Jamil if anything is done to me then I will involve you as the ringleader. I will say that whatever I have done was done under your instructions. I have proof. I will say how you arranged for me to be posted to 2nd Field Artillery to be with you in Dhaka after cancelling my transfer to the Gunnery School in Jessore'.

Rashid said Col. Shafat Jamil got the message. There was no further talk about action against him. But Rashid could see the danger signs. At any time there could be a knock on the door. Like Farook, he too, by then, had become totally committed to Mujib's assassination, if only for reasons of self-preservation. He told me, 'There was no turning back now. It was either him or us'. A few days later, before the end of July, Rashid sought an interview with Khandaker Moshtaque Ahmed, the Commerce Minister and the third ranking member of BKSAL after Chairman Mujib.

Khandaker Moshtaque was the least controversial of the Awami League ministers and generally considered to be the leader of the party's right wing—his Islamic leanings no doubt fostered by the fact that his father, Marhum Alhaj Hazrat Khandkar Kabiruddin Ahmed, known as 'Pir Sahib', was considered to be a Muslim saint in his time. Moshtaque was a year older than Sheikh Mujib. The two had been close comrades in the long struggle for Bengali emancipation during which he had been detained six times for a total of seven years in Pakistani prisons. In the process Moshtaque had also acquired a law degree from Dhaka University and built up a considerable reputation as an advocate in Dhaka High Court and the Supreme Court of Pakistan.

In 1971 during the freedom struggle, Moshtaque was Vice President of the Awami League. When he fled to India with his colleagues he was appointed Foreign Minister in the Mujibnagar government-in-exile based at Calcutta, headed by Tajuddin Ahmed. His right-wing views earned him a pro-American label. He did live up to that reputation when Henry Kissinger in the autumn of 1971 singled out Moshtaque in an abortive attempt to split the Awami

League and prevent the break-up of Pakistan. Because of this Moshtaque was abruptly sacked from his job as Foreign Minister when the Mujibnagar government moved to Dhaka after the formal creation of Bangladesh.

Khandaker Moshtaque served as Minister for Flood Control, Water Resources and Power in Sheikh Mujib's first Cabinet. In 1975 when Mujib switched to the presidential system of government Moshtaque became Minister for Commerce and Foreign Trade.

Moshtaque's political ability is underscored by his penchant for survival. Though always very servile and falling easily into line behind Mujib—even in the notorious BKSAL one-party system introduced just before Mujib was assassinated—Moshtaque did not share in the public odium which attended the other ministers. Nor was he ever accused of the blatant corruption that most of his Cabinet colleagues were. As such Khandaker Moshtaque Ahmed nicely measured up to Major Khandaker Abdur Rashid's ideas for a replacement for Sheikh Mujibur Rahman.

Rashid insists they are not related, though they come from the same general area of Daudkhandi in Comilla district. He also said they never had occasion to meet before then. But he was well aware of Moshtaque's reputation since they come from adjoining villages—Moshtaque from Dosphara, Rashid from Chandina. Rashid's uncle, Musharaf Hussain ('Mushu') had also befriended Moshtaque while he was escaping to India in 1971 and they had been close friends since then. Rashid asked 'Mushu' to arrange an appointment for him with Khandaker Moshtaque Ahmed in Dhaka. This was easily done.

Dressed in civvies to avoid attention Rashid accordingly turned up at Moshtaque's house in Aga Masih Lane in the old quarter of Dhaka at 7 pm on 2nd of August. He took the precaution of carrying with him an application for a permit to buy a scooter just in case he was noticed and someone wanted to know why an army officer was calling on a politician. Rashid was welcomed by Moshtaque in an upstairs room, and after the normal courtesies, Rashid steered the conversation to the political situation. They spoke for almost two hours.

Rashid recalls: 'We discussed political matters for some time as I was indirectly finding out how he felt. Then I asked him, being closest to Sheikh Mujib and one of the seniormost Awami League members, how did he feel? I asked him, "Can the nation expect progress under the leadership of Sheikh Mujibur Rahman?" He said, "No, they cannot". Then I said "If that is the case why don't you leave?" He said "That is also not so easy". It showed that they (the ministers) are quite afraid of taking such a decision though they know what he is doing. They are such cowards that they have accepted all his bad doings'.

Rashid continued: 'Then I asked, "Will there be any justification at this stage if somebody takes a decision to remove Sheikh by force?" He said, "Well, probably for the country's interest it is a good thing. But it is also very difficult to do it".'

I asked Rashid to squeeze his mind and confirm if that was exactly what Moshtaque said.

He answered: 'Yes. He said it was very difficult to do, but in the country's interest if somebody could do it probably it would be a great thing'.

Question: 'So he agreed?'

Rashid: 'Yes. Yes, he agreed. Then Moshtaque even asked me that if somebody removed him (Sheikh Mujib) who could be next? The alternative should be there'.

Rashid said his own reply was non-committal. He explained to Khandaker

Moshtaque that if anyone did think in terms of removing Sheikh Mujib he would also definitely think of a suitable replacement, particularly 'someone who could balance out the political side'.

Asked if Khandaker Moshtaque had got the message that he wanted Moshtaque as a replacement for Mujib, Rashid replied: 'He probably thought that as I went there to see him I would have chosen him as such. It's quite understandable'.

Rashid was satisfied that in Khandaker Moshtaque Ahmed he had found a willing replacement for Sheikh Mujib. He conveyed his impression to Farook who made no comment beyond, 'I hope you are right. That's your problem'. But in his own taciturn way Farook was happy that things were shaping up exactly as he wanted.

The revelations made by Rashid and Farook concerning Khandaker Moshtaque's prior knowledge of their plans to kill Sheikh Mujibur Rahman were made under oath in a series of separate tape-recorded interviews I had with them.

Moshtaque denies he was consulted. But I have no reason to disbelieve the two majors.

They make it clear that Moshtaque was brought into the plot to kill Mujib on 2nd August 1975, i.e. 13 days before the assassination. He thus had ample time to consult his cronies, particularly Tahiruddin Thakur, and to work out how they should proceed once the dire deed was done. Indeed, there are indications that that is what happened—and then someone in the group leaked the majors' plot to a contact in the American Embassy in Dhaka.

Farook has noted that he was surprised to find several American Embassy cars 'buzzing round the city' at the hour when his men were carrying out the killings. Then, Tahiruddin Thakur was at the Dhaka Radio station *before* Khandaker Moshtaque was taken there by Rashid. Moshtaque's speech—written by Thakur—was evidently thought out in advance. Thakur, in a post facto interview with a Western correspondent, also claimed that the assassination plot was 'finalised' in his house two nights before the event. Farook and Rashid swear they were NOT present on that occasion, and that they did not have any contact with Thakur before Mujib's killing; and at the time of the interview they were prepared to confront Thakur about his claim. So, if the former Information Minister is telling the truth, the meeting in his house on 13th August was obviously a private gathering of Moshtaque's men to 'finalise' their response to what the two majors had planned to do. This would confirm that Moshtaque had prior knowledge that Mujib was to be killed.

All this, of course, does not obviate the possibility that Moshtaque and Co. were plotting separately to overthrow Sheikh Mujib—as were many others at that time. The Maoist Sharbohara Party and another left-wing group, the JSD (Jatyo Samajtantrik Dal or Nationalist Socialist Party), it transpired, also had well-developed 'revolutionary' plans which were rudely overtaken by the majors' action.

A senior Bangladeshi intelligence officer told me that at the beginning of August 1975, his department had been investigating at least five concurrent 'possible plots' against Sheikh Mujib in addition to 'serious rumbling among young officers in the army'. One concerned a Bangladeshi politician who, on the pretext of buying Indian saris for his wife, had flown on a day-trip to Calcutta. He never left the Dum Dum airport and during that time had been observed having a lengthy meeting with a Western diplomat. Another was a report by Sheikh Moni who thought there was something sinister in the fact that a prominent politician had given a private dinner 'for some disgruntled elements and at least three senior military men of the rank of General and Brigadier'.

Lawrence Lifschultz, the author of 'Bangladesh, the Unfinished Revolution' told an interesting story of the plotting in the Guardian (of London) on 15th August 1979, the fourth anniversary of Sheikh Mujibur Rahman's assassination. He said:

'Knowledgeable Bengali and foreign diplomatic sources now claim that Moshtaque and his political friends had been involved more than a year in plans designed to bring about the overthrow of Mujib. According to senior US officials at the American Embassy in Dhaka and from well-informed Bengali sources, it appears that the United States had prior knowledge of the coup which killed Mujib, and that American Embassy personnel had held discussions with individuals involved in the plot for more than six months prior to his death.

'According to one highly placed US Embassy diplomat, officials at the American Embassy were approached by people intending to overthrow the government of Sheikh Mujibur Rahman. This Embassy source says that a series of meetings took place with the Embassy personnel between November 1974 and January 1975. These discussions were held with the purpose of determining the attitude of the US Government towards a political change in Bangladesh if a coup d'etat were actually to happen'.

Unfortunately Lifschultz does not—or cannot—identify the Bangladeshis who approached the American Embassy. The suggestion in the article is that it was some civilians, not the two majors. And I have it on oath from both Farook and Rashid that they did NOT make contact with any foreign Mission or, for that matter, any foreigner. But Lifschultz does say that a senior US official told him in January, 1975, as a matter of prudence 'we came to an understanding in the Embassy that we would stay out of it and disengage from those people'. Lifschultz continues:

'Although a decision was made at a high level in the embassy that there would be no further contact with the anti-Mujib group, what happened subsequently is a matter of controversy among US officials interviewed. Those who knew of the earlier meetings deny any personal knowledge of what happened after early 1975. Others allege that while contact was broken off at a level of diplomatic and foreign service officials, who wished to remain 'clean', liaison was taken over and carried on through the channel of the American Embassy's CIA station chief, Philip Cherry, and other station agents. When interviewed, Cherry categorically denied this allegation. "The Bangladeshis were doing it themselves" said Cherry. "It's a great canard to think any coup takes place because of a (outside) government involvement. Almost always coups take place because of the people themselves". When asked about the Moshtaque network's previous history of confidential contacts with the United States, Cherry stated: "There are politicians who frequently approach embassies and perhaps have contacts there. They think they may have contacts. But that's a far cry from any of those embassies involved in assisting them in or involvement in a coup".'

Lifschultz goes on to say that in April, 1975, 'Moshtaque and his political circle were in the process of discreetly checking military contacts whom they could adopt and integrate into their own strategy' and that they favoured 'a senior officers' coup d'etat.' He added:

'According to Bangladesh military sources with intimate knowledge of the events, approaches were made to the deputy chief of army staff, Major-General Ziaur Rahman (Zia) . . . and according to these sources, General Zia expressed interest in the proposed coup plan, but expressed reluctance to take the lead in the required military action'.

Lifschultz concluded that 'having failed to secure reliable leadership for the coup from the senior officer cadre, the Moshtaque group went forward with the junior officers' plot'.

Rashid is normally very slow to act. But once he had been jolted by Farook's determination to launch the coup on the following Friday he quickly began tying together his end of the arrangements.

At 2.30 pm on 13th August he called again at Aga Masih Lane for another meeting with Khandaker Moshtaque. This was done without appointment, and they spent about ten minutes together. According to Rashid the sole purpose of his visit was to find out whether Khandaker Moshtaque had any travel plans for the next few days.

Rashid recalled: 'I asked him if he is likely to go outside the country in the immediate future. He told me he will not be going anywhere. He will be in Dhaka.'

Question: 'He didn't ask you why?'

Rashid (laughing): 'No. After all he is a very clever man and he would have known . . .'

Like Barkis, Moshtaque is willing!

Having been assured that Khandaker Moshtaque would be available on the day, Rashid began to look around for officers who could assist in the strike. The failure of the earlier moves had shown they could not depend on serving army officers so Rashid craftily hit upon the idea of recruiting ex-army officers who had a grudge against Sheikh Mujib. Such men could be counted on to fall in with the plot. The man who really came to mind was ex-Major Sharful Huq, nicknamed 'Dalim', who had been prematurely retired following the incident involving Ghazi Gholam Mustafa, Mujib's city boss, at a wedding party eighteen months earlier. Rashid knew Dalim well since he had also been an artillery officer. He telephoned to invite Dalim for a chat.

Dalim arrived at Rashid's house in the cantonment around 10 pm (13th August). Rashid briefed him in general terms about the plot without giving details of the timing or the tactical plan and asked if he would like to join them. According to Rashid, Dalim was willing but at the same time wanted to talk it over with a friend. This was ex-Major Noor who had once been ADC to General Usmani the Defence Minister, and had subsequently been retired prematurely with Dalim and some other officers in the summer of 1974.

Dalim brought Noor to Rashid's house at 1 am (14th August) that night and they had a long discussion about the plot during which Rashid stressed that for an initial period it would be necessary for Khandaker Moshtaque Ahmed to replace Sheikh Mujib. Noor apparently was willing to join but was not convinced that Rashid had got Khandaker Moshtaque Ahmed to fall in with the plot to kill Sheikh Mujib. To reassure him, Rashid suggested that they met at 5 pm that day (August 14th) outside the Atomic Research Centre. He would take them to Khandaker Moshtaque's house to prove how friendly he was with him.

When Rashid turned up at the rendezvous, he was surprised to find Noor with another retired officer, ex-Major Shariar who he had not met before. Rashid began to have misgivings about his companions but decided that by that time he had no way out. So when Noor assured him that Shariar could be trusted, the three of them went off to Khandaker Moshtaque's house.

Though no appointment had been made, they were quickly ushered in to see the Minister. Khandaker Moshtaque received Rashid warmly and was introduced to the others. Rashid explained they had just dropped in to greet him and after a few pleasantries they left. Apparently the experience was enough to convince Noor and Shariar that Rashid had an understanding with Moshtaque. 'After that' Rashid said 'they told me that "any time you want our help we will be with you".'

Rashid asked Dalim, Noor and Shariar to join him and Farook at 10 pm at the new airport beyond the Cantonment where his unit would be on night training exercises. To make sure they would come he held out the bait that they could see at first hand the military preparations and could also have a fuller discussion about details of the plot. Even at that late stage Rashid was not prepared to trust the other conspirators with the whole truth that he had himself learnt from Farook only 48 hours earlier. Sheikh Mujib was to be killed the next morning.

VII

The Killing of Sheikh Mujib

His time has run out ... Do it very secretly.

Andha Hafiz

Sitting in a broken-down taxi in the middle of a Chittagong bazaar, Farook's wife Farida was bathed in a nervous sweat. For over an hour she had been trying to get to Hali Shaar with an urgent message for Andha Hafiz. It was a little after 11 am on 14th August 1975 and she was running out of time.

Farida had arrived in the port city the previous afternoon with her mother who was returning home from Dhaka after the mid-week anniversary party. Farook had sent her to consult the blind holy man, and his instructions were explicit: 'Tell him I'm going to do it on the 15th. That I'm doing it in the cause of Islam and the State, with faith in Allah that what I am doing will benefit the people. Tell him also that I'm not doing it for personal desire or ambition. I am prepared to follow the path of Allah, whichever way He wills. I want him to tell me if I'm doing wrong or right or if there is anything else I must do.'

Farook had asked Farida to telephone Andha Hafiz's answer to him in Dhaka by noon. She was not going to make the deadline. 'We had much difficulty in getting a baby taxi' (three-wheeler) she recalled, 'and the one we finally got broke down several times'. When she eventually reached the holy man's house the taxi driver, instead of apologising for the trouble, demanded 27 Takkas for the trip.

Farida found Andha Hafiz dressed in a lungi and cotton vest, sitting cross-legged on a low wooden bed. Assorted garments hung from a rope stretched across the single room. As she sat on a cane stool in front of him Farida remembered getting the scent of unseen flowers and a cooling breeze which quickly made her comfortable. Finding no sign of a fan, the thought crossed her mind that heaven had a way of keeping Andha Hafiz cool.

The blind man held her hand as he quietly listened to Farook's message. After what seemed to be an agony of waiting, he let out a deep sigh and with some emotion in his voice told her in Urdu: 'His time has run out. Do what you have to do but do it very secretly.' There was another long silence. Then he earnestly advised her to tell Farook that before he undertook his task he must pray with the fullest sincerity for God's support. His commanders must do likewise. He also gave her two 'Suras' which, he said, Farook must recite constantly 'so that his mind would be fixed with a holy zeal and he could think of nothing else.' One of these Suras was the Muslim prayer for the dead. The other was an invocation to ward off evil.

As she got up to leave Farida asked Andha Hafiz to pray for her husband and his companions. 'Don't worry,' he gently comforted her, 'I have placed them in the hands of God. It's His will. He will take care of them.'

Farida's troubles were not yet over. When she returned to her father's house she found the telephone lines to Dhaka were not working. Two hours later there was no answer from Farook's telephone. Farida then telephoned her sister's house and got a very bad connection. In desperation she called her father-in-law. 'Find Farook and ask him to telephone me urgently,' she implored him. Dr Rahman found his son at home fast asleep. Apparently the young major had returned home early and finding nothing to do had decided to take a nap. It was 5 pm before Farida finally passed on the fateful message.

Andha Hafiz was not the only one to see doom in Sheikh Mujib's stars. A senior member of the President's personal staff, Ruhul Quddus, was a well known amateur palmist. He had read Mujib's palm at the beginning of July. What he saw apparently alarmed him so much that he quickly set off with his wife for 'extended medical treatment' in Europe. The presentiment saved his neck. He was out of the country when Mujib was killed and the Bangladesh government for many months unsuccessfully tried to get him back.

Fate, it seemed, was also working against Mujib's family. The marriage of his niece, his favourite sister's daughter, on 10th August had brought the clan together in Dhaka. Serniabat's sons had come in from Khulna for the occasion bringing with them several close friends. They all stayed on in Dhaka because Serniabat on 14th August was observing his dead mother's 'Chelum', the 40th day ceremony which marks, for Muslims, the end of the period of mourning. Thus the entire family was concentrated within a half square mile of Dhanmandi when Farook and Rashid decided to strike.

Though the majors had not banked on it, Mujib was made even more vulnerable by a remarkable coincidence. Brigadier Nur Zaman, the tough commandant of the Rakhi Bahini, was on a visit to Europe. His second in command was a relatively junior officer who was acting independently for the first time. Thus Mujib's elite storm troopers were not geared, as they normally were, for instant action.

On that fateful day in August, Sheikh Mujib was blissfully riding a crest. The BKSAL apparatus for a one-party state was complete. The 61 District Governors would be in their posts after the weekend. Mujib himself had another trick up his sleeve. He was scheduled to make an important speech at Dhaka University next day, when it had been secretly arranged that by public acclamation he should be declared President for Life. With the Opposition shut out and his own position firmly nailed down, there would be nothing to touch him. Mujib was not to know what the majors were up to, although the reports he was getting suggested that something was cooking in the Cantonment. Mujib therefore concentrated his intelligence work where his Pakistani experience had taught him the danger lay—the army commanders. He did not bother about the junior officers. The mistake cost him his life.

Night training exercises for the 1st Bengal Lancers and the 2nd Field Artillery on 14th August began normally at 10 pm. None of the officers or the 600 men of the two units gathered at the yet incomplete new Dhaka airport beyond the Cantonment or in the tank garages nearby, had even a suspicion of the momentous operation their commanding officers had planned for them. Majors Farook and Rashid were observing Andha Hafiz's exhortation to secrecy in the strictest possible way.

The only thing out of the ordinary that night was the fact that one of the artillery regiments' three company-strength batteries had been ordered to dismount, arm themselves with rifles and proceed in 12 trucks to the exercise staging area. Even that order did not raise eyebrows since Major Rashid, on resuming command of the regiment, had often varied the training routine.

Rashid assembled six 105mm Yugoslav-made Howitzers with plenty of ammunition on the airport perimeter. The crews did not know it, but the guns, according to Rashid's 'practice' orders, were soon zero'd on the Rakhi Bahini headquarters barracks four miles away. Eleven other field guns were kept in the unit headquarters with crews at standby. The eighteenth gun in the regimental arsenal Rashid ordered to be taken with crew to the Lancers' garage a quarter of a mile away where Major Farook had started up twenty-eight T-54 tanks in the usual way. Due to mechanical failure he was that night two short of the normal complement.

Apart from the CO's there were only four officers from each unit present. Two other officers—not fully trusted—had been told to skip the exercise. The troops were another matter. Every available man of each unit had been mustered. It is significant of Mujib's faded image that both Farook and Rashid had not the slightest doubt that the troops—common men all of them—when ordered would not hesitate to come out against Mujib.

Rashid had till the last moment been trying to bring in an infantry unit so that the coup, for political reasons, could seem to represent a cross-section of the army. To this end he had that morning telephoned an old friend, Major Shahjehan, the acting commandant of the 16th Bengal Infantry stationed at Joydevpur, to bring his troops to the new airport in Dhaka for an unscheduled combined training exercise. He did not confide in Shahjehan but was confident that once the infantry unit had arrived on the scene he could talk it into joining the plot. The unsuspecting Major Shahjehan accepted Rashid's suggestion and promised to march his troops to Dhaka by 10 pm. Rashid was now anxiously waiting for the 16th Bengal Infantry and his fellow conspirators, ex-Majors Dalim, Noor and Shariar.

There was no sign of them at 10.30 pm when Shahjehan came through on the telephone to say his men were too tired and that he was calling off the rendezvous. When given this disappointing news Farook bitterly remarked, 'It seems that the Bengal Tigers have become pussy cats!'.

Meanwhile, there was still no sign of Dalim and his companions. They turned up at 11 pm bringing along Major Pasha and Major Huda. The latter was a serving military intelligence officer and a good friend of Dalim since they had once served together in the artillery corps. Rashid took the group and his 12 trucks to join Farook at the tank garages. It was only around midnight that the details of the operation were finally made known to all.

Farook, who was in overall command of the operation, quickly briefed them on the reasons and the purpose of the strike and asked if they would like to join. When they all agreed, he immediately got down to business.

With his well-worn tourist map of Dhaka City spread on the squadron office table, Farook ticked off the various points he wanted blocked. One tank would block the runway at Dhaka airport and the troops would control the bridge on the Mirpur Road. Other teams were sent to the radio station, to Bangababan and the New Market where the Pielkhana Barracks of the Bangladesh Rifles were located. Three big teams ranging from 75 to 150 men were assigned to the principal targets—Sheikh Mujib, Abdur Rab Serniabat and Sheikh Fazlul Huq Moni. Dalim was asked to lead the assault on Mujib's bungalow. He declined, probably because of his own family's close ties with the President's family. Instead he volunteered for Serniabat's house. Ex-Major Noor and Major Mohiuddin with one company of Lancers were assigned the task of knocking off Sheikh Mujib. Farook's trusted NCO, Risaldar Muslehuddin (nicknamed 'Muslim') was to lead the assault on Sheikh Moni. Their instructions were that they should kill Sheikh Mujib, Serniabat and Moni. Mujib's sons Kamal and Jamal were to be taken prisoner. No one else was to be touched. But they were given the latitude to proceed according to developments and, if necessary 'wipe out anything en route'. This opened the door for the subsequent massacre.

Rashid's job, according to Farook, was a 'political' one. When the operation got under way he had to rope in Sq. Leader Liaquat and have him stand by with the MiGs in case out-station army units tried to come into Dhaka. Rashid had two other responsibilities. One was to take Khandaker Moshtaque Ahmed to the radio station, announce the overthrow of Sheikh Mujib and introduce Moshtaque as the new President. The other was to try to win over Brigade headquarters and the top army brass after the assassination. Farook had a deep psychological insight into the mental processes of his fellow officers. He knew they would take at least two hours to mobilise any of the army units stationed in Dhaka. He was also certain that once it was established that Sheikh Mujib was dead, the army commanders would hesitate to make a move lest it endanger their own lives and jobs. So he did not bother to keep them covered. Instead he sent Rashid to win them over once the dreadful killing was done.

In the event Farook was proved remarkably correct.

At the same time Farook had no doubt whatsoever that he would achieve his principal targets. The three teams had been instructed to proceed expeditiously, 'wiping out anything en route' that tried to stop them. Even if the officers failed, he knew his Lancer boys would not. So he kept for himself the most difficult and dicey part of the whole operation—the containment of the Rakhi Bahini.

In normal circumstances, and given the element of surprise, it would not have been very difficult for 28 tanks to neutralise 3000 men of the Rakhi Bahini grouped in a single compound near the new Assembly Building. But the hard fact was that Farook's tanks were totally unarmed and sitting ducks for anyone who decided to stand up and fight. They did not have a single round of ammunition between them. Even the machine guns could not be operated. All tank ammunition, he said, was locked away safely in the Ordnance Depot at Joydevpur. Sheikh Mujib, who in the first place did not want to accept the gift of tanks from Egypt, had tried to make certain that they would never be used against him. Farook, however, had other ideas—and he was banking on an incredible bluff to pull it off.

'Few people really understand how effective the tank is as a psychological weapon', he told me 'When you see one coming towards you it takes a really brave man not to run away. We knew our tanks were unarmed. Not more than a handful of men in GHQ shared this knowledge but they could not be absolutely sure about it. So as far as everybody else was concerned the tanks were very lethal and ready to blast anything that moved'. And, he added with a laugh: 'Who would have thought I would be so mad as to take on the Rakhi Bahini and GHQ with a string of unarmed tanks!'.

By 4.40 am Farook had his strike group organised and ready to go. Rashid's artillery crews on the apron of the new airport and, in the unit area, stood by their guns. Lined up in the Lancers' garages were 28 tanks, 12 trucks, three jeeps and a 105mm Howitzer with a total of just over 400 men. Two-thirds of them were in the distinctive black uniforms of the Bengal Lancers which henceforth Bangladeshis would learn to dread.

Incredibly these massive preparations were made just 300 yards from the GHQ Field Intelligence Unit which was supposed to operate round the clock. As a precaution Farook had posted sentries outside its barbed wire fencing with orders to grab anyone who might venture out to investigate. No one did. Apparently the routine normality of the tanks' night training exercises had disarmed everyone.

Half an hour later as the column moved out with Farook in the lead tank he heard the 'Azan', the Muslim call to prayer, wafted on the heavy monsoon air by the loudspeakers of the Cantonment mosque. The undulating call was sweet music to his ears. He had been born on Friday at the time of the Azan. Now on another Friday with the Azan once more ringing in his ears he would either start a new life—or he would die. Again he repeated the Suras that Andha Hafiz had given. Then he waved his killer teams forward and breaking out of line they sped off on their dreadful mission.

Farook's only stop on the way out of the Cantonment was the Ammunition Sub-Depot. He had a sneaking suspicion that he might find some tank ammunition or at least some bullet belts for the machine guns stored there. So he swung his tank into the compound and with its gun bashed the door down. A quick search revealed nothing he could use. Now the only weapon he had available to him was the sten gun resting across his knees. The bluff would have to work!

The tank column drove slowly down Benani Road, turned right and proceeded towards the Cantonment check point. On the way it passed a group of men in white shorts and singlets. They were troops of the 4th and 1st Bengal Infantry on their morning P.T. The men interrupted their drill to wave to the tanks. Farook's men smugly waved back. Incredibly the large tank column outside its normal area had not aroused suspicion. The only person to take notice was Farook's father. Dr Rahman, who had just finished his morning prayers, looked out of the window as the tanks went by. He thought it odd that they should be out and that too so early. And he wondered where they were going.

Once clear of the Cantonment area, the tanks surged forward, crashing through the airport wall. One tank broke off to control the runway, another to the helipad where half a dozen helicopters were parked. Nothing was going to land or take off from Dhaka airport. The other tanks swung round the Plant Protection Centre and raced across the fields towards the Rakhi Bahini headquarters. Farook looked at his watch. It was 5.15 am. The killer teams should be on target.

On reaching the perimeter wall of the airport Farook discovered there was only one tank following him. Somehow he had lost the other 24. Undaunted he charged ahead. Crashing through the compound wall, he knocked down two trees and swung round the Rakhi Bahini barracks. What he saw took his breath away.

'Suddenly I found a brigade of 3000 Rakhi Bahini lined up six rows deep,' he recalled. 'They were battle equipped—steel helmets, rifles, packs, everything. There was no backing out after that.'

'The driver said, "What am I supposed to do?" '

'I told him, you just drive past them six inches from their noses. I ordered the gunner to keep the gun pointed straight at them. I told the other chaps in the turret to look brave.'

'As we slowly drove past them the Rakhi Bahini kept looking at us. We kept looking back at them. It was a tense moment. I told the driver if they start anything just steer right and run over them.'

'It was not necessary. They could hear gunfire in the distance and here suddenly were the tanks. No one moved a finger.'

Since the Rakhi Bahini had not reacted instantly and attacked the tanks, Farook was certain they would stay put. Once more his assessment was tellingly accurate. Supremely confident that he had won the day Farook left the other tank to menace Mujib's storm troops and drove on to Dhanmandi.

The scene at No. 32 Dhanmandi was chaotic.

The main killer team led by Majors Mohiuddin, Noor and Huda, had raced through the deserted streets getting to Sheikh Mujib's residence at approximately 5.15 am. They had 120 men squeezed into five trucks and the 105mm Howitzer which was quickly set up on the main Mirpur Road at the corner of the lake and diagonally opposite the house. Other troops in more trucks blocked off the surrounding area. Then the majors and the men went in.

The armed police guards posted on the perimeter outside the compound were taken completely by surprise and quietly submitted when they saw the heavily armed troops in black uniform. The Lancer sentries at the gate were not in the plot. But when they saw their colleagues and some officers in black uniforms, they quietly stepped aside and allowed them to pass. By this time, however, Mujib's personal bodyguards sleeping on the ground floor verandah were awakened by the commotion in the compound. Seeing strange men with guns pouring through the gate they grabbed their automatics and fired at them. Shamsul Islam of the Artillery was hit in the head and died on the spot. Another trooper, this one from the Lancers, was badly wounded. Seeing their comrades fall and realising from the heavy fire coming from the house that the game was up, the troops opened up with everything they had. Within minutes they killed Mujib's bodyguards and began systematically searching the rooms on the ground floor.

Meanwhile the Howitzer crew panicked when they heard the firing. Fearing that the resistance may be too great they opened fire with the big gun. Two rounds were fired, hitting the lake on both occasions. Then they elevated the guns and fired six more rounds missing the house each time. The shooting was so wild that one of the shells travelled four miles to Mohamadpur, killing two people and wounding several others in a Bihari household.

Mujib's older sons, Kamal and Jamal, momentarily held off the attackers with sten guns. Then Kamal was killed at the foot of the stairs. But before this he had injured two more of the attackers.

Mujib himself was quick to react. First he telephoned the Rakhi Bahini headquarters, but in the absence of their CO Brigadier Nur Zaman and Colonel Sabihuddin, he could not get through to any senior officer. In desperation Mujib phoned General Shafiullah, the Chief of Army Staff, and Brigadier Mashorul Huq, his Military Secretary, asking them to send help immediately. The last call was made to Col. Jamil, Director of Military Intelligence, who Mujib had specially selected for the job a fortnight earlier. Jamil responded quickly. Throwing a dressing gown over his pyjamas he hurried to the President's assistance in his red Volkswagen, but was stopped before he could turn into Road No. 32. There was a sharp argument and when he got out of his car and tried to push his way past the troops they shot him dead.

By this time the killers were swarming everywhere. Mohiuddin, Huda and Noor ran from room to room looking for Mujib. Mohiuddin unexpectedly found him. He was going up to the first floor and had just reached the landing at the turn of the stairs when he saw Sheikh Mujib standing not 20 feet above him. Mujib was wearing a white kurta and grey checked lungi and carried a pipe in his hand.

Although he had set out to kill him, Major Mohiuddin was thoroughly demoralised when face-to-face with Mujib. 'Sir, apne ashun' (Sir, please come) Mohiuddin stammered.

'What do you want?' Mujib asked him scornfully in Bengali. 'Have you come to kill me? Forget it! The Pakistan army couldn't do it. Who are you that you think you can?'

Mujib was obviously playing for time. He had made some telephone calls. Help must surely be on the way. Meanwhile he was putting on a bold face.

When relating the events to me in great detail later, Farook remarked: 'Mujib had quite a personality and Mohiuddin was completely dominated by him. I don't know what would have happened if Noor had not arrived at that moment'.

Mohiuddin kept repeating: 'Sir, apne ashun.' Mujib kept talking back rudely. Noor, who had stepped on to the landing, gun in hand, immediately sensed that Mujib was stalling. So brushing Mohiuddin aside and, according to Farook, screaming something unintelligible, Noor fired a burst from his sten gun. Mujib didn't have a chance. The bullets tore a huge hole in his right side. His body twisted backwards with the impact. Then it slipped, face down, towards the bottom of the stairs. The pipe was still gripped tightly in the right hand.

The time was 5.40 am. Sheikh Mujibur Rahman's tempestuous love affair with the Bengalis had come to an end.

Begum Mujib tried to follow her husband when the shooting flared. She was killed in front of her bedroom door by another burst of automatic fire. Then the massacre continued.

Officers and troops went from door to door, shooting the bolts away and spraying the rooms with sten gun fire. Mujib's second son Jamal, the young Sandhurst-trained army lieutenant, had gathered the rest of the family in the main bedroom for protection. Now it was his turn to die. He was blasted at close range by one of the officers. Nine years later the marks of his blood, bone and muscle tissue—and the bullets—could be clearly seen on a large section of the wall against which he was thrown.

The two young daughters-in-law, the new brides of Kamal and Jamal, were huddled on the bed with their arms round Russell, Mujib's 10-year-old son, who had been named after the great philosopher. They were roughly dragged apart and mercilessly shot dead at close quarters. So also was the young Russell who apparently tried to hide behind the furniture. Sheikh Nasir, Mujib's younger brother, who had made a vast fortune after independence, was killed in an adjoining bathroom where he had been hiding.

The evidence of the whole dreadful episode remains frozen in a nightmare tableau because Sheikh Hasina, the elder of Mujib's two daughters who escaped the killing since they were out of the country, has not yet disturbed anything in the house of death.

The attackers appear to have made a systematic search for valuables, much of which they looted. The rooms have been thoroughly ransacked. Every cupboard, drawer and receptacle has been broken open and their contents scattered about. There's a shambles everywhere and the lingering smell of death.

Mujib was to suffer a further ignominy after he was killed. According to Farook, one of the attackers had never seen Mujib at close quarters. So to get a good look at his face, the man slipped a boot under Mujib's body and rudely flipped it over. It was thus that the shattered remains of Bangabandhu, the friend of the Bengalis, was snapped four hours later by a photographer specially brought for the purpose from the Government's Information Department.

Not far from Sheikh Mujib's house, the Serniabats and Sheikh Moni were also under attack.

Dalim's team got to the Serniabats' residence at about 5.15 am. There was only a police guard at the gate and probably to frighten him off the troops started shooting. The gunfire awakened the household. Abu Hasnat, the Cabinet Minister's 30-year-old son, recalls looking out of his bedroom window and seeing soldiers in black uniforms shooting at the house. Grabbing the sten gun he always kept with him, Hasnat ran down to the first floor to awaken his father. Abdur Rab Serniabat was already on the telephone trying to call Sheikh Mujib for help. The line was busy. When he tried again he managed to get through.

'Father told Bangabandhu our house was being attacked by miscreants.' Hasnat recalled. 'My father told him to send help. At that moment I could hear someone shouting from the other end of the line. My father listened. He was shocked by what he heard. I got the impression that he had been informed that miscreants were also attacking Bangabandhu. My father didn't say another word. He put the phone down and sat on the bed. He just looked at me without talking.'

Hasnat went to a window and began shooting at the troops. 'I just pulled the trigger and emptied the magazine. When the bullets were finished I ran upstairs to the store to get some more bullets'. The action saved his life. Moments later troops burst into the bedroom and killed Serniabat where he sat. Then they herded everyone they could find into the drawing room on the ground floor.

Meanwhile Hasnat was in the loft desperately trying to break open the trunk where he kept spare magazines for his sten gun. As he tried to break the lock he could hear firing and the sound of boots approaching on the stairs. Leaving his gun on the floor Hasnat jumped and tried to squeeze himself through the skylight hoping he could escape onto the roof. He couldn't get through. So he jumped down and sat on the floor of the loft waiting for the men to come and kill him. Nothing happened.

For 20 minutes he could hear shouts and occasional bursts of gunfire. After a while the commotion died down and he could hear troops stomping out into the road. Hasnat waited a long time till everything was silent. Then very carefully he crept downstairs. He found the drawing room a shambles of blood, bodies and broken furniture. His wife, mother and 20-year-old sister were badly wounded and bleeding. His two young daughters, uninjured, were sobbing behind a sofa where they had hidden during the massacre. Lying dead on the floor were his 5-year-old son, two sisters aged 10 and 15 and his 11-year-old brother, the family ayah (maid) a houseboy and his cousin Shahidul Islam Serniabat. The latter wore a big moustache and looked a lot like Hasnat. Evidently the attackers had mistaken him for Serniabat's son and killed him. Of the 10 friends who had come along with the family from Barisal for the wedding of Mujib's niece four days earlier, one was killed and five wounded. Hasnat later slipped out of the house and escaped to India.

The attack on Sheikh Moni was brief and devastating. Apparently he was a light sleeper and when Risaldar Muslehuddin and his men drove up to the house in two army trucks, Moni quickly jumped out of bed. Seeing the troops he called out to inquire whether they had been assigned to guard him. Muslehuddin asked Moni to come out and when he did he tried to grab hold of him. At this point Moni's wife, who was seven months pregnant, jumped in front of her husband to protect him. Both were killed by a single burst from a sten gun. No other person was touched. Mission accomplished, Muslehuddin and his men drove to Mujib's house.

When the others had gone on their deadly mission, Rashid made straight for Sq. Leader Liaquat's house to alert him to stand by with his MiGs. It took a few minutes to get him out of bed and to brief him. Liaquat refused to do anything without orders from the Chief of Air Staff. So leaving him, Rashid dashed off to see Major Hafiz, Brigade Major of the 46th Infantry Brigade (Dhaka Brigade) who was involved in the earlier plotting but backed out at the last moment. Rashid wanted Hafiz to bring out the 1st East Bengal since Major Shahjehan and the 16th East Bengal had failed to come from Joydevpur. He hoped the Brigade Major would not now hesitate to act since the operation had already been launched.

Hafiz, however, refused to call out the infantry. He would not move without instructions from the Brigade Commander or the Chief of Staff. There was some argument and Hafiz tried to get his CO, Colonel Shafat Jamil, on the telephone. When he failed to get through Rashid got him into his jeep and drove off to Shafat Jamil's house. They were entering the compound when they heard the first salvoes from the Howitzer coming from the direction of Dhanmandi.

Rashid said he told the Brigade Commander about the strike. 'Sir, we have gone for action to remove Sheikh . . .' Shafat Jamil, he recalls, was shocked and very angry. He too could hear the guns booming in the distance. There followed loud exchanges between the two officers, when the telephone rang. It was General Shafiullah calling to say he had received a call from Sheikh Mujib that some soldiers were attacking his house and he wanted the Dhaka Brigade to mobilise immediately to go to his assistance.

'I told him (Jamil) that it's too late to do something since we have already gone for it,' Rashid said. 'Shafat Jamil put down the telephone. He was furious but did nothing. Then he told me, "I must go and see General Ziaur Rahman". I didn't bother to stop him.' Rashid got into his jeep and rushed to Dhanmandi.

After Rashid left, Shafat Jamil received another telephone call from General Shafiullah, who was crying as he informed him that Sheikh Mujib had been killed. The Army Chief appeared to have broken down completely and failed to give the Dhaka Brigade commander instructions to quell the mutiny. So quickly throwing on his uniform, Shafat Jamil walked over to General Zia's house. He found him shaving.

After recounting Rashid's visit and the telephone calls from General Shafiullah, Shafat Jamil told Zia: 'The President has been killed, Sir. What are your orders?'

Zia, he recalled, was quite calm, evidently aware of what had happened. Zia answered: 'If the President is no longer there, then the Vice President is there. Go to your headquarters and wait there.'

Zia clearly was not going to be pushed into any hasty action. Sheikh Mujib was dead. The situation was extremely fluid and unclear. So General Zia, like the other senior officers as Farook had suspected, decided to wait and see.

When he reached Sheikh Mujib's house Rashid found everything quiet. The troops were milling about outside and in answer to his query confirmed that Bangabandhu was indeed dead. Rashid said he was upset to hear that the family had also been slaughtered. His political perception made him keenly aware that this was a blunder of the first magnitude. It would turn public opinion against them and also disgrace them internationally. At the same time Rashid did not blame the troops because, as he put it, 'it was a military operation and civilians can get killed.' Nevertheless he was too squeamish to go inside the house. Instead he turned his jeep and returned to Brigade Headquarters in the Cantonment.

Rashid recalls: 'Colonel Shafat Jamil and the other senior officers were there. I told them that since it is confirmed that Sheikh has been killed there is no question of interference or any action by them. They should stay where they are and be prepared just in case the Rakhi Bahini move and they have to counter it.'

He said the officers were angry but also silent and afraid. 'Everybody was wondering what should happen to them now that Sheikh Mujib had gone and no one did anything.'

Meanwhile Farook, having confirmed Sheikh Mujib was dead, had secured the city. Taking 10 of his tanks he returned to Rakhi Bahini headquarters to confront the Acting CO. 'The man was shaking in his boots' he recalled. 'Seeing the tanks all lined up he thought I had come to get him'. Farook informed him that the Rakhi Bahini had been merged with the army and would be subject to orders from the army and army headquarters. Then he got on the phone and spoke to the Director of Military Operations, Colonel Noorudin. Farook talked him into bringing the Rakhi Bahini under military orders. Once that was accomplished Mujib's storm troops ceased to be a threat.

Later, going down Mirpur Road past Sheikh Mujib's house, Farook was flagged down by a Lancer picket. They had three men securely tied on the ground. 'We caught them going to the house' they told him excitedly. 'Shall we kill them'? Looking down Farook could not make out who the two younger men were. The third he recognised immediately. It was Brigadier Mashoorul Haq, Military Secretary to the President, the man who had presented Farida with the big bouquet three days earlier. Farook calmed his troops. There would be no more killing.

Farook continued: 'I then lined up my tanks and marched the column back via the 2nd Capital Road, Farm Gate, right into the Cantonment and parked them in front of Brigade Headquarters. I told them there: 'We are placing ourselves under your command'.

The officers in Brigade Headquarters were understandably non-plussed. What do you tell a brash young tank commander who has just knocked off the President? One or two congratulated Farook. The rest were angry, silent. 'I could feel their hostility' Farook said, 'as if they were telling me "you are a pariah, not wanted". When I tried to be nice to Colonel Shafat Jamil he turned on me savagely. "Who told you to give advice. You keep your mouth shut".'

Rashid said the success of their operation tempted him to consider making a grab for power, instead of installing Khandaker Moshtaque as President. He quickly took stock of the situation. The Rakhi Bahini had been cowed into submission by Farook's tanks. GHQ was in a state of paralytic shock. The army was in disarray but with a little persuasion now that the deed was done, it could be counted on to rally round the majors. He was also confident that the people were not shedding any tears for Mujib. But he was not sure what the public reaction would be once it became known that the families had also been slaughtered.

That was Rashid's main concern at the moment, and while giving it thought, he put off going to Moshtaque's house for about 20 minutes. Then he heard Dalim, contrary to instructions, announcing on the radio that Mujib had been killed and the army under Moshtaque had seized power. Dalim also said that martial law had been imposed on the country which henceforth would be known as the Islamic Republic of Bangladesh.

Apparently Dalim and some of the other retired officers—'with typical indiscipline and rashness' Rashid said—had rushed to the radio station after killing Sheikh Mujib and Serniabat. There they fought over the microphone, each wanting to be the first to break the news. Then Dalim grabbed it and made the announcement in his name.

The broadcast shocked Rashid into action. 'I knew it would create a problem for us', he said, 'because the brigades outside Dhaka would want to know how Dalim, a retired officer, had staged a military coup which could only be done by the army. How could such a man speak for the army? They would not accept it.'

Dismissing the thought of grabbing power, Rashid went post haste to Khandaker Moshtaque Ahmed's house.

VIII

Moshtaque Takes Over

I went into the toilet and while sitting there I began to prepare myself in my mind about what was to come.

—Khandaker Moshtaque Ahmed

At 7.30 am Rashid's jeep, followed by a solitary tank, snaked through one of Dhaka's older quarters into Aga Masih Lane and came to a stop outside Khandaker Moshtaque's house. It was an old-fashioned three-storey building sandwiched between even older houses in a tiny square. The clatter of the tank tracks had electrified the run-down neighbourhood. Hundreds of people, already staggered by Dalim's fateful radio broadcast, had instantly gathered to watch the drama unfold before their very eyes. They perched silently in windows, on the roofs and at other vantage points in the square, but keeping well away from the tank.

Looking through the top-floor balcony Moshtaque was shaken to find the venomous mouth of the tank's cannon pointing in his direction. Moments later, Rashid, dishevelled and carrying a sten gun, ran up the stairs followed by two armed soldiers.

Though the Major, during their three previous meetings, had made no secret of his intention to give him Sheikh Mujib's job, Moshtaque was too much a politician to fully trust another man, especially when he was a military officer in frightful circumstances such as these. The long wait after Dalim's radio announcement, and now the tank, had unnerved him. He was full of misgivings. Moshtaque gave me a vivid account of the episode in two lengthy interviews on 11th and 12th December, 1975, after he had been thrown out of office by the counter-coups.

'I was not sure whether they had come to kill me,' he recalled. 'They were looking very disturbed and had guns in their hands. I kept looking at their hands to see what they were going to do. When I saw that instead of pointing their guns at me one or two of them were saluting, I felt relieved. So I took courage and asked. "What brings you here?"' If nothing else, Moshtaque is an excellent actor.

Rashid told Moshtaque he wanted him to take over as President and for that purpose must accompany him to the radio station. The words were music to Moshtaque's ears. Still he was hesitant. He did not yet fully trust Rashid and decided to test him. 'How do we go?' he asked the major. 'Do we go in your jeep or in my car?' The intention here was to ascertain whether he would drive with dignity in his own car or as a prisoner in the military jeep. Rashid told Moshtaque they could use his car if the driver could be trusted. Now even more relieved, Moshtaque said he told the major: 'Alright, give me some time. I have something to do and I have to put on my clothes.'

He continued: 'I went into the toilet and while sitting there I began to prepare myself in my mind about what was to come. This gave me some time to think.'

When they went down to the car, Moshtaque, still a little apprehensive, put Rashid to another test. 'I was wondering who would open the door?' he told me. 'My anxiety was to make sure they were not bluffing me. If I was made to open the door myself it would have meant one thing—they were in fact taking me to be killed. If someone else opened it for me then I would be sure they were being respectful. So I waited for a few moments.'

The matter was resolved when one of the soldiers, saluting smartly, opened the door of the car and politely indicated he should get in. Moshtaque's doubts were swept away. He had, at last, made it to the top. 'It was,' he recalled, 'a wonderful drama'.

On the way to the radio station, Moshtaque was even more gratified to find no display of public resentment at the killing of Sheikh Mujib. 'People appeared to be shocked and bewildered,' he said, 'but as we went along I could see some of them cheering. You know, success has many parents!'

Though oozing confidence when they reached the radio station Moshtaque still had one nagging fear in his mind. The majors had engineered the coup and had chosen him to replace Mujib, but how would the Service Chiefs and the rest of the army take it? He knew he would not be fully secure till they also had been nailed down. He therefore suggested to Rashid that the Service Chiefs be brought in. Rashid thought it was a good idea. He went off to the Cantonment, leaving Moshtaque with Tahiruddin Thakur, the Minister of State for Information, who was finalising his speech. In the headquarters of the 1st Bengal Regiment Rashid found Brigadier Khalid Musharraf, the CGS, along with Colonel Shafat Jamil and some other officers. He asked the CGS to arrange for the tank ammunition and found him most willing to oblige. Khalid Musharraf also assured Rashid he would muster the Service Chiefs for him. Within half an hour he brought in Major General Shafiullah, Air Vice Marshall Khondkar, and Commodore M. H. Khan. Major-General Ziaur Rahman, the Deputy Chief of Staff, also arrived with them.

Rashid briefed the Service Chiefs about what they had done and asked for their cooperation. 'We have done it for the greater interest of the country' he told them. 'We are not seeking power for ourselves and we don't disown you. Rather we want your leadership. So you come to the radio station and do what you have to do.'

As Farook had anticipated, once they knew Mujib was dead the military brass quickly fell into line. At that stage no one dared to take on the majors.

What transpired next was vividly described to me by Khandaker Moshtaque: 'I am a good lawyer and know how to trap a man' he gloated. 'Since I was being pushed into the saddle I had to get the allegiance of the Forces. So I shouted at Shafiullah, "Tell me have you done this?". Now Shafiullah was in a very awkward position. In front of him were the majors who had killed Sheikh, and he couldn't back out for fear of his own life. So he told me quietly "Yes, we have done it." Then I proceeded one by one to ask the same question of the other Chiefs of the Services. One by one they admitted they had done it. I could see they were very frightened. They had no alternative.'

Moshtaque continued: 'I then asked them: "What do you want me to do?" They told me: "Please take over. You are the only acceptable person in Bangladesh." I told them I am a civilian and a democrat and not an army person. I will only take over if we have a purely civilian and a democratic government and you will not have anything to do with it.' (Moshtaque didn't try to explain—and in the circumstances I didn't want to embarrass him by asking—by what mental gymnastics he was conferring the dignity of 'democratic government' on a regime brought to power by treachery, assassination and military coup.)

The military officers, Moshtaque said, went into a huddle in another room, returning about half an hour later to confirm acceptance of his terms. He then quickly put them on the air one by one to swear allegiance to his government. By 11.15 am when he finally made his own broadcast, Moshtaque had gained complete mastery of the situation. The majors may have made him President, but he bottled them up with the army. He was not going to be anyone's puppet.

In his first broadcast President Khandaker Moshtaque Ahmed excelled even Sheikh Mujib in bombast and in exploiting the people's gullability. He described the killing and the coup as 'a historical necessity.' He said 'everybody wanted to change the administrative system but since it was not possible through available means that armed forces had come forward to change the government . . . they have opened the golden gates of opportunity before the people.' Moshtaque also solemnly pledged 'in unambiguous terms that this government will never compromise with any type of corruption, nepotism or social vices.' But he was lying in his teeth. For even as he spoke he was compromising with the most heinous of crimes—murder.

Moshtaque was guilty of another public deception which some Western newspapers dubbed as 'The case of the Missing Islamic Republic'.

Dalim's announcement early that morning had led everyone to believe that Bangladesh was now an 'Islamic Republic'. Farook and Rashid also intended it to be so. Moshtaque, however, had his own ideas. He had no intention of changing the country's secular character. But very cleverly he did not announce his unpopular decision at that time. Instead he fooled everyone by liberally lacing his speech with invocation to Allah and concluded with the exhortation 'Bangladesh Zindabad', the Urdu equivalent of 'Joi Bangla' (Long live Bengal) which had been Mujib's rallying cry to the Bengalis. At the end of it all the people, 85% of whom are Muslim, were left with the impression that a new Islamic dispensation had been installed. It was only later that they would learn the bitter truth. Bangladesh was not an Islamic State. Sheikh Mujib's international commitments and his professed domestic objectives were also unchanged. In essence President Moshtaque was carrying on in the traditions of the Awami League. But by that time Khandaker Moshtaque had consolidated his position and it was too late to complain.

Moshtaque's speech caused tremendous confusion in Britain where there is a sizeable Bangladeshi community. Pious Muslims who had exulted when Dalim first announced the establishment of the Islamic Republic, were crestfallen when the text of Moshtaque's broadcast was known. Hundreds of telephone calls were made to the High Commission in London for clarification.

One caller asked Deputy High Commissioner Farook Chowdhury, 'Is it or is it not an Islamic Republic?'. When the official said there was no change, he was disgustedly told, 'If this is the case then why did you kill Sheikh?'.

The Bangladeshis were not the only ones to be fooled by Moshtaque's adroit reversal of the declaration of the 'Islamic Republic'. Saudi Arabia was also taken in. Though they had repeatedly expressed goodwill for the people, the Saudis had resisted recognition of Bangladesh for three and a half years because they felt the Muslim people should have an Islamic state. Justice Abu Syed Chowdhury, Bangladesh's first President, who later became Sheikh Mujib's travelling envoy, explained the Saudi position to me when recounting a meeting he had with the late King Faisal in January, 1974.

According to Justice Chowdhury, King Faisal wanted clarification of what was meant by the Article in the Bangladesh Constitution relating to secularism. 'I told the King' he said with semantics that would have amazed King Solomon, 'that, as President of the Republic of Bangladesh, on various occasions I had referred to this particular Article and said that it did not mean irreligiousness. It merely meant that all persons professing different faiths would be treated with equality in the affairs of the state, i.e. they could profess and practice their own religion and maintain their religious institutions and should have equal opportunities in life. Since a very small minority does not profess the faith of Islam, Your Majesty might treat it as an Islamic country.'

Justice Chowdhury continued: 'For a time it looked as if the King was impressed by my argument. But then he said he would be happy if the word 'secularism' was omitted from the Constitution and it is declared as an Islamic Republic of Bangladesh. He further met my point about tolerance of other religions by saying an Article specifying that the minorities would not be oppressed would be an adequate protection for them.' King Faisal was not fooled. He did not grant recognition to secular Bangladesh. But the Saudi government under King Khalid on hearing the news of Mujib's assassination and Dalim's declaration of an Islamic Republic, rushed in with the long-denied recognition. I have not been able to discover by what verbal gymnastics Justice Chowdhury, as Moshtaque's Foreign Minister, was able to mollify the Saudi embarrassment—if indeed he did—when the new President retained the country's secular status.

Meanwhile on that fateful day, events were moving swiftly in Dhaka. With fore-knowledge of what the majors had planned, Khandaker Moshtaque Ahmed had ample time to formulate his plans and thus was able to move with precision and purpose in the midst of the general confusion.

First he imposed martial law, and ordered an indefinite curfew throughout the country. But here again, as a sop to religious sentiment, he took pains to ensure that there was a three-hour break in the curfew so that the faithful might go to the mosques for Jumma (Friday) prayers. Next he appointed a Vice President and a 10-men Cabinet which excluded members of Sheikh Mujib's inner circle. Among the new appointees were Justice Abu Syed Chowdhury and Dr. A. R. Malik, Farook's uncle who was a university Vice Chancellor. He was made Finance Minister. The new President suspended some of Mujib's most trusted officials and placed them on the transfer list. Moshtaque also arrested several politicians, among them Ghazi Gholam Mustafa and Abdus Samad Azad, the man who had replaced him as Foreign Minister when he was dumped from the job a few days after independence. He also granted interviews to ambassadors, and the press, radio and TV were quickly orchestrated to praise the new dispensation and denounce the old.

The sycophants needed no encouragement to switch loyalties. They went in droves to the President's house to fawn on Moshtaque, and any of the majors they could find. Congratulatory telegrams and letters poured in from everywhere.

No tears were shed for Sheikh Mujibur Rahman. Maulana Bashani, who had a few months earlier pledged 'total support' for Mujib's 'Second Revolution', quickly issued a statement welcoming the historic change and offering fullest support to Khandaker Moshtaque's government. In London a group of young Bangladeshis stormed the High Commission tearing down Mujib's photographs and assaulting his personal intelligence officer. The High Commissioner, Syed Abdus Sultan, who had always shown himself greatly devoted to Mujib, and was one of his most trusted appointees, instead of having the boys arrested for trespassing and vandalism, entertained them to tea in his office after removing the many photographs of Mujib which normally adorned the room.

In Dhaka Khandaker Moshtaque lost no time in tidying up the evidence of the massacre in Dhanmandi. Mujib's family, along with the Serniabats and the Monis were quietly buried in Benani graveyard in the Cantonment. Mujib's body alone was flown by Air Force helicopter to Tungipara and buried in the village graveyard. It was there that Bangabandhu's final humiliation took place. According to Brigadier Manzoor, when the news of the coup and assassination became known some villagers broke in and looted Mujib's ancestral home.

A few hours after installing Khandaker Moshtaque Ahmed as President, Farook and Rashid placed themselves at the disposal of the Army Head-quarters, but were not allowed to rejoin their units. Not only were they a source of embarrassment and fear to the military commanders but they were also the target of much hostility from those officers who had earlier conspired with them for the overthrow of Sheikh Mujib, but had backed out at the last moment. The problem was solved by Khandaker Moshtaque. For his own security he insisted that the two majors remain with him in the President's house at all times.

Although he had connived with the majors in the overthrow of Sheikh Mujibur Rahman and now clung to them for protection, Khandaker Moshtaque, like his predecessor, had a basic mistrust and dislike for all things military. He too was after all basically an Awami Leaguer who had suffered at the hands of Pakistan's military rulers. The military 'monster' that Mujib feared had now reared its head. Moshtaque was quick to perceive that unless he demolished it by restoring military discipline and re-establishing civil authority over the armed forces, he would not be able to consolidate his position as President. To put down the military, therefore, became Moshtaque's pre-occupation during his 83 days in office.

But he faced many obstacles to his plans. The most important was Farook and Rashid's insistence that Major General Ziaur Rahman should replace Major General Shafiullah as Chief of the Army Staff. Later, despite Moshtaque's reservations, they brought in another man of their choice to head the Bangladesh Air Force. He was Group Captain Towab, a former Pakistan air force officer who had for a time served as the senior air officer with the Mujibnagar government-in-exile in Calcutta. Towab was living in retirement with his German wife in Munich when Rashid went there to recruit him.

Moshtaque was disinclined to appoint General Zia as Chief of Army Staff for two reasons. First, he did not trust him. It was essentially a gut feeling, but Moshtaque was not the one to invalidate his intuition. Time would prove how right it was. Secondly, Zia, unlike the other senior army officers, was popular with the troops. This was anathema to Moshtaque for he firmly believed that such a commander must be regarded as a potentially dangerous rival. So he did the next best thing. While appointing Zia as Chief of Army Staff, Moshtaque made sure he was tightly boxed in and made ineffective by his own nominees.

Rashid was supposed to be advising him on army matters. But without consulting the major, Moshtaque created the post of Chief of Defence Staff—ranking above the three Service Chiefs (and above Zia)—and appointed Major General Khalilur Rahman, Commandant of the Bangladesh Rifles, to the job. Major General Ershad, who was on a staff course in India, was given his second promotion in four months and brought in as Zia's deputy. Brigadier

Khalid Musharraf had been Zia's rival for promotion. Moshtaque retained him in the sensitive position as CGS (Chief of General Staff) under Zia. On top of all of them he placed General M. A. G. Osmani, Mujib's first Defence Minister, as his own Defence Adviser. Known as the 'Papa Tiger' because he was Colonel-in-Chief of the Bengal Regiment, Osmani was an old-style officer and a gentleman who lived by the Military Manual. Moshtaque found him the ideal person to oversee what he grandly described as the restoration of discipline in the Armed Forces.

In fact Moshtaque was doing the opposite.

Recalling his actions, Brigadier Manzoor regretfully told me later: 'Moshtaque outdid Mujib in his mistreatment of the Forces. He was clever and cunning. He played one against the other and he set up the bureaucrats against the Army'. General Zia, who was present on the occasion, nodded his head in agreement.

On 26th September Moshtaque indemnified Mujib's killers against punishment for their crimes. It took the form of 'THE INDEMNITY ORDINANCE, 1975' issued on the authority of the President of Bangladesh and published in a Gazette Extraordinary—but without the usual publicity in the media. There was good reason for the secrecy for surely there would have been a public outcry had its contents been known.

Hidden by the legal verbiage was total exculpation for the Majors, their men and all those involved with them not only in respect of the killings and the coup of 15th August, but also in the planning and abetment of it. In effect it was a comprehensive pardon for the men who had slaughtered the Founding Father of the nation and 21 members of his family.

In the circumstances, no one expected Moshtaque to prosecute Mujib's killers. But to formally pardon them is an entirely different thing. I was told later that not even Farook and Rashid expected it or thought it necessary. But Moshtaque, ever the casuist, was playing it safe for his was more than a casual role in the grisly affair. I don't know whether he issued himself an 'indemnity certificate' like the others were promised. Certainly the terms of the Ordinance were broad enough even for this purpose.

The pardoning of the killers, the promotion of Farook and Rashid from major to Lt. Colonel, and the most extravagant praise he heaped on them—in a radio broadcast on October 3 he called them 'the sons of the sun of the armed forces'—had the most shattering effect on the morale and discipline in the armed forces. Clearly established for officers and men was the precedent that anything is permissible—mutiny, mayhem, murder—only don't get caught doing it. All this would foster widespread unrest and Bonapartism, attempted coups and counter-coups, and General Zia Rahman's assassination in Chittagong seven years later.

Sheikh Mujibur Rahman, by his free-wheeling ways, broke the sequence of crime and punishment in Bangladesh and for betraying the people brought down upon himself and the country a terrible legacy of blood. Khandaker Moshtaque, during the brief 83 days of his stewardship, formally cemented the break and multiplied the legacy many times over.

Despite the bombast of his first radio broadcast, Moshtaque had few innovations to his credit during the first ten days in office. One, which was given front-page coverage in the government-controlled press, was the introduction of a new form of national head-dress—a black 'nehru' cap similar to the one he wore, but used by few others in Bangladesh at that time.[1]

However, during this time Moshtaque took steps to remove all possible rivals in the political field. He reckoned the main threat, apart from the unstable army, came from his old party, the Awami League. Its leaders could become a rallying point for the opposition. So as soon as he was satisfied that the country had accepted Mujib's killing, Moshtaque quickly rounded up the four men who had been most prominent in the Mujibnagar government in Calcutta—Tajuddin Ahmad, Syed Nazrul Islam, Mansoor Ali and Kamruzzaman. Here again, Moshtaqaue acted with extreme guile to disarm public opinion.

Mansoor Ali, till recently the Prime Minister, was invited to Bangababan where he was photographed being effusively received by Moshtaque. While the pictures were being shown on TV that night, poor Mansoor Ali was quietly whisked off to jail. Syed Nazrul Islam, the former Vice President, and Kamruzzaman, who had been Mujib's confidant, were then jailed without fuss. So was Tajuddin, who had been dismissed for publicly criticising Mujib and still enjoyed countrywide respect.

Peter Gill, who was the last journalist to see Tajuddin alive, recorded the event in the Sunday Telegraph:

'As I approached his house I saw Mr Ahmad being escorted to a military jeep by an army officer. The house was ringed by about 30 soldiers and more soldiers were crammed into an army Land Rover. I walked to the jeep and with all the naivety at my command asked Mr Tajuddin Ahmad whether he was about to join the new army-backed government of President Ahmed. "I don't think so," he replied. Then after a glance at the army officer in the driving seat he added: "I'm being taken to an army detention camp,"'[2]

While in jail these four political leaders became the object of a diabolical 'contingency plan' which would ultimately result in their massacre there two months later.

Farook told me three people—Farook himself, Rashid and Khandaker Moshtaque—were privy to the plan which was intended as a contingency in the event of a counter-coup. They had decided on it when Moshtaque made his first visit to his village home in Dhospara because they felt he would be extremely vulnerable when he left the safety of the tanks in Bangababan.

'If we could bump off Sheikh Mujib,' Farook explained, 'then we reckoned others could do the same to Khandaker Moshtaque. You must remember that the possibility of a counter-coup was very real. In that case the four politicians in jail would have been the obvious choice of anyone trying to form an alternative government, probably backed by India. So they had to be removed.'

Accordingly it was agreed that should Moshtaque be killed or there be a counter-coup, two things would be done immediately. One, the Chief Justice (at that time Justice Abusadat Mohammad Sayem) would be immediately sworn in as President to avoid a governmental vacuum. Simultaneously, a 'combat' team from the President's House would rush to Dhaka central jail and kill Tajuddin, Syed Nazrul Islam, Mansoor Ali and Kamruzzaman. Assigned to the latter task was one of Farook's 'hunter-killer teams'—the three- to five-man specially trained and motivated squads he had earlier boasted about. This was one put in charge of Farook's most trusted men, Risaldar, now Hon. Lieutenant, Muslehuddin. He was the Lancer who led the killer team to Sheikh Fazlul Huq Moni's house on 15th August. Thus the diabolical murders were planned in the most cold-blooded way.

'The contingency plan was expressly designed to operate automatically,' Farook added. How true his words! Operate it did with the most baleful results on 3rd November when Khalid Musharraf launched his counter-coup.

On 6th September 1975, just three weeks after Sheikh Mujibur Rahman's death, a dapper, middle-aged Bengali, wearing a spotless silk achkan (knee-length shirt) over white 'churidar pyjamas' (Jodhpur-style cotton pants), flew into London from Islamabad, the capital of Pakistan, and checked into the plush Carlton Towers Hotel at Knightsbridge. He had an expensive penthouse suite, but money was no consideration. Mahmood Ali was in London on a special mission which he hoped to turn into the crowning glory of an otherwise disappointing life: the undoing of Bangladesh and the reunification of Pakistan.

As Special Adviser to Prime Minister Zulfiquar Ali Bhutto, Mahmood Ali had come out to establish contact with the new Bangladesh regime. Specifically it was to sound out how far Khandaker Moshtaque Ahmed would go in establishing the 'link'—special relationship—with Pakistan that Mr. Bhutto had suggested to Sheikh Mujib when he released him from prison in December 1971.

Mahmood Ali, however, had plans of his own, a grand design, far exceeding his official brief. No one, not even his boss, Mr. Bhutto, I was to learn, would stand in his way. 'I want reunification of Pakistan,' he told me in an interview in his hotel, 'This Bangladesh thing must be finished with.'

As an old Muslim Leaguer, Mahmood Ali, like some other Bengalis living in Pakistan, had never accepted the fact of Bangladesh and was dedicated to its undoing. He had always worked for the reunification of Pakistan and, he explained to me, had for four years 'tenaciously clung with great faith to this eventuality'. Now apparently, he felt the great moment was at hand. He was in constant touch with Dhaka by telephone and was patiently 'waiting for the great news'.

Mahmood Ali's jubilation was understandable. Khandaker Moshtaque Ahmed, though not wanting reunification, by his actions had encouraged such wishful thinking. On assuming office after Mujib's death Moshtaque had given Bangladesh a decidedly pro-Pakistan posture. Justice Abu Sayed Chowdhury, his Foreign Minister, told me: 'Our foreign policy was pro-Pakistan, pro-Islamic countries, pro-America.' Moshtaque sent Pir Muslehuddin (Dadu Miah) as a special emissary to Islamabad and quickly established diplomatic relations with Pakistan—something that Sheikh Mujib had refused to do till Pakistan agreed to give Bangladesh its share of the national assets. Furthermore, Moshtaque had surrounded himself with government officials who had been closely identified with Pakistan during the Liberation movement. Among them were Shafiul Azam, Tabarak Hussain, Salhauddin and A. B. S. Safdar.

Shafiul Azam was intensely disliked by the FFs and Awami Leaguers because he had continued to serve as Chief Secretary of East Pakistan province after the Pakistan army had cracked down on the Bengalis in March, 1971, at the start of the Liberation War. Moshtaque appointed him Cabinet Secretary of the new Bangladesh government. Salhauddin, who had been Home Secretary of East Pakistan provincial government in 1971, was brought back from a foreign job to become Home Secretary of Bangladesh. A. B. S. Safdar, a former senior office in the Pakistan intelligence service, was appointed Director General of the National Security Intelligence (NSI), the country's top intelligence agency.

Tabarak Hussain, a senior Pakistan foreign service officer, had a family connection with the former Pakistan President, General Yahya Khan, who had ordered the genocide in Bangladesh in 1971. Tabarak served the Pakistan government through most of the Bengali freedom struggle. After repatriation to Bangladesh in 1973 he was mercilessly ostracised by his colleagues in the Foreign Office in Dhaka. He lingered for several months as an O.S.D. (Officer on Special Duty which in the bureaucratic parlance means 'Officer without responsibility'). I had known him well in Pakistan and when we met again in Dhaka in February, 1974, Tabarak was lying with a broken leg in the corridor of an open ward in a local hospital totally neglected by his colleagues. He was hoping that Mujib would ultimately give him 'a small embassy in one of the Gulf states'. Khandaker Moshtaque brought him in as Foreign Secretary, the most senior position in the Foreign Service.

Later, when he took over, General Ershad would drop them one by one. But at that time all those appointments had encouraged Mahmood Ali and others like him to hope that Khandaker Moshtaque, with some encouragement, would take the decisive step for the reunification of Pakistan.

Mahmood Ali told me that although Khandaker Moshtaque, 'because of immaturity', had failed to endorse the re-naming of Bangladesh as an 'Islamic Republic', he was confident that it was Moshtaque's intention 'to reverse the course set in December, 1971'. He had therefore proposed to Moshtaque through intermediaries a loose form of confederation which would unite Bangladesh and Pakistan 'under one name and one flag' while leaving the details of other relationships to be worked out in due course. Mahmood Ali felt Moshtaque was very vulnerable 'because the army could demolish him at any time'. He thought it would be to Moshtaque's advantage 'to come out soon with the one thing that could make him unassailable—the re-establishment of the link with Pakistan which 80 per cent of the people want'.

'I told him (Moshtaque) waiting would be dangerous and he must act now,' Mahmood Ali confided. 'What I want from him is a simple declaration of intent. Let him say that Pakistan is one again and no one on earth will be able to contradict it. The details can be worked out later.'

I asked Mahmood Ali if he seriously believed that the Bangladeshis would want to go back to Pakistan after all that they had suffered in 1971. There were other obstacles. A confederation pre-supposed a paramount authority and either Bhutto or Khandaker Moshtaque would have to step down to a junior position. That was something that neither would be inclined to do. Mahmood Ali admitted that Prime Minister Bhutto was an 'obstacle' to the reunification of Pakistan. He said, however, that Mr. Bhutto was seriously troubled by a revolt by his party stalwarts such as Mustafa Khar and Hanif Ramay and he would go the way Mujib did 'unless he can sweep away the opposition by giving them Bangladesh back'.

Bhutto, it was clear, had no such intention. At about the time Mahmood Ali was talking to me in London, Foreign Minister Aziz Ahmad was telling his Bangladesh counterpart during the UN General Assembly session in New York that Pakistan wanted close ties with Bangladesh, a state-to-state relationship, even a special one, but nothing more. According to Justice Chowdhury, Aziz Ahmad told him: 'There are certain over-enthusiastic persons who want many things but we are not encouraging them. We have to keep them under restraint.'

Mahmood Ali waited three weeks in London for the fateful announcement from Dhaka. It never came. Evidently someone in Bangladesh had strung him along. Khandaker Moshtaque would never have dared to put the clock back. Had he tried to do so he would have been immediately killed by the Majors Farook and Rashid, both staunch nationalists. Farook told me: 'If anyone wanted to hand over Bangladesh to someone else, I would have blown his bloody head off'.

Three months later, when we had occasion to discuss it, General Ziaur Rahman told me he had been 'extremely suspicious about Moshtaque hob-nobbing with Pakistanis' 'Immediately after Mujib was killed,' he said, 'several Bengalis who had been living in Pakistan rushed to England and started wangling how they could come to Bangladesh which they called the "new Pakistan". Similarly some Bengalis who had been underground for some years in Bangladesh suddenly surfaced in London all intent on resuming relations with Pakistan. All of us were quite amazed and were wondering what they were trying to do—but really, the answer was obvious,' Zia added.

China's long overdue recognition gave Moshtaque's ego a big boost. But otherwise things were not going well for him as the summer made way for autumn. Despite the best efforts of the government's propaganda machinery, Information Minister Tahiruddin Thakur (who had earlier slaved with equal diligence for Mujib), was unable to dispel widespread public confusion about Moshtaque's policies. On the one hand Moshtaque hob-nobbed with pro-Pakistan elements and lost no occasion to speak out loudly about Islam and Islamic practices. On the other, he also paradoxically clung to Mujib's secular line. The absurdity of this stance was highlighted by a government White Paper on the economy issued on 12th September, 1975.

Moshtaque had appointed an Economic Task Force to identify the economic problems in an obvious attempt to expose Mujib's wrong-doings. The Task Force completed its work in a record 12 days. The report was then incorporated in a White Paper which staggered the country by recommending: 'The immediate task is to put the economy on an even keel and bring back sanity, rationality and discipline in economic policy and management . . . keeping in view the four basic state principles, namely DEMOCRACY, SOCIALISM, SECULARISM and NATIONALISM . . .' Surely there was something wrong. The 'Four Principles' they referred to had been the 'Four Pillars of Mujibism', the self-same banners that brought Sheikh Mujibur Rahman to an early grave. Yet here was Khandaker Moshtaque, the self-proclaimed product of the 'historical necessity' to change the system, clinging with the same pomposity to Mujib's jargon in his government's first White Paper. No wonder people were bewildered. Why had Sheikh Mujib to die? Seeing this, the Majors who had put Moshtaque in power became daily more restive.

On the 3rd October, the 50th day of his regime, Khandaker Moshtaque went on TV and radio to announce 'the decision to restore to the people their lost democratic rights'. Restrictions on political activity would be lifted from 15th August (1976) and General Elections held on the following 28th February (1977) for a parliament and parliamentary form of government. This shrewd political move was widely acclaimed. Also well received was the announcement that the government had decided to release political prisoners and Moshtaque's flat assurance that 'There is now no warrant of arrest pending against political leaders only for their political beliefs'. Moshtaque again was not exactly telling the truth. At least four senior politicians—Tajuddin, Syed Nazrul Islam, Mansoor Ali and Kamruzzaman—were still locked up in Dhaka Central Jail with no hope of early release.

Moshtaque took the opportunity in his broadcast to apply a soothing balm to the ruffled feathers of the Majors and their men by extravagantly referring to them as 'the valiant sons of the sun of the armed forces'. Cynical Bangladeshis however derided this remark. They had in the past seven weeks come to know only too well the dark side of the Sons of the Sun! The courtier sycophants, the corrupt and corrupting bureaucrats and businessmen had gone to work again within hours of Sheikh Mujib's murder. With their well-developed antennae they had accurately homed in on the real source of power, the Majors and their men. Farook recalled: 'I could have made millions of dollars, leave alone takkas, within a week. But I refused to see any of those chaps'. Rashid confirmed he had received reports that some of the retired officers involved in the coup 'were making money left and right'. Not to be outdone, some of the Lancers and Artillery men had also run wild. Military intelligence reports at that time indicated that these jawans and NCOs and some of the retired Majors and Captains had set up extortion and protection rackets. 'They began to sport expensive watches and gadgets,' I was told, 'and lots and lots of money.' Acton's dictum—All power corrupts. Absolute power corrupts absolutely—had begun to exert itself. So Farook's 'revolution'—the great cleansing operation he had undertaken—and specifically his reasons for killing Sheikh Mujib had all come to naught!

Farook and Rashid also had other reasons for concern. First, their attempts to programme Moshtaque were clearly falling on deaf ears. He shamelessly used them, but their 'advice' was adroitly diverted to the bureaucratic maze 'for action', it was said, and invariably got buried there. Secondly, it was particularly galling for Farook and Rashid to find that Moshtaque and Tahiruddin Thakur were secretly but nonetheless effectively fostering the legend that they, not the majors, had been the principal factors in the 15th August coup. Thus Farook and Rashid found themselves not only isolated and bottled up by Moshtaque, but also denied what they felt was well-deserved public recognition and acceptance.

'Suddenly they (Moshtaque and Tahiruddin Thakur) were the heroes and we were the killer dogs,' Farook complained. Rashid was equally bitter. 'He (Moshtaque) should have been a little grateful to us as we have picked him for the President's post. But he was a politician and it's in their blood and nature to betray. He has never been a straightfoward chap.'

The majors decided to remedy this with a 10-page document highlighting their deeds and intentions which they decided to make public. Explaining the move in fractured English, Rashid said: 'First thing we wanted to clarify is why it was essential to kill Sheikh and why we gave power to Moshtaque. Otherwise if things turned out good, he would claim benefit. If they turned out bad, we would get the blame. In both ways he was riding our backs. We did not want to go down in history as assassinators.'

Moshtaque was not amused by Rashid and Farook's plans to publicise themselves. However he tactfully suggested that Tahiruddin Thakur could improve upon the draft, perhaps do a better job for the Majors. So the draft Rashid had made was handed over to him. Somehow it was never completed.

Although he kept them in limbo in Bangababan without any official position, Moshtaque did allow the two majors to stand on equal terms with the generals and to join them in discussions of high policy. On one such occasion, four days after the killing of Mujib, the Chief of Army Staff, General Shafiullah, called a conference of Formation Commanders and Principal Staff Officers at Army Headquarters. Farook and Rashid were also present. Shafiullah informed the assembled officers that President Moshtaque had sent the two majors to 'explain why they killed Sheikh Mujib and we will have to listen'. Rashid started off recounting the law and order situation and why Sheikh Mujib had to be replaced by President Moshtaque. Before he could proceed further, he was angrily interrupted by Col. Shafat Jamil shouting: 'Moshtaque is not my president. He is a self-made president, not elected, and I owe no allegiance. He is a usurper, conspirator and murderer and at the first opportunity I'll overthrow him.' The Dhaka Brigade commander who told me about the incident said his outburst caused consternation among the officers and a speedy end to the conference. The majors did not attempt to address the Formation Commanders again, but they did make their presence felt at Army Headquarters. Moshtaque allowed them to do so. And he turned a blind eye to the depredations of Farook and Rashid's men and some of the retired officers from the group that killed Sheikh Mujib. Thus instead of stamping out indiscipline as he publicly promised, Moshtaque in fact kept the army in turmoil.

General Zia would later tell me: 'He (Moshtaque) used the majors for his own protection and did not mind if he destroyed them in the process. He played on their fears and the fears of the Bengal Lancers and Artillery men, thus dividing and creating indiscipline in the Army.'

It was an uncomfortable situation all round. Here were two majors, still formally within the army, yet outside its discipline and chain of command, with powerful armoured and artillery units at their disposal. Rashid periodically descended on General Zia at the Chief of Staff's office to 'discuss' problems or to make 'suggestions'. At the same time the commander of the Bengal Lancers, Col. Momin, received his instructions from Major Farook Rahman, still nominally his second-in-command. Farook's arrogance was particularly galling to the army brass. Having complained to Moshtaque about the lack of personal transport, he had been given the run of the President's motor pool. So Farook used to sport about in the President's Cadillac or Mercedes limousines to the immense irritation of his seniors. Inevitably these anomalies became intolerable. Plotting in the army against Moshtaque and the Majors developed in earnest.

Towards the end of September a young infantry officer was caught trying to subvert some of the Lancers who were guarding Bangababan. The matter was promptly reported to Farook and Rashid who interrogated the man and, so they claimed, discovered he had been put up to it by Brigadier Khalid Musharraf and Colonel Shafat Jamil. Rashid took the 'evidence' to General Zia with the request for appropriate action. Zia promised to look into it. Nothing happened. Rashid said he had the same experience on many other occasions when he reported such incidents to the General.

'Zia kept telling me, "Rashid don't you worry. If anything happens it will be over my dead body." I think he was either a coward or very clever,' said Rashid. 'He may have been hoping we will knock out each other and give him the benefit.'

Khandaker Moshtaque, who also accused General Zia of ignoring his warnings, was even more caustic in an interview he gave me at Dhaka on 12th December, 1975, a little more than a month after he had been forced out of office. 'Before 2nd November,' he said, 'even the rickshaw men were knowing that something was going to happen. I knew it. Everybody knew it. Yet they couldn't see it. What were they doing?'

Who are the 'they' you are referring to, I asked Moshtaque. He replied: 'Those fellows in the Cantonment. Those men who call themselves generals and who really are small majors. What were they doing? Ninety-eight per cent of the officers were with me, yet they couldn't protect the President against the two per cent? They are miserable failures.' Then, in a pointed reference to General Zia, Moshtaque added: 'Let me tell you again, he (Zia) is like a small major, inexperienced, unintelligent, ambitious-minded. He couldn't defend the Cantonment. How can he defend the country? Yet he is ambitious.'

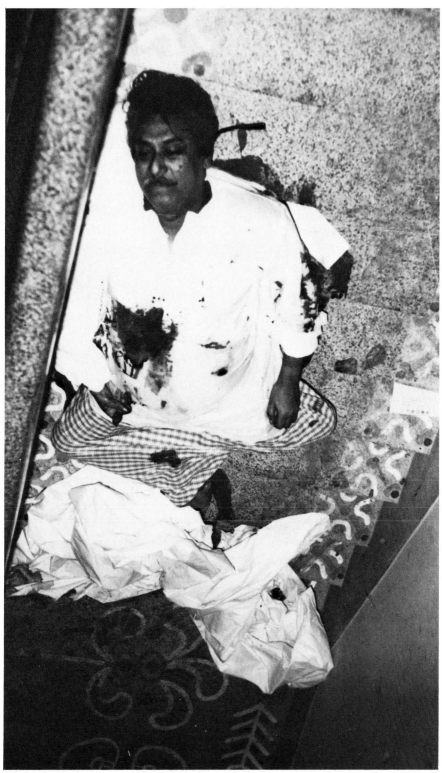

Sheikh Mujibur Rahman after he had been killed by the majors. His body lies sprawled on the staircase of his home in Dhaka with the right hand still clutching his favourite pipe.

General Ziaur Rahman, assassinated President of Bangladesh.

Major Farook Rahman, 2nd in charge, Bengal Lancers, who masterminded Sheikh Mujib's assassination.

Major Khandaker Abdur Rashid, CO of 2nd Field Artill Farook's brother-in-law and partner in Mujib's assassina

Sheikh Mujibur Rahman and Zulfiquar Ali Bhutto in Dhaka in 1974. Once implacable political foes, they got together as fairweather friends after Pakistan broke up – with Mujib becoming the Founding Father of Bangladesh and Bhutto President of what remained of Pakistan.

On returning triumphantly to Dhaka after the liberation war, Sheikh Mujibur Rahman receiving a Judas kiss from Khandaker Moshtaque Ahmed who connived at his assassination and succeeded him as President for 83 days in 1975.

BATMEN EXTRAORDINARY: Air Vice Marshal Towab and Admiral M. H. Khan, the Air Force and Navy Chiefs, pinning new badges of rank on Khalid Musharraf, leader of the short-lived coup in November 1975, who promoted himself to Major General. A day later Khalid was killed during the Sepoy Mutiny and the Air Force and Navy Chiefs switched loyalty to the new Army strongman, Major General Ziaur Rahman.

Andha Hafiz, the blind holy man in Chittagong, who gave Major Farook a talisman for the killing of Sheikh Mujib.

Registered No. DA-1

THE
BANGLADESH GAZETTE

Extraordinary
Published by Authority

FRIDAY, SEPTEMBER 26, 1975

GOVERNMENT OF THE PEOPLE'S REPUBLIC OF BANGLADESH
MINISTRY OF LAW PARLIAMENTARY AFFAIRS AND JUSTICE
(Law and Parliamentary Affairs Division)
NOTIFICATION
Dacca, the 26th September 1975.

No. 692-Pub. – The following Ordinance made by the President of the People's Republic of Bangladesh, on the 26th September, 1975, is hereby published for general information:—

THE INDEMNITY ORDINANCE, 1975
Ordinance No. XLX of 1975
an
ORDINANCE

to restrict the taking of any legal or other proceedings in respect of certain acts or things done in connection with, or in preparation or execution of any plan for, or steps necessitating, the historical change and the Proclamation of Martial Law on the morning of the 15th August, 1975.

WHEREAS it is expedient to restrict the taking of any legal or other proceedings in respect of certain acts or things done in connection with, or in preparation or execution of any plan for, or steps necessitating, the historical change and the Proclamation of Martial Law on the morning of 15th August, 1975;

AND WHEREAS Parliament is not in session and the President is satisfied that circumstances exist which render immediate action necessary;

(2705)

NOW, THEREFORE, in pursuance of the Proclamation of the 20th August 1975, and in exercise of the powers conferred by clause (1) of article 93 of the Constitution of the People's Republic of Bangladesh, the President is pleased to make and promulgate the following Ordinance:

1. SHORT TITLE – This Ordinance may be called the Indemnity Ordinance 1975.

2. RESTRICTIONS ON THE TAKING OF ANY LEGAL OR OTHER PROCEEDINGS AGAINST PERSONS IN RESPECT OF CERTAIN ACTS AND THINGS – (1) Notwithstanding anything contained in any law, including a law relating to any defence service, for the time being in force, no suit, prosecution or other proceedings, legal or disciplinary, shall lie, or be taken, in, before or by any Court, including the Supreme Court and Court Martial or other authority against any person, including a person who is or has, at any time, been subject to any law relating to any defence service, for or on account of or in respect of any act, matter or thing done or step taken by such person in connection with, or in preparation of execution of any plan for, or as necessary step towards the change of Government of the People's Republic of Bangladesh and the Proclamation of Martial Law on the morning of the 15th August, 1975.

(2) For the purposes of this section, a certificate by the President, or a person authorised by him in this behalf, that any act, matter or thing was done or step taken by any person mentioned in the certificate in connection with or in preparation or execution of any plan for, or as necessary step towards, the change of Government of the People's Republic of Bangladesh and the Proclamation of Martial Law on the morning of the 15th August, 1975, shall be sufficient evidence of such act, matter or thing having been done or step having been taken in connection with, or in preparation or execution of any plan for, or a necessary step towards, the change of such Government and the Proclamation of Martial Law on that morning.

KHANDAKER MOSHTAQUE AHMED
President

DACCA;
The 26th September, 1975.

M.H. RAHMAN
Secretary.

Printed by the Special Officer, Bangladesh Government Press, Dacca.
Published by the Assistant Controller-in-charge, Bangladesh Forms & Publications Office
Dacca

POST-MORTEM REPORT ON THE DEAD BODY OF THE LATE PRESIDENT ZIAUR RAHMAN

Post-Mortem Report in respect of Lt. Gen. (Retd.) Ziaur Rahman, BU, psc, President of the People's Republic of Bangladesh.

Body Identified by—Lt. Col. Mahfuz, P.S. to President.

Time of Death—04·00 hrs. on 30-5-81.

Time of Post-mortem Examination—10·00 hrs. on 01-6-81.

Brief History.—The President was allegedly assassinated by the miscreants on Saturday the 30th May, 1981 at 04·00 hrs. in Chittagong Circuit House. He sustained multiple bullet injuries on his person and died on the spot. It is stated by Lt. Col. Mahfuz that his body was buried with another two dead bodies at about 14·30 hrs. on 30th May 1981 near Chittagong Engineering College. Lt. Col. Mahfuz with others of the Sta. HQ. Ctg. exhumed his body from that mass grave on 01-6-1981 morning and brought to CMH Ctg. Cantt. for necessary P.M. examination at about 10·00 hrs. on 01-6-1981.

On Examination.—The body was partially decomposed but the configuration was intact to be identified as the body of the late President Ziaur Rahman. There were about twenty separate bullet wounds on the body. The details of the wounds are as follows:—

a. One bullet entered through right eye and was out through the left occiputo-parietal region with the extrusion of the brain matter.

b. Another 8″×3″ oblique lacerated wound present extending from the left angle of the mouth up to the left lower neck. The mandible was shattered and all the neck structures

c. There are about ten bullet wounds over the chest and abdomen probaly entrance wounds.

d. There were equal number of corresponding bigger wounds on the back of the trunk also. These were probably exit wounds.

e. There was big lacerated 4″×3″ wound on the perineum and left groin with corresponding wounds of the back of pelvis and buttock left. Probably due to the effects of brush fire.

f. There were two bullet wounds in the rt. arm.

g. There were few scattered small wounds on both lower limbs.

The body was cleaned and reconstructed. Formalin Solution was injected in all the wounds and the body was soaked by the same. The whole body was then bandaged with soft cotton wool. and wrapped in new white sheet. Cedar wood oil. Eucalyptus oil and "Atar" were sprinkled over the whole sheet. Then the body was preserved in a coffin by tea leaves. The coffin was wrapped by the National Standard and handed over to Brig. A.K.M. Aziaul Islam. Lt. Col. Mahfuz and Lt. Col. Mahtabul Islam at 13·00 hrs. by CO, CMH. Chittagong.

Sd/- Lt. Col. A. Z. TUFAIL AHMED
Gd. Specialist in Pathology.

POST MORTEM REPORT: MAJ. GEN. M.A. MANZOOR

Body identified by Lt. Col. Shamsur Rahman of EBRC.
Reported time of death: 23.30 hours on 1st June, 1981.
Time of post mortem: 07.30 hours on 2nd June, 1981.

History: Dead body of Major General M.A. Manzoor was brought
         to CMH Chittagong at about 04.00 hours on 2nd June.
         No history available.

External Examination: Rigour Mortis had set in. There was a big
                      gaping hole 4"x 2" with ragged margin on
                      the right occipital region. The bullet
                      crushed the bone and shattered it completely.
                      A big chunk of bone was blown away and the
                      brain matter extruded through the gap. There
                      was no other injury on the body.
                      No internal examination was carried out
                      because the cause of death was obvious.

Cause of death: Shock and haemorrhage from bullet injury, head.

                    Signed: Lt. Col. A.Z. Tufail Ahmed

                    Dated: 2nd June 1981.

                              Copy

          Government of the People's Republic of Bangladesh
                        Ministry of Defence
                      Old High Court Building
                              DHAKA

                          NOTIFICATION

No 7/3/D-I/75-160.   Dated, the 28 February 1979.

     BA-69 Major General Ziaur Rahman, BU,psc is promoted to the
rank of Temporary Lieutenant General with immediate effect.

                    By order of the President,

                    Sd/ xxxxxxxxxxxxx
                    (A H F K Sadique)
                    Defence Secretary

No 7/3/D-I/75-160   Dated the 28th February 1979.

Copy forwarded for information and necessary action to :-

1. Chief of the Army Staff, Bangladesh Army, Army Headquarters,
    Dhaka Cantonment, Dhaka

2. Chief of the Naval Staff, Bangladesh Navy, Naval Headquarters,
    Dhaka Cantonment, Dhaka

3. Chief of the Air Staff, Bangladesh Air Force, Air Headquarters
    Dhaka Cantonment, Dhaka.

4. P. S. O. to the Commander -in- Chief, C-in-C's Secretariat,
    Dhaka Cantonment, Dhaka.

                    Sd/ xx x x xx
                    (M A Hena)
                    Joint Secretary

The
Bangladesh  Gazette

Published by Authority

THURSDAY, APRIL 19, 1979

PART III

Notifications issued by the Ministry of Defence other than those included in Part I,

MINISTRY OF DEFENCE

NOTIFICATIONS

Dacca, the 9th April 1979.

No. 7/8/D-I/75/270.—BA-69 Major General Ziaur Rahman, BU, psc is promoted to the rank of Temporary Lieutenant General with effect from 28th April 1978.

2. This cancels this Ministry's Notification No. 7/8/D-I/75/160, dated 28th February 1979.

No. 7/8/D-I/75/271.—BA-69 Temporary Lieutenant General Ziaur Rahman, BU, psc is retired from the service of the Bangladesh Army with effect from 29th April 1978.

By order of the President
A. H. F. K. SADIQUE
Defence Secretary.

প্রজ্ঞাপনসমূহ

ঢাকা, ৬ই এপ্রিল ১৯৭৯।

নং ২জ-৩/৭১ /ডি-১/:৬৪—গণপ্রজাতন্ত্রী বাংলাদেশ সরকার প্রচলিত বিধি মোতাবেক বি এস এস-৩৬৫ সহসী মো: মোহাম্মদ মফিজুল ইসলাম, ইঞ্জিনিয়ারকে বাংলাদেশ সেনাবাহিনীর চাকুরী হইতে বরখাস্ত করিয়াছেন।

২। উক্ত অফিগারকে ২৮শে মার্চ ১৯৭৯ তারিখ হইতে দেহাই (এস ও ডি) এবং সেনাবাহিনী সংখ্যা বহির্ভূত (এস ও এস) করা হইল।

ঢাকা, ৭ই এপ্রিল ১৯৭৯।

নং ৪/৩৩/[ডি-১/৭২/(অংশ)/২৬৭— বাংলাদেশ সেনাবাহিনীতে সহকারি ২য় চাকুরী কমিশন প্রদান সম্পর্কিত ৭ই নভেম্বর ১৯৭৬ তারিখের প্রজ্ঞাপন নং ৪/৩২/[ডি-১/৭২ (অংশ)/৮৫৮-এর ক্রমিক নং খ-এর নিচে বহিতে সংশোধনী আনী করা হইল :

পরিবর্তে

ক্রমিক নং।	নাম।	কমিশনের তারিখ।	কোর।
৭।	মো: মাহবুবুর রহমান	১৪-৯-১৯৭৬	আর ভি এ ও এস সি।

পঠন

ক্রমিক নং।	নাম।	কমিশনের তারিখ।	কোর।
খ।	মো: মাহবুবুর রহমান	১০-৬-১৯৭৬	আর ভি এ ও এস সি।

রাষ্ট্রপতির আদেশক্রমে

মো: শামসুল ইসলাম
সিনিয়র স্টাফ অফিসার

By the end of October Moshtaque, Osmani, General Khalil and Farook and Rashid were convinced that a coup was imminent. General Khalil said that according to the reports they were receiving the finger of suspicion pointed equally at Khalid Musharraf and General Zia. 'We used to meet every night to try to find out who was the more dangerous,' Khalil told me. 'At first the boys (Farook and Rashid) wanted to arrest both of them. Then they suggested we quickly form a brigade that was loyal to us and get everybody arrested. But that too was discarded as not being feasible.'

Whatever the reason, General Osmani apparently was convinced that General Zia presented the greater danger. On the night of 2nd November, accompanied by General Khalil, Osmani informed Moshtaque that Zia must be removed from his job as Chief of the Army Staff. Rashid, who was present on the occasion, gave me an interesting account of the incident. The cabinet sub-committee had been convened on the evening of 2nd November to finalise the arrangements for restoring the Constitution and political rights. After a lengthy discussion the meeting broke up a little before midnight, leaving the Law Minister, Manoranjan Dhar, the task of drafting the required legislation. Osmani had attended the meeting. Before going home to the Cantonment he had got hold of General Khalil and went in for a chat with the President. Rashid joined them. The nub of the discussion was that Osmani had serious misgivings about General Zia and wanted him removed from his job. Rashid objected strongly. He said it was not Zia, but some other senior officers such as Khalid Musharraf and Shafat Jamil who were the real threat to the government. And in couching his argument, Rashid said he took pains to slyly convey a warning to Moshtaque that Osmani may have a deeper motive for wanting Zia out. Moshtaque was quick to grasp the point. Though he had never been happy with General Zia, this was a new situation and he was not going to throw his hand away so easily. Furthermore, there was the possibility that what the new man Osmani had in mind was even less acceptable to him than Zia. So Moshtaque temporised. He told Osmani: 'Alright, if you want to change General Zia tell me who is to replace him? Give me some names.' Osmani promised to do the needful the following day. The two generals then bid them goodnight and left Bangababan for their homes.

Rashid recalls sitting for more than half an hour with Moshtaque in the President's private quarters chewing over the bombshell that Osmani had dropped. It's symptomatic of the miasma of suspicion and intrigue that permeated Bangladesh at that time that the two of them began to suspect that, of all persons, the grand old soldier, General Osmani, may be working hand-in-glove with Khalid Musharraf's group. 'We decided to wait and see whether he would recommend Khalid as General Zia's replacement,' Rashid said. 'If he did, then we would have been sure he was doing some mischief.'

Rashid was returning to his own bedroom further down the corridor when a very agitated police officer ran up to tell him breathlessly in staccato bursts: 'Sir ... those infantry men ... those who were guarding ... they have run away. They said ... we must go also as there's to be trouble ... serious fighting. They said we must run away.'

Rashid's worst fears had materialised. The counter-coup had begun.

Notes
1. The Sunday Telegraph, 25.8.1975.
2. ibid.

IX

'Counter coup' and the Jail Killings

In the middle of the confusion, the telephone rang. When I picked it up I heard a man say: I'm DIG Prisons. I would like to talk to Hon'ble President.

—Major Abdur Rashid

Bangababan, the President's House in Dhaka, is not built to withstand a seige. The splendid colonial-style building with wide carriage-ways and acre upon acre of tropical flowers and foliage—the colours somehow always seem more vivid in Bengal—has an old-world charm about it, quite removed from the pressures of everyday. It belongs to another world; a world of pomp and circumstance, of unhurried movement, a world of orderliness. Yet on that fateful night of 2nd November, 1975, Bangababan looked like a military camp gearing to beat off an invader.

The roar of tanks starting up had startled hundreds of crows roosting in the trees and they flew about cawing wildly in the night. But within moments even their raucous noises were drowned out as the rest of the tanks sprang to life. Farook had eight tanks in Bangababan. He had another eight at Suhrawardy Udhyan, the old racecourse ground, conveniently placed to control the radio station and intercept anything coming from the Cantonment and the old airport. Twelve other tanks awaited his orders in the Bengal Lancers' lines in the Cantonment itself.

Farook had been sleeping in an adjoining bedroom when Rashid awakened him to break the news of the defection of the infantry guard, the 1st East Bengal Regiment. The two of them had a hurried conference with Khandaker Moshtaque. Farook wanted to implement immediately a plan he had prepared for such an eventuality. It involved seizing Dhaka Airport (the old one), the 46th Brigade Headquarters and other key army installations. How he hoped to do this with tanks alone—and without the necessary infantry back-up—Farook did not explain. But he did say that Moshtaque and Rashid reacted sharply to this 'hot-headed' scheme. They told him they would rather try to talk their way out of the crisis than provoke a civil war. So Farook undertook an alternative plan, a defensive one. He ordered the tanks in all three locations to start and take up previously designed defensive positions. In Bangababan this meant some of the tanks moving outside the walls to control the approach roads. Others stayed within the compound like enormous growling mastiffs waiting to savage any intruder. Men with machine guns and sten guns took up positions on the long perimeter wall.

Before leaving for Suhrawardy Udhyan to take personal command of the tanks there, Farook made one telephone call. It was to a friend, an army officer overseeing the government's telecommunications system. Farook requested a total communications black-out with the outside world. It is not known whether this officer did indeed oblige Farook or instead choose to look the other way, as Rashid found so many other officers doing at that crucial moment for the Majors and Moshtaque.

Sitting in the President's office with Khandaker Moshtaque, Rashid had been burning up the telephone with calls for help. First he phoned General Zia, Chief of the Army Staff, and found him asleep. He briefed the general about the developments and requested his presence in Bangababan. 'I'll look into it,' was Zia's brusque non-committal reply. Then, to the major's chagrin, Zia abruptly hung up.

Rashid telephoned Brigadier Khalid Musharraf, Chief of the General Staff. 'Sir, what's happening?' Rashid asked. 'You tell me,' said the Brigadier. Rashid briefly told him about the infantry withdrawing from the President's House. Then he asked: 'What do you think?' 'What's there to think,' Khalid retorted. 'What was expected earlier has started. I'm going out now. You wait there. I'll call you back later.'

Rashid's third call was to the headquarters of the Bangladesh Rifles. But he got no joy from them. Then he telephoned Air Vice Marshal Towab, the Chief of the Air Staff who was billetted in the VIP rest house next to Hotel Dhaka Sheraton. Towab owed his appointment to Rashid. Two months earlier the major had flown all the way to Munich with a letter from General Osmani to offer him the job. So Rashid was counting on a positive response at least from this Air Force officer. Once again he was disappointed. According to Rashid, Towab didn't think there was any point in rushing to Bangababan. He felt he would be of little use there. Towab said he would, instead, see what he could do about getting help from some Air Force personnel. Rashid got the message: Towab would not be coming. 'Perhaps he didn't think he should risk his life,' the major added wryly.

Rashid, in desperation, then telephoned General Osmani at his Cantonment residence. After explaining what had happened, Rashid told him that the President would like to have his Defence Adviser with him in Bangababan as soon as possible. Osmani readily agreed to come. But he did not have a car. Looking out of the window he also noticed a lot of troops moving about. Osmani wasn't sure it was safe to venture out. But the old general did try to help. While waiting for a lift, he telephoned an order to the Bangladesh Rifles to send two battalions to guard the President. Apparently these instructions were aborted somewhere down the line because no BDR units turned up at Bangababan.

Osmani also telephoned General Zia. 'His wife picked up the telephone,' he told me, 'and said Zia can't come to the telephone . . . there's some difficulty. When I insisted on talking to him, she told me in a hushed sort of voice that there were some men in the hall with him and he couldn't come to the phone. I realised then that Zia was under some sort of restraint,' Osmani added.

Calling Khalid Musharraf's house a little later Osmani was informed that the CGS was 'in the lines' i.e. with the 4th East Bengal. He telephoned him there. When the brigadier came on the line, Osmani recalled, they had a brief but sharp exchange that indicated that by this time Khalid Musharraf had taken charge of the operation.

Osmani: 'Khalid, what the hell's going on?'

Khalid; 'The tanks are adopting threatening postures.'

Osmani: 'What threatening postures? You pull back your infantry and I assure you the tanks won't do anything.'

Khalid: 'Don't worry. I'll sort it out.'

Khalid Musharraf and Shafat Jamil had been waiting a long time to sort out the majors in Bangababan. In fact on the day Sheikh Mujibur Rahman was killed, Khalid had personally contacted Shafat Jamil, the 46th Brigade (Dhaka Brigade) commander, to 'prepare for action against the mutineers'. The troops had accordingly been prepared to strike at midnight, but the action was never carried out because Khalid was called to Bangababan and did not contact Jamil again till three days later. The CGS then told him: 'We want no further bloodshed. Stand down your troops.'

Shafat Jamil had never accepted this situation. From time to time he went to General Zia, who had been promoted to Chief of Army Staff in place of General Shafiullah, complaining: 'The majors are ruining the country. Let's re-establish the chain of command. If you allow me, I'll sort them out.'

'Zia never shut me up or gave me orders,' Jamil recalled. 'He was playing both sides.'

However in the middle of October, General Zia suddenly ordered the Bengal Lancers to return to the Cantonment, leaving only four tanks in Bangababan. The order was not carried out and rescinded next day when the majors intervened. Farook and Rashid had asserted their supremacy again.

On 25th October, General Zia summoned Shafat Jamil to his office in Army Headquarters. The brigadier found Air Vice Marshal Towab closetted with Zia. When Jamil entered and exchanged courtesies with his Chief, General Zia got up and went to the toilet leaving Jamil alone with Towab for more than 10 minutes. They sat in silence because Jamil did not like Towab since he was connected with the majors. When Zia returned, without further ado, he told Jamil to go back to his headquarters, leaving the brigadier perplexed about the reason for being summoned in the first place. Then he realised that Zia had wanted to give them an opportunity to speak.

Towab confirmed the incident in his own way. He told me he had been getting reports of an imminent coup and indications were that General Zia was behind it. So to test him out Towab had gone to Zia to say: 'General, I've been hearing things and I want you to know that if you are planning anything, please note that I am fully behind you.' Zia was not at all taken in by Towab. He never trusted the Air Force Chief and he correctly assumed that it was more than possible that Towab was trying to trap him. Zia strongly denied he was plotting. But he cunningly put Towab and Shafat Jamil together. This could have been either to compromise Towab since Jamil's opposition was well known, or to quietly promote their intrigue from which he could benefit. In any case the effort failed.

On the 1st November Khalid Musharraf asked Shafat Jamil: 'Are you still keen to streamline the chain of command?' Jamil replied in the affirmative. Then Khalid told him: 'Things have gone beyond the limit. We must strike now.' A secret meeting was arranged for that afternoon in a Chinese restaurant near Dhaka Stadium. Khalid and Jamil were joined there by two trusted junior officers when they discussed the plan of action. The juniors suggested that General Zia should be killed as part of the coup. But this was vetoed by Khalid because he did not want any bloodshed. The decision was taken to strike the next day at Bangababan to take out the majors and their tanks and to seize control of the government. They would simultaneously arrest Zia and forcibly retire him. After that the conspirators were confident they would not have trouble from any of the other officers.

Accordingly on the evening of 2nd November, Shafat Jamil ordered Major Iqbal, company commander of 1st East Bengal regiment guarding Bangababan with about 300 infantry men, to withdraw his troops to the Cantonment after midnight—and to keep the move secret. Major Iqbal complied. He had the troops back in the barracks by 1 am on the morning of the 3rd November. That was the start of the counter-coup. A detail under Capt. Hafizullah of the 1st East Bengal was sent to detain and isolate General Zia in his residence. Hafizullah stormed into Zia's house. Zia, who had been awakened earlier by Rashid's telephone call, asked the young officer: 'What are you doing, Hafiz?' The captain, nervously pointing his gun at the general, told him, 'Sir, You are under arrest. Please don't do anything.' Hafizullah detained Zia in the living room with an armed guard. But in attempting to isolate Zia by ripping out the telephone in that room, Captain Hafizullah didn't realise that it was only an extension of the one in Zia's bedroom. It was on the bedroom telephone that Begum Zia received her calls from General Osmani and Major Rashid.

By 3 am, General Osmani said, 'I was getting reports from all over that the infantry had taken over the airport, parts of the city and the radio transmitter on the outskirts of Dhaka. Tanks were confronting the infantry. A civil war situation had developed.'

In Bangababan, Major Rashid was anxiously awaiting some word from General Zia. It was more than an hour since they had spoken and the situation had deteriorated rapidly. He called Zia's home a second time. Begum Zia said her husband was being held captive in the living room. She was evidently crying and quite overcome with anxiety for her husband's safety. Rashid tried to reassure her. 'Don't worry. If they haven't done anything to him so far it's not likely they intend to harm him. But pray to God. Only He can help us now.'

Indeed, God was now their only recourse. Man had failed the majors. The fantasy world of power, pretention and politics they had built up since August on the dead bodies of Sheikh Mujibur Rahman's family, was now crashing all around them. Rashid didn't blame himself or Farook for their tragic miscalculation. Instead he put the blame on Zia, silently cursing his hesitancy, his refusal to act against those who had been conspiring against them, and even more, Zia's inability to trust them or anyone at all. Rashid was still very bitter a year later when he recounted the incident in an interview. 'He (Zia) was a cowardly man who couldn't be trusted and couldn't trust anyone,' he said. But that night as he sat silently cursing the general, Rashid's reverie was interrupted by a call from Khalid Musharraf.

Khalid: 'We are in action now, so why don't you come and make a compromise?'

Rashid: 'What compromise?'

Khalid: 'Come and join me. You have nothing to fear.'

Rashid: 'So far as I'm concerned, I trust only once . . . I may make mistakes, but I don't change and I don't compromise especially in such circumstances.'

Khalid: 'We are coming for the counter . . . I will see you till the end.'

Rashid: 'If you have started the action, it's your luck. I will also see you till the end.'

The two officers traded verbal abuse and insult for several minutes before Khalid Musharraf hung up. Bangladesh may have been on the brink of civil war but for the moment at least the battles were being fought by telephone.

By that time Bangababan was very tense and ablaze with activity as the Bengal Lancers prepared to meet the impending assault. They could see elements of Shafat Jamil's 46th Brigade infantrymen coming towards them in the first glimmer of light before dawn. Yet the foot soldiers always kept a safe distance from the tanks which every now and then made quick, menacing movements and swung their guns about.

The President's office reflected the frenetic atmosphere outside. Telephones rang. Orders were shouted. Men dashed in and out with messages. Rashid himself kept making quick sorties outside the main building to keep an eye on the troops. Then some time after 4 am, as he recalled in a tape-recorded interview, 'In the middle of the confusion the telephone rang. When I picked it up I heard a man say: "I'm the DIG Prisons speaking. I would like to talk to hon'ble President".'

Rashid handed the telephone to Moshtaque.

Rashid continued: 'The President listened for some time to what the man was saying. Then he spoke quietly and listened some more. Then I heard him say, "Yes . . . Yes . . . Yes . . ." several times. I couldn't make out exactly what he meant, but it seemed he was giving some sort of OK.'

Rashid was only telling part of the truth. It will be recalled that Majors Farook Rahman and Abdur Rashid, two months earlier, had formulated a diabolical 'contingency plan' which, in the event of Moshtaque's assassination or a 'counter-coup' would pre-empt the restoration of an Awami League government by killing the four top party leaders who had been detained in jail. The plan had been expressly designed to be self-executing. Now, in the early hours of 3rd November, the 'contingency plan' had, indeed, been automatically activated at the first real sign of trouble for Moshtaque's government.

When Khalid's 'counter-coup' got under-way, the previously designated 'combat team' led by Naik Risaldar Muslehuddin went straight to Dhaka Central Jail and demanded admission. Seeing the armed men in uniform the jailor refused. An argument developed and the Deputy Inspector General (DIG) of Prisons—i.e. the head of the Dhaka Central Jail—was brought from his quarters to deal with the matter. What transpired next has been well-documented in a series of depositions and tape recordings made by the jail authorities when, on the orders of Khalid Musharraf and Shafat Jamil, Brigadier Aminul Huq, a senior army officer, interviewed them on the evening of the 4th November, 1975.

According to these records, Muslehuddin and his men said they had been sent by Rashid and Farook and demanded that Tajuddin, Syed Nazrul Islam, Mansoor Ali and Kamruzzaman be handed over to them. On hearing this the DIG prisons got very scared but nevertheless refused to comply because it was against prison regulations. Muslehuddin then insisted on telephoning Rashid in Bangababan and was allowed to do so. In the course of the call Rashid ordered the DIG prisons to do whatever Muslehuddin told him. Despite these instructions, the DIG was reluctant to comply. After consulting his superiors, the officer then telephoned Bangababan to obtain clarification and instructions from President Moshtaque himself. Moshtaque verified Rashid's orders. Accordingly Muslehuddin and his gang were admitted to the jail proper and allowed to go to the cells.

Tajuddin and Nazrul Islam shared one cell; Mansoor Ali and Kamruzzaman an adjoining one. They were all brought together in Tajuddin's cell and killed by automatic fire from close range. Three of them died immediately. The fourth, Tajuddin, had bullet wounds in his abdomen and leg. He seems to have slowly bled to death. Horrified prisoners in adjacent cells later told the family that they could hear him moaning and calling out for water from the cell that Muslehuddin and his gang had locked shut before leaving.

The savage slaying of these hapless men is an act of infamy on par with the massacre of the Bengali intellectuals by the departing Pakistani troops on the eve of Bangladesh's independence in December, 1971. Yet, whereas the Bangladeshi martyrs are revered and mourned nationally each year on their death anniversary, the Jail Four remain a national embarrassment, unmourned and unremembered except in private by a selected few.

There is much confusion about the jail killings—who did it? How? and Why? The conventional wisdom has it that they were bayonetted to death. Clearly this is untrue for the official record shows they were killed at close range by automatic fire. This was verified by the families. It has also been advanced by a number of writers that somehow from their jail cells Tajuddin and his companions managed to plot and plan with Khalid Musharraf and his men to launch the 3rd November coup. The jail conditions and the extreme hostility of their environment made this impossible. Also the writers clearly are not aware of the 'contingency plan' hatched by Moshtaque, Rashid and Farook two months earlier to kill the Jail Four.

Lifschultz in 'The Unfinished Revolution' quotes the Reuters correspondent in Dhaka, Atiqul Alam, about possessing a hand-written letter from Tajuddin to the Indian High Commissioner Samar Sen concerning 'coup plans and preparations'. Alam has stoutly denied he had any such 'letter' and no one else has heard of it. While I am prepared to accept that Atiqul Alam may have told a different story to Lifschultz and others, he is in the circumstances hardly a credible witness since he was jailed for 'collaboration' by the Awami League government in 1972 and only released six months later when he cited a list of senior officials who were gravely embarrassed to be called upon to give evidence on his behalf at his trial.

Zillur R. Khan, the noted academician, in his book, 'Leadership Crisis in Bangladesh', also makes the statement (page 151) that 'the most damaging evidence supporting the contention that the coup (led by Khalid Musharraf) was originally pro-Mujib was the FACT that the four closest associates of Mujib, who were languishing in jail, knew about the coup and were preparing to come out as heroes.' This is an astonishing assertion. The real FACTS based on jail and government records, backed up by the testimony of independent witnesses, some of Khalid's chums and the Tajuddin family, gave a contrary picture.

Tajuddin was arrested on 22nd August, 1975, and his family was kept under house detention for several weeks thereafter. He was not allowed any visitors till 15th October when his wife was permitted to see him for half an hour in the presence of five officers of the jail and intelligence services. The second and final visit granted Tajuddin was on 1st November, just 36 hours before he was killed. Mrs. Tajuddin was allowed to see him for less than 20 minutes in the presence of four men, some of whom were military officers in civies. She recalled that Tajuddin was in a 'very depressed mood'. He had been keeping a diary and that day had hoped to fill in the last of the 560 pages. Mrs. Tajuddin said her husband also had a premonition of death. 'The situation,' he told her at that last meeting, 'seems to be very bad and I don't think we will be allowed to leave this place alive.'

Apart from these two visits, Tajuddin had no communication at all with the outside world. An official who saw him at that time confirmed that he had been very gloomy before the end and certainly was not expecting to come out of jail a hero.

All this could have been cleared up by a proper inquiry.

A Judicial Commission consisting of three Supreme Court judges was in fact appointed in November, 1975, to inquire into these jail killings. For reasons yet unexplained, General Zia, during the five and a half years he ruled in Bangladesh, did not allow the Commission to function or fulfill its purpose. The Commission thus quietly withered on the vine. That episode will always shame General Zia's memory. It did not matter that some of the Jail Four were corrupt or brutal or that they all once belonged to the team that tore the heart out of the Bangladeshis. What did matter is the fact that a most horrible crime was committed and that once again the sequence of crime and punishment was broken—principally by official connivance; to a lesser degree by public silence. For that reason we are all diminished. And Bangladesh continues to wallow in its legacy of blood.

The situation began to hot up as dawn broke on the morning of 3rd November. Two MiGs of the Bangladesh Air Force made threatening passes over Bangababan, forcing Khandaker Moshtaque to temporarily hide in the basement air raid shelter. Then a tank commander reported that one of the Air Force's ageing Russian-built helicopters was flying in tight circles over the tanks in the compound. 'I've got it in my sights. It's a sitting duck,' he radioed excitedly. 'Request permission to bring it down.'

General Osmani sternly ordered him to hold his fire. The general had reached the President's house just in time after hitch-hiking all the way from the Cantonment. He wasn't going to be the first to start the shooting—and a civil war. A few minutes later a small delegation from the Cantonment turned up at the gates with a list of demands from Brigadier Khalid Musharraf. There were two colonels, another officer and ex-Majors Dalim and Noor. Apparently at the first sign of trouble that morning these two men from the group that killed Mujib had rushed off to the Cantonment and were now involved with Khalid in negotiating Farook and Rashid's surrender!

Khalid's demands were, first, that the tanks must be disarmed and returned to the Cantonment. Second, a new Chief of Army Staff must be appointed to replace General Zia. Third, Moshtaque could stay on as President, but there must be a change in foreign policy to make Bangladesh more closely aligned with the countries that had proved to be its friends in the past. Curiously omitted was the first thing that Khalid Musharraf had been trying to obtain on the telephone all night, i.e. Farook and Rashid's surrender. Perhaps the Brigadier expected that it would follow the disarming of the tanks. But no one was assuming anything at that time. Moshtaque himself refused to countenance the demands. Instead he told the officers that they should inform the CGS that he, Moshtaque, would 'cease to be President at 0600 hours' that morning.

Moshtaque's sudden decision to resign has not been explained. But if it was intended as an act of brinkmanship, it failed to work. The officers returned two hours later with another message. This time Khalid Musharraf demanded only two things: the tanks must be disarmed and returned to the Cantonment and a new Chief of Army Staff must be appointed. He did not volunteer for the job. He didn't have to. Neither Khandaker Moshtaque nor General Osmani or Major Rashid had any doubt whatsoever about Khalid's intentions.

What transpired next would have been more appropriate in a Bengali stage farce.

Moshtaque told the officers he could not accept the demands because he had ceased to be President after the 0600 hours deadline. When they turned to General Osmani, he told them that since Khandaker Moshtaque had ceased to be President, he himself had no authority to do anything as he had also automatically ceased to be the President's Defence Adviser. 'Go to hell and do what you damn well want,' Osmani stormed, his moustache bristling and once more the Papa Tiger.

Non-plussed by the turn of events, the young officers kept pleading alternately with the two men. Then Dalim turned to Osmani: 'Tell them to sur-render,' he shouted. 'I know why Ayub Khan called you an old mule. But don't you be stubborn now.' Moshtaque got the excited major to simmer down. The negotiations dragged on for another three hours. The officers shuttled between Bangababan and the Cantonment and there were exchanges of defiance on both sides. And every now and then Khalid and Rashid traded insult and invective on the telephone.

At around 10 am there was another telephone call to Bangababan, one which would have a profound effect on the decision of the majors and Moshtaque to capitulate to the forces led by Khalid Musharraf and Shafat Jamil. The event was described to me by Major General Khalilur Rahman, Chief of the Defence Staff, who was in Bangababan at that time.

General Khalil said: 'Nurul Islam, the Inspector General of Police, who was a close friend of mine, telephoned to give me the news of the killing of Tajuddin and the others in the jail during the night, I was horrified by the news and immediately went over to Chashi (Mahboobul Alam Chashi, Secretary to the President) to tell him so that he could inform Moshtaque. Chashi immediately got up and went to the President's room. He came back within a minute to say in an awed voice: "He knows!"'

General Khalil said the realisation that Moshtaque was involved in the jail killings so horrified him that he decided from then on that he would do nothing to protect him or the majors. But, for reasons yet unexplained, the general did not tell another soul about the killings that day. (For this reason Brigadier Shafat Jamil would 36 hours later try to arrest him, claiming his silence had allowed the killer majors to escape.) Moshtaque and evidently Rashid, who was constantly in Moshtaque's room that morning, were not to know of General Khalil's decision to remain silent. All they knew was that the grisly secret was out and that they were now extremely vulnerable to an angry public reaction which would surely come when the news percolated into the city. Their attitudes thereafter showed a remarkable change. The effort now was not to fight but to extricate themselves from the mess as quickly as possible.

Till then Rashid had been putting on a bold front, telling those around him that they 'would fight it out to the death'. Now he began to talk about a 'standoff' and their reluctance to 'precipitate a civil war'. For his part Moshtaque, with Rashid's approval, requested the other side to allow the two majors to leave the country safely with their families. The only one not party to these goings on at that time was Farook, sitting with his tanks at Suhrawardy Udhyan. Farook was itching for a fight. But the signal from Rashid in Bangababan never came.

Khalid Musharraf and Shafat Jamil agreed to Moshtaque's request that the majors be allowed to leave the country. It was then left to Air Vice Marshal Towab and the Bangladesh Foreign Office to work out the modalities of their safe conduct to Bangkok along with those who elected to go with them.

At one stage Moshtaque himself insisted on going into exile with the majors. (Brigadier Manzoor would tell me a month later that it was 'an attempt to get out of the country while the going was good'.) But Khalid Musharraf would not hear of it. Eventually 17 members of the group immediately involved in the killing of Sheikh Mujib—including Dalim, Noor, Huda, Pasha and Shariar—went into exile with Farook and Rashid.

The departure was marked by emotional scenes in Bangababan. Some of the Bengal Lancers and artillery men wept openly. 'Don't leave us or we will be killed,' they wailed. Farook tried to reassure them with the promise that they would not be victimised. But the apprehensions remained. This would be a major factor in the Sepoy Mutiny four days later.

As Farook was waiting in the airport terminal building to board the Fokker aircraft that would be taking them to Bangkok, the 'azan' (call) for Magreb or evening prayers rang in his ears. He looked at his watch, noting the time, the date and the day. Then he smiled ruefully to himself. The 3rd of November was a MONDAY—not his lucky day! And Friday's Child was tasting his first defeat.

After the departure of the majors there was an angry argument in Bangababan about what should be done next. Moshtaque wanted no further part in the proceedings, saying he had resigned and was going home to his private residence. Khalid Musharraf wanted him to continue as President, perhaps hoping he could use him to advantage. The argument continued. Ultimately Moshtaque agreed to remain on two conditions. The first was that the Army pledge allegiance to him and promise to obey his orders. The second was that the Cabinet be allowed to meet formally to express support and confidence in him. Khalid wasn't very happy about these conditions. He countered with the demand that he be appointed Chief of Army Staff in place of General Zia. This demand, according to General Osmani, was actively supported by Air Vice Marshal Towab and Commodore M. H. Khan, the Chief of Naval Staff. The evidence is that these two officers, who were heading their respective services, blithely abandoned General Zia in favour of Khalid Musharraf when he appeared to be leading the winning side. Two days later, they would, like glorified batmen, pin the general's Star and Ribbon on Khalid Musharraf's uniform. The picture of that happy event—Towab and Musharraf wore big smiles—was splashed across five columns at the top of the front page of the Bangladesh Observer. Then two days later, when Khalid had been killed in the Sepoy Mutiny, Towab and Commodore Khan switched sides again to back General Zia. No wonder the sepoys and the navy and air force rankers had such utter contempt for their officers at that time.

For the moment, however, there was no hint of all this. General Osmani told me Khandaker Moshtaque and Khalid Musharraf had a big argument in Bangababan after the majors left for Bangkok. Moshtaque appeared to be playing for time—what exactly for, no one explains. But at about 11 pm he finally got Khalid and his men to disperse and meet again the following day (4th November). It was very late, Moshtaque explained. They were all very tired and, in any case, nothing could be done without the approval of the Cabinet.

'We had a little food,' Osmani recalled, 'the first in more than 20 hours. Then we went to sleep that night wondering what new trauma the day would bring.'

When he turned up at about 10 am on Tuesday, Khalid Musharraf was accompanied by Major General Khalil, Towab and Commodore Khan. They brought with them the first shock of the day. It was General Zia's resignation. It was a short letter, Osmani recalled. Zia said he was resigning because he did not want to become involved in politics. And he asked for full pension and the normal gratuity and benefits an officer gets when he retires. Osmani remembered this last request with some derision. 'How could he, a General and Chief of Army Staff at that, go down so placidly clutching on to his pension rights?' Osmani asked.

Whatever Osmani's opinion of him, Zia was a survivor. The resignation clearly had been obtained under duress because he was still being held prisoner in his own home. And if Zia was anxious about the future it was because he would have to live on his pension alone. Unlike some of the others he had not made money on the side. Indeed, after resigning Zia asked one of his junior officers to find him a small house with a monthly rent of about 300 Takkas. 'But Sir,' the embarrassed officer replied, 'you can't find a place even in Mohammadpur (a Dhaka suburb) for less than 800 Takkas.'

General Zia's resignation had cleared the way for Khalid, the coup leader, to become Chief of Army Staff. Accordingly at his insistence Moshtaque summoned the Cabinet to meet after evening prayers that day to consider the appointment and also to formalise his own position as President. Osmani told Khalid, Towab, Commodore Khan and General Khalil to be on hand in Bangababan when the Cabinet met. They were about to disperse when Air Commodore Islam, Director of Forces Intelligence, hurried in with the report about the massacre of Tajuddin and his companions in jail. Islam made no secret of the affair, babbling at the top of his voice. Now finally, 30 hours after the event and long after the majors and their men had left the country, the tragic news was at last made public.

'There was a terrible commotion,' General Osmani recalled. 'Some ministers who had come in were overcome with fear. Others were shouting. We were all taken aback. I felt sickened by the thought that we had once more lapsed into barbarism.'

Moshtaque, the consummate actor, was protesting as loudly as the others and as though he didn't know about it all along. He said the Cabinet must meet immediately to consider the situation. Accordingly an emergency meeting was called which even junior ministers were invited to attend. The 26 members of the government who quickly assembled in the Cabinet Room on the ground floor of Bangababan didn't take long to appoint a Judicial Commission to inquire into the jail killings. The Commission had three Supreme Court judges and was required to complete its findings 'expeditiously'. Then they all went on to a heated discussion about the 'counter-coup' and why Farook, Rashid and the rest of the group had been allowed to leave the country.

Khalid, General Khalil, Towab and Commodore Khan were brought in for questioning. They assured the government of their loyalty and promised to obey the President. But some of them were visibly annoyed when the ministers demurred about appointing Khalid Musharraf as the new Chief of Army Staff in place of General Zia. Moshtaque cunningly passed the buck to General Osmani. 'I can only act on the recommendation of my Defence Adviser,' he said. Osmani, taking the cue from Moshtaque, loudly announced that 'normal procedures' i.e. the selection process, would have to be followed to make the appointment and that would take some time. This did not please Khalid Musharraf and his friends. Angry exchanges followed.

Suddenly they were interrupted by a loud banging on the door. Col. Shafat Jamil, waving a stick and accompanied by five officers with sten guns, forced their way into the Cabinet Room. It caused consternation, with ministers fleeing in panic from their chairs. At one stage President Moshtaque was seen sprawled on the floor with a young major holding a sten gun at his head. General Osmani went to his rescue, pleading with the young officers: 'For God's sake don't do anything. This is madness. You will destroy the country.'

Shafat Jamil demanded Khandaker Moshtaque's resignation. 'You are a murderer,' he screamed at the President. 'You have killed the Father of the Nation. You have killed the four leaders in jail. You are a usurper. Your government is illegal. You have no right to stay in power. You must resign immediately.' Then turning on General Khalil, the Dhaka Brigade commander accused him of hushing up the jail killings. 'You are under arrest,' he told him.

Recalling these events a month later, General Osmani told me: 'I kept telling myself, "My God, this is going to be another bloody massacre". Anything could have happened. If just one shot had been fired by accident it would have been the end of all of us.'

The commotion continued for a while. Every time the young officers surged forward pointing their guns at the ministers, Osmani kept pushing them back. Finally in desperation, Osmani told Moshtaque: 'It's getting too dangerous. You had better resign.' Moshtaque nodded his head in agreement. With that the moment of madness seemed to pass.

When the ministers had settled down once more, Shafat Jamil proposed that the Chief Justice should be made President in place of Moshtaque. One of the ministers (Osmani identified him as Manoranjan Dhar, the law minister; Shafat Jamil said it was Yusuf Ali) interrupted to say that that would not be the correct procedure. Legally, he added, the Speaker of the National Assembly should act as President if Moshtaque resigned. Whoever it was, Shafat Jamil turned on the man savagely: 'Damn him and damn you all,' he screamed. 'You changed the Constitution to justify one killing. So you can change it again. I tell you the Chief Justice will be President.'

That settled the matter. Having had their way the military officers allowed all but four of the ministers to leave Bangababan. The four—all Ministers of State—were Tahiruddin Thakur, Shah Moazzam Hussain, Nurul Islam Manzoor and K. M. Obaidur Rahman. They were told to write out their resignations. 'Are you going to arrest us?' Tahiruddin Thakur asked. No one bothered to answer him. But two of them, Thakur and Shah Moazzam Hussain, were indeed arrested soon afterwards and charged with corruption and the misuse of power. No one has explained why they were singled out for such treatment.

Osmani recalled there followed several hours of hectic activity in Bangababan as the officials prepared for the change of government. Khalid Musharraf also drafted several letters for Moshtaque to sign. One of them concerned his resignation as President. Another was to make Moshtaque responsible for the majors leaving the country along with their killer team. The third, according to Osmani, 'was something to do with the jail killings'. He would not say what exactly this was.

Osmani continued: 'Khalid kept insisting that Moshtaque sign the last two letters and pre-date them to the 3rd November. Moshtaque kept refusing. Things were getting out of hand again so I told him (Moshtaque) "You may sign if you have to and if there's a court case I'll come as a witness".' Asked what he meant by that, Osmani replied: 'Oh, I would say he signed it under duress.'

It was 1.00 am on the 5th November when Chief Justice Abusadat Mohammad Sayem was finally brought to Bangababan. Seeing Osmani in the corridor the judge asked why he had been brought there. Osmani told him: 'You are to be President.' When the Chief Justice smartly declined the honour, Osmani advised him: 'For God's sake do it. You have to be President otherwise there will be no law and the country will be finished.'

Justice Sayem, however, still wanted no part of the arrangement. He turned around and went home, to be followed by Khalid, Shafat Jamil, Osmani, Khalil and the Air Force and Navy Chiefs. They finally persuaded him to accept the job. Thus on the 6th November, 1975, Justice Abusadat Sayem became Bangladesh's fifth President in the fourth year of the country's independence.

102

X

A Night to Remember

Sephai, Sephai, Bhai Bhai
Officer de Rakta Chai.

(*All Sepoys are brothers*
We want the blood of officers).

—Sepoy Mutiny slogan

For three days, the 3rd, 4th and 5th of November, 1975, Bangladesh was without a government. Khandaker Moshtaque Ahmed, the out-going President, was still nominally in charge. Things were done in his name until the morning of the 6th when Chief Justice Abusadat Mohammad Sayem was sworn in to replace him. But Moshtaque in fact was a prisoner in Bangababan, held securely in his first floor apartment by Brigadier Khalid Musharraf and Col. Shafat Jamil.

During this time the two coup leaders showed themselves to be indecisive and politically inept. They got hopelessly snarled in the effort of overcoming an obstacle entirely of their own making. This was the absurd attempt to give a semblance of legitimacy to the coup and to their own positions. It was as if they were undertaking an orderly transfer of power when the reality was the opposite. As a coup it was a farcical affair with few comparisons.

After the majors had been sent off to Bangkok on the 3rd, Khalid Musharraf spent the rest of that day and half of the next coaxing Khandaker Moshtaque and General Osmani to appoint him Chief of the Army Staff in place of General Ziaur Rahman who had been arrested. Khalid went through the rigmarole of issuing a Presidential Proclamation enabling the Chief Justice to succeed to the office of President instead of the speaker of the National Assembly, as the Constitution required. Ironically, the Proclamation was signed by Moshtaque who had himself been installed as President three months earlier by the majors' coup. I can't imagine who they were trying to impress by this adherence to mock constitutionality. But in the circumstances the whole thing was utterly ridiculous, totally unnecessary and, ultimately, entirely self-defeating. Khalid should have made public acceptance of the coup his first consideration. It would have saved his life.

Although they had seized the government, Khalid Musharraf and Shafat Jamil showed themselves to be ignorant of the first imperative of power: that might is right and a successful coup is its own authority. They did not need President Moshtaque or General Osmani's say-so for anything. Backed by the guns of Jamil's 46 Infantry Brigade, at that time the dominant force in Dhaka, Khalid could have appointed himself Chief of Army Staff, even President—or both. By failing to grasp the leadership with both hands he precipitated his own downfall. For three days people wondered who was in charge—Moshtaque or the coup leaders. The political vacuum that developed was quickly filled by his enemies who smartly turned the tables on him. By the time Khalid got round to explaining the reasons for the coup and its objectives—in a broadcast made by the new President, Justice Sayem, on the evening of the

6th—the situation was beyond recall. Already ignited were the fires of the great Sepoy Mutiny. It would destroy him in a matter of hours and go on to cast a long and terrifying shadow on the country's other military leaders.

Khalid's coup, even more than 20 or so coup attempts and mutinies that plagued Bangladesh between 1975 and 1981, was ineptly planned, short-sighted and pressed with a surprising lack of vigour for a soldier who had such a creditable record during the Liberation War.

When they met in the Chinese restaurant near Dhaka stadium on the 1st November, the conspirators were under pressure to pre-empt action by someone else. The air was thick with rumours about the imminent overthrow of Moshtaque's government. Any number of groups were known to be plotting. The left-wing JSD (Jayto Samajtantrik Dal) and the Sharbohara (proletarian) party were known to be actively forming revolutionary cells among the army jawans preparatory to a bid for power. General Ziaur Rahman, the Chief of Staff, was also the central figure of much gossip concerning another coup. There were freedom fighters, resentful of the elevation of former Pakistani officials to key positions in Moshtaque's government, who were threatening 'corrective' action. At the same time Pakistan-oriented parties wanted a man more pliable than Moshtaque was to promote their designs for a 'New Pakistan'. The word in Dhaka was that something was about to happen. But this time Khalid Musharraf didn't want to be caught napping as he had been the previous August by the majors' coup. So when he told Shafat Jamil and the other officers, 'We must strike now', he was echoing a desperate need for action.

The Chinese restaurant plot therefore was a hasty one and strictly limited in its objectives. Essentially these were to seize the government by taking out the majors and their tanks, peaceably if possible, by force if necessary. Secondly, to simultaneously arrest General Ziaur Rahman and force him into retirement. Once this was accomplished the conspirators thought they would play it by ear. There was some disagreement about what they should do about President Moshtaque. For political reasons Khalid wanted to retain and use him as Rashid had previously tried to do. But Col. Shafat Jamil could not stomach Moshtaque. He insisted that he be replaced by the Chief Justice. After some discussion the decision was left to Khalid. Ultimately on the 3rd of November Khalid asked Moshtaque to stay on as President. When the jail killings were discovered the next day, Khalid had no option but to get rid of him. This seemed to have upset Khalid's plans.

In this context it is noteworthy that at no time during the plotting—before it or subsequently—did Tajuddin or any of the others of the Jail Four figure in the conspirators' plans for an alternative government. One of the survivors from Khalid's group, who does not wish to be identified, told me in an interview: 'If, as it's been alleged, Khalid wanted to install Tajuddin or any of the other chaps as Head of Government, wouldn't we have gone to the jail to release them immediately after the majors surrendered? If we didn't do so it was for the simple reason that they did not figure at all in our plans. We forgot about them entirely until the forenoon of the 4th when we learned that they had been killed in Dhaka Central Jail 30 hours earlier. Had we wanted Tajuddin and found him dead while trying to rescue him on the 3rd, then neither the majors nor Moshtaque would have survived and the coup would have had a totally different outcome.'

The logic of this argument is indisputable. But it did not help Khalid Musharraf. He got lumped with the odium of attempting a sell-out to India and restoring a Mujibist government in Bangladesh. 'SAMYABAD', the journal of the JSD, has summed up the conventional history of Khalid's four-day coup: 'When Khalid Musharraf and his faction came to power they immediately engaged themselves in bringing about an increase in Indo-Soviet political dominance over the country. The Awami League and its tail—the parties of the Moni-Muzzafar circle—came out openly and made all efforts to re-establish the image of Sheikh Mujib.' The fact is that it's not what Khalid did but what he failed to do in the face of some adverse circumstances that enabled his opponents to tar him with the Indian brush and so turn public opinion in Bangladesh against him. The overthrow of Moshtaque and Sheikh Mujib's killers, for one, was received with tremendous exultation and gloating in India. The Indian press and official radio outdid each other with the most egregious reports and commentaries about the event. That understandably created misgivings and some alarm in Bangladesh whose people are always chary of the attention of their big neighbour. They began to wonder whether India was behind Khalid's coup. Unfortunately for Khalid this suspicion was fostered by what was happening in the country at that time.

With the ousting of Moshtaque and the majors, jubilant Awami Leaguers, students and pro-Moscow groups who had supported Mujib in the past came out on the streets in large numbers to celebrate. Tuesday, the 4th of November, was observed as 'Mujib Day'. Remembrance meetings were held in the main towns and in the capital, at Dhaka university campus, the Shaheed Minar (Martyrs memorial) and other public places. A number of processions were taken out from different parts of the city to Road No. 32 Dhanmandi where Mujib's house was filled with garlands and flowers. Next day a half-day 'hartal' (business closure) in memory of Tajuddin and his companions shut down the city. 'Namaz-i-Janaza', the public prayers for the dead, were said as the four murdered Awami League leaders were ceremonially laid to rest, three of them in Banani graveyard, Dhaka, in plots adjacent to the unmarked mass grave in which Sheikh Mujib's family lies. Then another mass observance with prayers in Mujib's memory was called for Friday, the 7th. All this gave the impression that the coup heralded the return of Mujibism, when the people had barely got over the nightmare of Sheikh Mujib's prodigality, and the return of the allegedly pro-India Awami League when sentiment against India was running high because of a dispute over the Farakka Dam. What made it all the more damning for Khalid was the public outrage when they discovered that his mother and brother, both staunch Awami Leaguers, had led the main procession to Mujib's house on the 4th. The left-wing JSD and the right-wing Muslim League seized on their presence in the Awami League procession as 'proof' that India was behind Khalid's coup. The charge was hammered home in hundreds of thousands of leaflets, 'shabnamas' (anonymous night letters) and posters that flooded the military cantonments and main cities. The results were devastating.

Col. Shafat Jamil told me later in an interview that Khalid was very upset when he saw the papers that Wednesday morning. Picking up the telephone he asked his mother: 'What have you done? You have been in the procession and your picture is in the paper. For this you may have shortened my days and I may not survive.' According to Jamil, 'Khalid felt this would go against us very much.'

Curiously neither of them did anything to counter it. The coup leaders neither encouraged nor discouraged or dissociated themselves from the Awami League demonstrations. For the first three days when it mattered most they unaccountably remained silent and so let their case go by default. This is all the more surprising in view of the attractive presentation made on their behalf

by the new President, Justice Sayem, in a nationwide broadcast on the evening
of the fourth day, i.e. Thursday the 6th of November. Sayem made clear that
the new government was 'neutral, non-party and interim'; one dedicated to 'an
active foreign policy' which included 'unqualified support' for the Muslim
world. Compared to Moshtaque's bombastic pronouncement in similar circumstances three months earlier, Sayem's broadcast was a remarkably prosaic,
forthright declaration of intent. It dissociated the armed forces from the killing
of Sheikh Mujib. It also promised the return of law and order and a clean and
impartial administration. The objectives were so fair and so eloquently stated
that General Ziaur Rahman, who succeeded Khalid Musharraf as the new
military leader a day later, had no hesitation in adopting them without change
for the first year of his rule.

All this was the work of Justice Abusadat Mohammad Sayem, who at 59
was by any standards a remarkable man. He had served as a junior to A. K.
Fazlul Huq, the towering Bengali Muslim leader venerated as the 'Lion of
Bengal'. After a distinguished practice, Sayem joined the Bench and had risen
to become the first Chief Judge of the Bangladesh High Court in January,
1972. A year later when the Supreme Court was created, he became its first
Chief Justice. Justice Sayem had been most reluctant to step into Moshtaque's
shoes. But once he was persuaded to accept the job in the national interest, he
filled the role of President with dedication and sincerity. As Head of the new
government President Sayem gave an immense dignity to Khalid's coup. But
the appointment and his guiding hand came too late to matter. Before the text
of Sayem's broadcast was printed in next morning's newspapers it was overtaken by the Sepoy Mutiny and Khalid himself was dead.

A major consideration for Khalid during his short-lived coup was the improvement of his military position. He didn't feel entirely secure although he
controlled the major fighting units in Dhaka. Shafat Jamil's 46 Infantry
Brigade consisted of two infantry regiments, the 4th East Bengal which he had
raised and was supposed to be personally loyal to him, and the 1st East Bengal.
They were a powerful force. But within the same cantonment at that time were
two important disaffected units—Farook's Bengal Lancers and Rashid's 2
Field Artillery. Although they had been disarmed, they could be dangerous
and needed to be 'blocked' at all times. For this purpose Khalid summoned
the 10th and 15th East Bengal regiments from Rangpur where they made up
the 72 Infantry Brigade. He had raised both regiments and they had fought
under him during the Liberation War as part of 'K (for Khalid) Force'. Now
he was depending on these freedom fighters to bolster his strength. The 15th
East Bengal commanded by Major Jaffer Imam for unreported reasons failed
to reach Dhaka in time. But the 10th East Bengal under Major Nawazish
rapidly moved into Sher-i-Bangla Nagar, the new capital area of Dhaka, by
the morning of 5th. Col. K. S. Huda, the 72 Infantry Brigade commander who
was related to Khalid, also came post-haste to join him in Dhaka.

On the 5th Khalid called a conference of military Formation Commanders
to drum up support among the out-station brigades. But neither he nor Shafat
Jamil made any attempt to address or to motivate the rest of the officers and
the troops in Dhaka. They ignored them completely. In the circumstances this
was an inexplicable lapse and it hastened their undoing. Ironically, two of the
officers of the 10th East Bengal, on whose support Khalid depended, were
responsible for his death during the Sepoy Mutiny.

There is no evidence of foreign-related action by Khalid Musharraf between
the 3rd and 7th of November; no attempt to tilt Bangladesh this way or that;
certainly nothing even remotely suggesting, as the JSD's 'SAMYABAD' journal

did, 'an increase in Indo-Soviet political dominance over the country'. Only two events concerning foreign countries were recorded during this period. One was a £10,000,000 grant-in-aid agreement with Britain for the supply of industrial spares and raw materials. The other was a US $30.9 million agreement with Turkey for 49 meter-gauge passenger coaches for the Bangladesh railways. In both cases the agreements were negotiated much earlier and signed by senior officials in Dhaka. The coup leaders had nothing to do with them. It must be noted that in the circumstances the allegation that Khalid Musharraf had sold out to India is also a calumny of President Sayem. But no one has made such a ridiculous suggestion against Sayem.

The sepoy mutiny erupted in Dhaka a little after midnight on the night of the 6th of November. For two days there had been ominous signs of unrest in the Cantonment as sepoys of the Bengal Lancers and 2 Field Artillery watched with mounting anxiety, first the arrest and resignation of General Ziaur Rahman, then the arrest and resignation of President Moshtaque. Before leaving for Bangkok, Farook and Rashid had assured them that they would not be victimised in any way. Now those assurances were wearing thin with the exit of Moshtaque, Zia and General Osmani, the 'Papa Tiger' and Colonel-in-Chief of the Bengal Regiment who had been a reassuring father figure as the President's Defence Adviser. There was no one left to protect them. The troops were now at the mercy of Brigadier Khalid Musharraf and Colonel Shafat Jamil, both well known to be arrogant, harsh disciplinarians. Jamil on several occasions had publicly threatened retribution for Mujib's killing. Now the reckoning had come. The jawans became even more apprehensive when word got around that the 10th and 15th East Bengal were on their way to Dhaka from Rangpur to 'sort them out'.
   Playing on the soldiers' perturbation at the same time were thousands of leaflets and posters which descended like confetti on the cantonments and main cities of Bangladesh on the 5th and 6th of November. They were the work of extreme right-wing groups such as the Muslim League, and the left-wing JSD. The former had once been accused of collaborating with the Pakistanis. It had resurfaced under Khandaker Moshtaque and now once more faced the prospect of being suppressed by Khalid Musharraf. The latter, officially banned and with its principal leaders in jail, was operating under the cover of the Biplobi Sainik Sangstha (Revolutionary Soldiers' Organisation) and the Biplobi Gono Bahini (People's Revolutionary Army). The leaflets from the political right and left had a common theme. In effect it was that Khalid was a traitor, an Indian 'stooge' promoting the return of the hated Mujibism and Baksal.
   The JSD appeal went one significant step further. The jawans, it argued, were being used as pawns on the chessboard of power by ambitious senior officers who really had no interest in the plight of the soldiers or the oppressed masses. Calling for a general uprising, the JSD proposed a list of 12 demands. Among them were the ending of the much-abused 'batman' system where soldiers were employed as officers' body-servants; the removal of all differences between officers and men in the matter of uniforms and status; the recruitment of officers from among the jawans rather than from the privileged classes; improved pay and housing; a crackdown on corruption and the release of all political prisoners. Loaded as they were in favour of the military under-dog, the demands found instant favour among the aroused soldiery because they had in the past suffered terribly outside the established military pecking order.
   This finely-calculated gambit was the brain-child of a remarkable ex-army

officer. He was Lt. Colonel (retired) Abu Taher who would later be hanged by General Zia but nevertheless became a legend in Bangladesh for his integrity, patriotism and egalitarian concepts of a productive people's army based on the jawan or common soldier. Abu Taher trained as a commando in the USA, first at Fort Benning, Georgia and then at the Special Forces Officer Training Institute, Fort Brag, North Carolina. As a member of the Special Services Group (SSG), an elite Pakistani para-commando unit, Taher found himself stranded in West Pakistan at the start of the Bangladesh War of Liberation. His first attempt at escaping to join the struggle ended in failure. But in June of that year he managed to cross over to India in the company of two other officers. Like him they went on to carve their names in the history of the Bangladeshis. One was Lt. Colonel Mohammad Ziauddin, a legendary left-wing figure, the first man to publicly condemn Sheikh Mujib in 1972. The other, Mohammad Abul Manzoor, as a major general would be responsible for the assassination of President Zia at Chittagong in May, 1981.

Taher had served with distinction in the Liberation War, losing a leg during an assault on Kamalpur, a river port on the Brahmaputra. In 1972 he was made Adjutant General of the Bangladesh Army, then commander of the 44 Infantry Brigade at Comilla before being forced into retirement along with Col. Ziauddin for publicly airing irreconcilable differences with the establishment about the shape and content of the Bangladesh Army. The two colonels wanted the inherited British pattern replaced by a Chinese-style productive 'People's Army'. Sheikh Mujib and the military establishment would have none of it. Taher was given a civilian job as director in charge of the Dredger Organisation. But he maintained his links with the troops through secret membership of the JSD which was infiltrating the armed forces.

According to A. S. M. Abdur Rab, general secretary of the JSD, Taher formed the Biplobi Sainik Sangstha (Revolutionary Soldiers' Organisation) in July, 1974, as a 'vaguely socialist and egalitarian study group, not well organised'. But after Khalid's coup 15 months later, 'Taher grasped the opportunity and quickly gave the organisation an organised, activist shape and a pro-people programme linked to the students'. Thus were the jawans made aware that if for a combination of reasons it had become a question of 'them or us', now was the time to rise up against Khalid Musharraf and the officer class.

They did exactly that a little after midnight, i.e. in the early hours of the 7th November. With an infectious spontaneity the jawans began breaking into the 'kots' or armouries and looting sten guns, rifles and all available weapons and ammunition. Then they spread rapidly through Dhaka cantonment chanting 'SEPHAI, SEPHAI, BHAI BHAI. OFFICER DE RAKTA CHAI' (All sepoys are brothers. We want the blood of officers), and 'SEPHAI, SEPHAI, BHAI BHAI. SUBEDARAR UPPERE OFFICER NAI' (All sepoys are brothers. We don't want officers above the rank of subedar). Clearly the JSD's call for class conflict was being interpreted literally by the troops as an exhortation to kill their officers. Thus Abu Taher, by cleverly manipulating the sepoy's pre-disposition to mutiny brought on by the fear of victimisation, was able to promote his own revolutionary ideas.

The first to feel the effects of the mutiny were 10 young army officers billetted in the Officers' Mess near the 2 Field Artillery barracks. The 'batman' or body-servant of one of the officers ran down the bedroom corridors shouting 'Run for your lives. The sepoys are coming to kill you.' Hastily discarding their uniforms for unobtrusive civies, the officers climbed over the back wall and proceeded to wade through the paddy fields behind the Combined Military Hospital. With the help of a villager they ultimately made it to the Mirpur Road where they dispersed for safety. One of them was 2nd Lt. Syed Eskander, the younger brother of General Ziaur Rahman's wife, Khalida. Even he wasn't taking any chances.

Khalid Musharraf was given the news of the Sepoy Mutiny in a telephone call to Bangababan from the 4th East Bengal headquarters. Evidently he had anticipated trouble because he had earlier in the day sent his wife and family to a secret hide-out in the city. Accompanied by Shafat Jamil, Khalid had gone to Bangababan around 11.30 pm for a late night meeting with Towab and Commodore Khan. Having switched support from Zia to Khalid at the start of the coup, the Air Force and Navy chiefs were now demanding a major role in the government that was to be sworn in on the morrow by President Sayem. Specifically they wanted equal status with Khalid as Deputy Chief Martial Law Administrators (DCMLAs). The President would be CMLA or Chief Martial Law Administrator, however nominally. Khalid refused their demands. He wanted to control all the forces and be CMLA. They argued acrimoniously for more than an hour until the meeting was abruptly broken up by the report of the mutiny.

Khalid decided to leave Bangababan immediately. Shafat Jamil chose to stay behind. The coup leader drove off in his private car accompanied by Col. Huda, the 72 Infantry Brigade commander, and Lt. Colonel Haider, CO of the 8th East Bengal based in Chittagong who had been visiting him while on leave in Dhaka. They proceeded down the Mirpur Road. The general assumption is that they were trying to escape across the river in the direction of India. Jamil disputes this. He said they were on their way to the 10th East Bengal at Sher-i-Bangla Nagar, the new capital area of Dhaka. Whatever the truth, it was unfortunate for them that the car broke down near the Fatima Nursing Home. Khalid telephoned 10th East Bengal headquarters from the clinic, asking whether they had the situation under control and if it was safe for him to come. He was assured on both counts. The three officers then walked down to Sher-i-Bangla Nagar and spent the night with 10th East Bengal.

Short after breakfast next morning (7th November), some jawans from the Bengal Lancers and 2 Field Artillery came over to urge the 10th East Bengal troops to join the mutiny. The trouble seems to have spread rapidly. A few minutes later Khalid Musharraf and Colonels Huda and Haider were gunned down in the CO's room by two company commanders, Captain Asad and Captain Jalil. It's not clear what prompted them to do this. Some allege at least one of them was directly influenced by Abu Taher. Shafat Jamil, however, said the two captains had developed a 'fear complex'—that things would go against them because they had come all the way from Rangpur to bolster Khalid's strength. So they killed him to clear themselves and to curry favour with the mutineers.

Public opinion in Bangladesh has been unkind to Khalid Musharraf. He was neither the traitor who tried to sell his country as his detractors suggest, nor the hero who attempted to right a grave injustice, as his friends would have it. The evidence suggests that this handsome, mercurial man was merely an ambitious military officer, an unlucky opportunist who, because of his political ineptitude, didn't quite make it.

Farook and Rashid are the most unlikely admirers of Bangladesh military brass. Yet they have paid Khalid a surprisingly fulsome tribute in 'The Road to Freedom', a book published in Dhaka in 1984. Describing Khalid as a 'true patriotic hero', they say he 'became a victim of circumstances while trying to avert the danger to the nation created by the conspirators'. The real conspirator, Farook and Rashid claim, was General Ziaur Rahman 'whose attempt to capture power on the night of 2nd November, 1975, was foiled by Khalid Musharraf'. According to the majors, General Zia exploited the misunderstanding created by the presence of Khalid's mother and brother in the Awami League procession and 'so a devilish combination of misfortune and conspiracy brought about the tragic end of a great patriot, General Khalid Musharraf.'

The mutiny spread rapidly in Dhaka.

By 1.00 am the troops had fully taken over the Cantonment. Some fired at random in the air; others milled about excitedly, shouting slogans and searching for officers. A group of jawans led by Havildar Sarwar of the Bengal Lancers, scattered the guard at General Zia's house, ending his four-day detention. Zia, still in his night clothes, was loudly cheered as they carried him on their shoulders to the headquarters of the 2 Field Artillery nearby. The general appeared to be overwhelmed by the sudden turn of events. For long moments he could only shake the outstretched hands of the nameless young men who had rescued him or lightly press the shoulders of those who embraced him in the manner that Muslims do. When fully recovered, one of Zia's first acts was to telephone General Khalil to say: 'I am free. I am okay. There's nothing to worry about. Please inform the American and British and Indian ambassadors.'

General Khalil told me he was thrilled to hear that General Zia was safe. But he could not immediately pass on the information to the foreign missions as requested because he was too busy monitoring the developments. When he finally got round to telephoning the diplomats later in the morning, Khalil discovered that Zia had already been in touch with them.

Zia asked his rescuers to bring him some officers, notably General Mir Shaukat Ali, General Abdur Rahman and Col. Aminul Huq. When the troops ushered them in, Zia embraced each of them. He asked for help in controlling the troops. 'I don't want bloodshed,' he told them. A little later Zia telephoned Col. Shafat Jamil at Bangababan asking him to 'forgive and forget and unite the army'. Jamil, however, would have none of it. 'I was rude to him,' he recalled. 'I said "nothing doing". We'll sort this out in the morning.' Zia hung up without another word. 'I thought our troops would support us,' Jamil added, 'but they didn't because they were not motivated. That's the blunder we made.' A little later about 150 jawans and civilians, the latter Abu Taher's men, stormed into Bangababan without resistance in search of the coup leaders. In trying to escape Shafat Jamil fell and broke a leg and spent the next three months in hospital. But somehow the accident saved his life.

The jawans took over the radio station at 1.30 am, announcing to the night staff on duty that 'Sephai Biplob (sepoy revolution) has begun and will continue under General Ziaur Rahman.' The astonished radio staff didn't quite know how to take it. When they realised that the jawans were not threatening them and that Khalid Musharraf had been defeated, they all joined with the wildly-celebrating troops. Some Lancer tanks, piled high with exuberant soldiers and civilians, showed up in the middle of the city. The sight of these mechanical monsters had always sent people running for their lives. Now crowds filling the streets cheered them on. As the radio continued proclaiming 'Sephai Biplob' and that General Zia had taken over, thousands of people who had at first been alarmed by the firing in the Cantonment, poured into the streets to celebrate. For three days they had believed that India through Khalid Musharraf was threatening their hard-won independence. Now that

that nightmare was over, they hailed the troops as liberators. Everywhere jawans and civilians exchanged salutations, embraced one another, danced in the streets. The night was filled with cries of ALLAH HO AKBAR, BANGLADESH ZINDABAD, SEPHAI BIPLOB ZINDABAD, and GENERAL ZIAUR RAHMAN ZINDABAD— God is great, Long Live Bangladesh, Long Live the Sepoy Revolution, Long Live General Ziaur Rahman. It seemed that the people were re-living the heady moments of the Bangladesh upsurge in March, 1971. It was a night to remember.

In a short speech over Radio Bangladesh, General Zia announced he had temporarily taken over as Chief Martial Law Administrator. He had done so at the request of the armed forces and because of the situation in the country. He said he would discharge his responsibility to the best of his ability. Zia also called for unity, hard work and dedication to getting the country moving again. He ordered offices, courts, airports and mills—closed since Khalid's coup on the 3rd—to reopen and resume working at once. 'May Allah help us all,' he added.

The brief, emotional appeal, eloquently stated in Bengali and with just the right timing, sent a current of nationalistic fervour surging through the country. Zia, the hero, the man who had proclaimed the independence of Bangladesh at the start of the Liberation War, was once more the man of the hour. No one who heard him broadcast that morning of the Sepoy Mutiny will ever forget the experience. 'I was lying in bed,' an old friend recalled, 'when the radio announcer said "Stand by for General Ziaur Rahman the Chief Martial Law Administrator". Then his voice came over—simple, sincere, reassuring. Suddenly the darkness was pushed back and there was hope again for us. I told myself I must go to work today; I must go early and do my bit. I began preparing for the day, all the time crying emotionally to myself. Allah had been Merciful. Allah had indeed answered our prayers.' Thus was Bangladesh born again—its peoples' hopes raised once more, however temporarily.

There is some controversy about how General Zia made his broadcast. Abu Taher and the JSD claim he took Zia to the radio station after responding successfully to a personal appeal from the general to rescue him. This is disputed by some of Zia's associates who were present at 2 Field Artillery headquarters on the morning of the 7th. One of them, a military officer who does not wish to be identified because he is still in the army, told me Abu Taher turned up around 5.30 am. Zia embraced him warmly, just as he had embraced the others before him. They had, after all, been comrades in the Liberation War and subsequently had kept in touch. After exchanging pleasantries, Abu Taher requested and obtained a private word with Zia. But when the retired colonel tried to take Zia to the radio station the other officers 'for security reasons' refused to let him go. Abu Taher was furious. The others, however, had their way. Instead of Zia going there, these officers summoned a recording unit from Radio Bangladesh. My informant insists it was Zia's recorded speech that was broadcast early that Friday morning.

Later Abu Taher wanted Zia to address a meeting of jawans he had called for 10 am at the Shaheed Minar (Martyrs' memorial). Evidently the left-wing retired colonel was hoping that once he had Zia in front of a mass gathering of troops he could conveniently put to him the 12 Demands. At that point Zia would hardly be in a position to refuse them. The demands themselves had by now acquired a crucial new dimension that proposed a radical alteration of the decision-making process in Bangladesh. The new leaflet now proclaimed:

'Our revolution is not for changing the leadership only. This revolution is only for the interest of the poorer class. We have accepted you (Zia) as our leader in this revolution. For that reason you are to express very clearly that you are the leader of the poorer class. And for that you have to change the structure of the armed forces . . . From today onwards the armed forces of the country will build themselves as the protector of the interest of the poorer classes . . .'

To this end the Demands document proposed a system of pyramiding soldiers' councils. A Revolutionary Army Organisation with Revolutionary Soldiers' Cells would be formed in each unit of the army throughout the country. In Dhaka a Central Revolutionary Army Organisation would decide all policies and 'link up' with the revolutionary students, workers, peasants and masses. Most importantly, it was emphasised that General Zia 'should NOT take any decision without first consulting this body'.

Clearly Abu Taher and his group wanted an entirely new system of government. And they were trying to ride General Zia's back to achieve this objective. The gambit had been tried before on a notable previous occasion. In 1971 Bengali student leaders—among them A. S. M. Abdur Rab, now general secretary of the JSD—had transfixed Sheikh Mujib with a public re-assertion of the famous 'Six Points' for Bengali autonomy. They ultimately led to the creation of Bangladesh. If Col. Abu Taher could now inveigle General Zia, popular new military leader, into public endorsement of the 12 Demands, Bangladesh would be pushed irrevocably into radical, revolutionary channels. Taher did not succeed because other officers at 2 Field Artillery headquarters saw through his game and persuaded Zia to decline the invitaion to speak at the meeting of the jawans. Taher thereupon abruptly cancelled the meeting.

He did, however, manage to get Zia along to the radio station in the afternoon. There, in the presence of a room full of excited troops, Taher confronted him with the 12 Demands. Zia diplomatically signed the paper on which they were inscribed. In the circumstances he couldn't have done otherwise. But when invited to broadcast again to the nation, Zia carefully steered clear of any reference to the 12 Demands. Instead he thanked the people for their support, emphasising he remained a soldier and not a member of any political group or party. And he appealed to the troops to return at once to their places of duty.

Taher made one more attempt to get Zia to publicly commit himself to the sepoys' 12 Demands. This was at an 11 am conference Zia had called at 2 Field Artillery headquarters on the 7th to decide on a course of action. Present on that occasion were General Osmani, General Khalil, Towab, Commodore M. H. Khan, Mahboobul Alam Chashi (Secretary to the President) and Abu Taher. Col. Taher's presence was a gesture to the jawans because his followers were the most vocal among the mutineers. Taher in turn was the most vocal at the meeting. The first item on the agenda was who should be President. Moshtaque's time had run out, but Osmani and Chashi pleaded that he should be re-instated. In this they were echoing a substantial public demand. Khandaker Moshtaque, after General Zia, was the most popular figure during the Sepoy Mutiny. A number of troops and civilians were chanting slogans in favour of him being made President. Moshtaque's portrait decorated military vehicles and private cars. A group of jawans had also taken him in the morning to the radio station. When they got there Taher's men, who had astutely controlled it from the start, would not let him broadcast. Now Osmani and Chashi wanted Moshtaque to be made President again 'in the national interest'.

General Khalil and Abu Taher opposed the move. Zia himself had had enough of Moshtaque's slights and intrigue in the previous months. So when he quietly threw his weight behind Justice Sayem, who had been sworn in the day before by Khalid Musharraf, it was quickly decided that Sayem should continue as President.

The meeting didn't go entirely General Zia's way. Earlier in the day he had assumed the role of CMLA. Zia obviously felt it was his by right because he was the designated leader of the counter-coup and head of the Army which was by far the most important of the defence services. Now, however, after they had agreed that Justice Sayem should continue as President, General Khalil sprung a surprise on everyone by insisting that it was inappropriate that anyone should appear to stand above the Head of State. He argued that the President, for reasons of precedence, must also be the CMLA. Put that way General Zia could not very well demur, especially as all but Taher supported Khalil's argument. So President Sayem was made CMLA. General Zia was reduced to the position of Deputy CMLA, a rank he shared with the Air Force and Navy Chiefs. The three of them formed the President's advisory council. Zia swallowed his humiliation, but he never forgave General Khalil for it.

Other matters agreed at the conference were the need to move rapidly towards the restoration of democracy and the release of all political prisoners. The JSD was particularly interested in this last point because its principal office bearers and a large number of party workers were in jail. But when Abu Taher proposed that the conference endorse the sepoys' 12 Demands—he called it 'the programme of the 7th November uprising'—he received not a single gesture of support from any of the others. Taher too would not forget this rebuff in the days to come when the JSD and its Revolutionary Peoples' Army tried to topple Zia.

Troops had also mutinied at Chittagong, Comilla, Jessore and other brigade headquarters. Some came to Dhaka to join the 'Biplob'. There were some tense moments when officers were threatened by their troops. But apart from the murder of Khalid Musharraf and his two companions at Sher-i-Bangla Nagar in Dhaka, there was no significant violence reported anywhere on the 7th. The killing of officers started next day, i.e. from early in the morning of the 8th. At least 12 officers were killed that day. Some were murdered out of grudge; others because they happened to belong to the 'hated officer class'. An Army lady doctor nicknamed 'Cherry' and Major Karim, a dental surgeon, were among the former group. Among the latter were Captain Anwar Hussain and Lt. Mustafizur Rahman who were attending a hockey camp at Dhaka stadium. They were caught by some 'revolutionary' soldiers as they attempted to flee, taken to a spot near the TV station and shot dead. Another officer, Major Azim, was caught and killed at Dhaka airport while boarding a flight to Chittagong.

General Zia blamed the JSD for the killings. In an interview six weeks after the event, Zia told me the JSD had 'tried to destroy the army for its own narrow purposes'. Discipline had been wrecked and, he added confidentially, the country's security was endangered because the army 'had been reduced to only 30 per cent of its officer strength'. The others had 'disappeared'—'a few had been killed; the rest had just run away.'

The killings convinced General Zia and the army commanders that they were now facing a determined attempt by a group of radicals to seize power by turning the spontaneous uprising against Khalid Musharraf into a fully-fledged military insurrection. The JSD in fact made no secret of this intention after the 8th. Once it had supported Khalid's overthrow as the first move in the step-by-step advancement of the proletarian cause. Now the party called for immediate and uninterrupted revolution. Its national leaders such as A. S. M. Abdur Rab, retired Major M. A. Jalil and Mohammad Shahjehan, who had been released from jail on the 7th, quickly denounced Zia and tried to rally the jawans for class war. A new wave of leaflets and posters flooded the cantonments. This time, under the banner of Col. Abu Taher's Revolutionary Soldiers Organisation the troops were urged to form 'BIPLOBI SAINIK PARISHADS' (revolutionary soldiers' councils) to press the sepoys' 12 Demands. They were also instructed to hold tight to their weapons until their demands were met. Thus the stage was set for a showdown with General Zia.

Army Headquarters in Dhaka Cantonment resembled a mini fortress under seige. Zia and his headquarters staff worked, ate and slept in their offices for almost two weeks. This was not for convenience, but as a matter of necessity. The headquarters, I was told by one of the officers who lived through the ordeal, 'was the only secure place in the country for officers'. Nevertheless apart from Zia, Brigadier (later general) Mir Shaukat Ali, who temporarily took over Khalid's job as CGS, and one or two other officers were still nervous in front of the soldiers and prudently removed all badges of rank from their uniforms. 'This was a measure of prudence,' my informant said. 'It was that sort of situation.'

Security was provided by a hastily-assembled commando group chosen from the 7th, 9th, 11th and 12th East Bengal regiments, all based at Jessore. Each of these units had a specially-trained commando company. Zia brought them together in Dhaka on the 9th to guard and support Army Headquarters while he faced up to the continuing upsurge and JSD threat. It was a courageous effort and, in retrospect, one of the bright moments of the Bangladesh Army. In the capital at that time were four infantry regiments, the Bengal Lancers and 2 Field Artillery. The latter were in an uproar but were not the major threat because their principal weapons—the tanks and the field guns—had been disarmed. The men had only the rifles and other guns they had managed to loot. The infantry was another matter. Zia wasn't immediately aware of how deeply affected were these fighting units and he had no way of disarming them. So he played it cool. He bought time to identify and neutralise the troublemakers by pacifying the troops with non-political sweeteners from their 12 Demands: improved pay, accommodation and kit and the ending of the invidious 'batman' system of body servants. Zia also went on the radio and TV to warn the country against the insidious activities of 'interested quarters'. He re-asserted that both he and the armed forces were 'absolutely neutral'; that the government was non-party and non-political and dedicated to the return of democracy. In many ways the broadcast was an echo of what President Sayem had said on behalf of Khalid Musharraf on the 6th of November.

Zia would not have succeeded were it not for the remarkable character of the Bangladeshis. However volatile their politics and violent their political changes, Bangladeshis are paradoxically middle-of-the-roaders, eschewing extremism in both religion and politics. What else would explain the persistent eclipse of the left or the rejection of Ayatollah fundamentalism of the right whenever it reared its head? Their basic chemistry is constituted in equal measure of burning nationalism, unobtrusive piety in the practice of Islam, and an aggressive sense of equality combined with a penchant for instant outrage when confronted by injustice and wrong-doing in others.

Sheikh Mujibur Rahman, perhaps better than anyone else, understood these character traits of his people. He was remarkably presentient when he warned his Baksal party three weeks before he died that '. . . the cause for alarm nowadays is that the people of Bangladesh react too much . . . You make devoted efforts throughout (your) whole life, but if you do one wrong you will perish . . . This is the rule of Bangladesh'.

Abu Taher and the JSD failed because they tried to push the Bangladeshis beyond their natural desire. The mistake would cost Taher his life. Once they received their financial demands and Sepoy dignity had been restored by the ending of the 'batman' system, most of the jawans quickly lost interest in 'biplob' or revolution. The Cantonment quietened down. By the 23rd November General Zia was ready to crackdown on the JSD. While he was broadcasting a warning that night—'We shall not allow any more disorder . . . We shall not tolerate any more bloodshed . . .'—armed police fanned out in the city. Among the first to be arrested were Rab, Jalil, Hasanul Huq Inu and Flight Sergeant Abu Yusuf Khan, Abu Taher's elder brother. Taher himself was arrested next morning from a hide-out in Dhaka University hostel. That effectively ended the great Sepoy Mutiny.

Two days later a dramatic bid was made to rescue Abu Taher and the other JSD leaders. It took the form of an attempt to kidnap and take hostage the Indian High Commissioner, Mr. Samar Sen. Six armed JSD 'commandos', two of them Taher's brothers, grabbed Mr. Sen outside his office in the Dhanmandi area of Dhaka. Reacting instantly, the High Commissioner's bodyguards opened fire killing four of the attackers, including one of the brothers, and wounding the other two. In the process Mr. Sen received a bullet wound in the arm. Mercifully for both Bangladesh and India this daft scheme did not have more serious consequences. What India would or would not have done had the kidnap attempt succeeded is a matter of conjecture. The fact remains that the incident convinced many Bangladeshis that Taher and the JSD were a lunatic group of adventurists who had gravely imperilled the country. General Zia took advantage of this feeling in the next few months when he hounded the JSD till an estimated 10,000 of its members were locked up in jail.

Col. Abu Taher was brought to trial on 21st June, 1976, seven months after his arrest, before a specially-constituted military tribunal which sat in Dhaka Central Jail. Charged along with him were 33 others. Among them were the top echelon of the JSD and more than 20 soldiers, some of whom were absconding. It was clear from the start that Taher was the principal accused. He never denied his leadership of the BIPLOBI GONO BAHINI (Revolutionary Peoples' Army) or BIPLOBI SAINIK SANGSTHA (Revolutionary Soldiers' Organisation). By his own admission he had also attempted and failed to change the system of government by a military insurrection. In these circumstances Col. Taher could have been tried—and probably been convicted—by due process before the ordinary courts. But to make sure he hanged, General Zia resorted to what unquestionably was one of the most outrageous judicial farces perpetrated in Bangladesh.

For a start, there was an amazing absurdity about one of the main charges against Taher: the overthrow of the 'duly constituted' government on 7th November, 1975. This, it will be recalled, was Khalid Musharraf's four-day regime which had usurped power from Khandaker Moshtaque; and Moshtaque himself had been installed by the majors after they had killed the President, Sheikh Mujibur Rahman. General Zia had ultimately been the principal beneficiary of this chain of assassination, coup and counter-coup. Now, ironically, Zia had brought Taher to trial for the very mutiny that had placed him in power on the 7th of November. Taher was also not given a reasonable opportunity to defend himself. The charges were first made known to him on the day the trial started. It was only then that he was allowed access to lawyers. The rest was done with appalling haste, as though Zia was anxious to be done with it as quickly as possible. Taher was sentenced to death on the 17th of July, 1976. His mercy petition to the President was rejected on the 20th. Next morning, the 21st, he was hanged at dawn in Dhaka Central Jail.

It was murder by fiat; a grotesque distortion of the judicial process. No one deserves to die that way, whatever the crime, unless we are all to be stained with the guilt of the injustice. The action shamed General Zia and all those who had a hand in it.

I tried, unsuccessfully, to interview President Sayem about the circumstances in which he so promptly confirmed Abu Taher's death sentence. Sayem was the only one of more than a score of people I interviewed in connection with this book who declined to talk to me. But some idea of his version of the event is given by Zillur Rahman Khan in his book 'Leadership Crisis in Bangladesh'. Zillur Khan, who interviewed Sayem in Dhaka in June, 1981, has recorded: 'At Taher's trial, due process of law was clearly violated by the government to such an extent that Justice Abusadat Sayem, then President of Bangladesh, indicated off the record that he had reservations about the trial's fairness . . . Sayem felt that the government evidence at the trial was insufficient for a death sentence but that Taher had received just punishment because of his treasonous attempt to sacrifice the sovereignty of the country.' After such double-faced reasoning, President Sayem should not feel aggrieved—as he indicated to me on the telephone—about the chicanery and hypocrisy of military leaders and politicians. With such private misgivings he was wrong to confirm Taher's death sentence whatever the pressure from General Zia. It must remain a blot on his otherwise admirable record.

Taher's last moments are poignantly described by his wife, Lutfa, in a letter from Kishorgang dated 18th August, 1976, reproduced in Lifschultz's book 'Bangladesh: the Unfinished Revolution'. It said:

'On the 20th in the evening, Taher was informed that on the 21st early in the morning at 4 o'clock, the death sentence would be carried out. He accepted their news and thanked those who had to deliver the message. And then he took his dinner completely normally. Later the Moulvi (priest) was brought and asked him to seek absolution for his sins. He said "I am not touched by the evils of your society, nor have I ever been. I am pure. You may go now. I wish to sleep". He went to sleep quietly. At 3 o'clock in the night he was woken up. He asked how much time was left. After knowing the time he cleaned his teeth and shaved himself and bathed. All those present came forward to help him. He forbad them to do so, saying "I don't want you to touch my body which is pure". After his bath he told the others to prepare tea and to cut the mangos we had given him. He himself put on the artificial limb, shoes and trousers. He put on a beautiful shirt, his wrist watch and combed his hair carefully. After that he took tea, mangoes and smoked cigarettes with all those present. Looking at his courage all burst into tears about the death sentence on such a man. He consoled them saying, "Come on, laugh. Why are you so gloomy? I had wanted to make the face of death bloom with smiles. Death cannot defeat me". He was asked whether he had any wish. He said, "In exchange for my death, the peace of the common man". After that Taher asked: "Is there any time left?" They answered a little bit. He said in that case I shall recite a poem to you. He read out a poem about his duty and his feelings. Then he said, "Alright, I am ready. Go ahead. Do your duty". He went towards the gallows and taking the rope in his own hand he put it around his neck. And he said "Goodbye countrymen. Long live Bangladesh! Long live Revolution!"'

A. S. M. Abdur Rab, the JSD's general secretary who was sentenced to 10 years rigorous imprisonment at the same trial but was released later in an act of clemency, said of Taher's hanging: 'Zia couldn't afford to let Taher live because he was the symbol of the patriotic left jawans and the young, junior officers'. Taher himself saw his death as martyrdom for the cause and embraced it as such. In a short valediction he told his wife and brothers: 'If lives are not sacrificed this way how will the common people be liberated?' Things didn't go the way Abu Taher wanted. But his ghost did haunt Zia for the next five years in more than 20 mutinies, insurrections and attempted coups until Zia was finally brought down in a hail of bullets from the guns of young officers, perhaps equally disenchanted but less imaginative than the volatile, one-legged ex-army colonel.

XI

Zia: The Man and the Myth

I did not capture power. I was made to assume power.

—Gen. Ziaur Rahman

He was a man who could kill with one hand and eat with the other.

—A Zia colleague during the Liberation War in Chittagong

In the morning of the 26th of March, 1971, a small group of radio script-writers, artistes, producers and a solitary technician got together in Chittagong 'to do something' for Bangladesh. In the circumstances it was an extraordinarily courageous decision by gentle, soft-handed men who had never before raised their fists in anger. Only hours earlier the Pakistan army had launched its campaign of genocide, massacring more than 1000 previously disarmed Bengali soldiers in Chittagong Cantonment alone. This alarmed, but did not deter, the brave little band—not more than 10 men in all. First they stopped the Chittagong radio station at Agarabad relaying the Pakistan army's Martial Law orders broadcast from Dhaka. Then they decided to set up the SADHINI BANGLA BIPLOBI KENDRA or Free Bengal Revolutionary Radio to rally the Bangladeshis and broadcast defiance against the Pakistanis from the Chittagong radio transmitter located at Kalurghat well outside the city. (The term Biplobi or Revolutionary would be dropped two days later).

To operate effectively, Belal Mohammad, one of the founders of the group explained, they sought protection from Captain (later Major) Rafiq-ul-Islam of the East Pakistan Rifles who was leading the fight against the Pakistanis from a 'tactical headquarters' on Railway Hill inside the city. Rafiq promised to help but did not do so, perhaps because he was already over-committed elsewhere. Next day Belal and his friends got the news that another group of Bengali soldiers were holed up at Patya, 16 miles from Chittagong down the Kalurghat road. This was the 8th East Bengal Regiment which had revolted after being ordered to unload arms and ammunition for the Pakistan army from the supply ship *Swat*.

'We went to Patya in a white Toyota car belonging to one Mahmood Hussain of Bogra,' Belal Mohammad recalled, 'and we found a lot of soldiers with guns. We asked them, "Who is in charge?" and were told it was one Major Zia. Till then we had never even heard of the man. But when we asked him for help he readily agreed and we returned to Kalurghat at about 4.30 pm in a convoy of three trucks with troops, Major Zia in his jeep and we in the Toyota.'

Belal and his friends were impressed by the confident manner in which Zia told the groups of Bengalis they met on the way: 'We will take no more than two days to destroy the Pakistan occupation army . . . Those who speak Urdu are also our enemies because they support the Pakistan army. We will crush them . . .' They were even more impressed by the way he quickly deployed his troops in defensive positions around the radio transmitter station. So when they gathered in the station manager's office, as a courtesy to Major Zia they offered him the boss's chair.

Then, Belal Mohammad recalls, 'I told him, "Major Sahib, we are all minors and you are the major. Why don't you broadcast something for us in your own voice?" I said this out of pleasantness, almost a joke,' Belal Mohammad told me, 'but he took it seriously. Pulling a fountain pen out of his pocket Zia proceeded to draft his statement: 'I Major Ziaur Rahman do hereby declare the independence of Bangladesh . . .'

Thus did Zia, by seizing on a chance invitation, talk himself into the history books as the man who supposedly proclaimed the independence of Bangladesh at Chittagong on 27th March, 1971.

The incident was typical of the man. Ruthless opportunism combined with a series of lucky breaks is the story of his remarkable rise from an unknown Major to Lt. General and President of Bangladesh in a mere seven years. The record shows that Zia never stuck his neck out; and he always rode someone's back. There are numerous instances of this, but the major ones are the pillars that mark his progression along the road to power.

* Zia did not lift a finger to stop Major Farook when he told him he was going to knock off Sheikh Mujibur Rahman five months before the event.

* After Sheikh Mujib was killed, Zia readily accepted the job of Chief of Army Staff from his successor, but after that he once more conveniently shut his eyes while Khalid Musharraf and Shafat Jamil plotted and finally toppled President Moshtaque and the majors.

* Zia thanked the jawans for saving his life and making him Chief of the Army Staff during the Sepoy Mutiny; then he hanged their leader Lt. Col. (rtd) Abu Taher.

* In November, 1976, Zia used President Sayem to call off the elections that the government had so solemnly promised the nation. Then he unceremoniously stripped Sayem of authority and grabbed power for himself.

* Zia even took the credit for being the first to announce Bangladesh's independence on 27th March, 1971, when in fact someone else had made the announcement over the same radio station 30 hours earlier.

Belal Mohammad recalls that Mohammad Abdul Hanan, general secretary of the Chittagong district Awami League, had turned up at Kalurghat transmitting station a little after noon on the 26th of March to broadcast what he claimed was a 'message' from Sheikh Mujibur Rahman. They suspected that the 'message' had been fabricated by Hanan himself and for that reason refused to let him broadcast. But the man persisted. So at 2.30 pm on 26th of March, 1971, Hanan was allowed to tell the world: 'There is fighting in Raja bazar (police headquarters) in Dhaka and in Peelkhana (headquarters of the East Pakistan Rifles) where there was a sudden attack by Pakistanis. In these circumstances I, Sheikh Mujibur Rahman, do hereby declare the independence of Bangladesh. Joy Bangla. Khuda Hafiz.' [1]

It was a bold, imaginative effort, on par with anything Zia did the next day. But by a curious twist of fate Hanan's broadcast went largely unnoticed, except by a very few people in Chittagong. Belal Mohammad and Major Rafiq think this was due to the fact that the 10 kW transmitter had a radius of only 60 miles and that anyway most people on the first day of the Pakistan army crackdown were listening to the more powerful Dhaka Radio station broadcasting Martial Law announcements and the momentous news of Pakistan's determined bid to crush Bengali nationalism. It must also be remembered that Belal and his group had themselves switched off Chittagong Radio for a time as they moved to Kalurghat and as a result people had turned from that frequency to the Dhaka radio broadcasts.

Zia, however, was infinitely more fortunate. When he went on the air next day at 7.30 pm everyone in the area was tuned in again to the old frequency of Chittagong Radio after they discovered that SADHINI BANGLA BIPLOBI KENDRA, the revolutionary Free Bangladesh Radio, was screaming defiance at the Pakistanis from Kalurghat. By lucky chance Zia's broadcast was also picked up clearly in India and when it relayed the news around the world, the hitherto unknown Major Zia became an instant sensation. Zia did nothing to correct the record. Quite typically, he hogged all the glory and Hanan died an embittered man for having lost his place in the history books. This is all the more ironic because up to the 26th of March Zia had resisted getting involved in the Bangladesh movement, considering it to be a political, non-military affair.

Major Rafiq-ul-Islam, who was Zia's contemporary in the army at Chittagong at the start of the Liberation War, recounts an interesting story he heard from Khalid Musharraf which provides an insight into Zia's attitude to the Bangladesh liberation movement before the Pakistan army crackdown. Tension had been building up in Dhaka as the confrontation between West and East Pakistan developed over the Awami League's right to form a government after winning the elections. The Pakistanis had quite ominously been building up their military strength in the province. In these circumstances Khalid Musharraf, who was then a Brigade Major in Dhaka, went to Chittagong to consult the other Bengali officers about their attitude to the gathering storm. One of those he talked to was Major Zia. He is reported to have told Khalid: 'These are political problems and politicians' headaches. We as soldiers have nothing to do. You must keep away.'[2] Then again, according to Rafiq, when on the 24th of March he personally appealed to Zia to support a pre-emptive strike against the Pakistanis in Chittagong ('We must hit them before being hit . . . otherwise they will butcher us all') Zia dissuaded him with the remark, 'Don't worry. They will not go to that extent.'[3]

Rafiq also claims that Zia was actually on his way to the port area of Chittagong on the 26th of March to supervise the unloading of arms and ammunition from M.V. *Swat* against the strong opposition of the Bengalis in Chittagong when he got a message to him that the Pakistan army had attacked the East Bengal Regimental Centre and killed a large number of Bengali troops.[4] Zia, to his credit, immediately turned back and joined the revolt, taking his troops to Patya where Belal discovered him a day later. Thereafter Zia was a model of patriotism. Zia never denied Rafiq's revelations made in 'A TALE OF MILLIONS', a book widely circulated during Zia's lifetime.

Clearly Zia wasn't the type for hasty action; a man not given to impulse or the grand gesture. He always displayed an elemental caution and patience in everything he did, taking no risks, ruffling no feathers, trusting no one. He went to extreme lengths to conceal his emotions. He wore dark glasses even at night so that no one could read his eyes peering through the inflexible mask that was his face. These dominant personal traits would later make him concentrate all power in his own hands and work alone as far as possible. All this was perhaps the result of Zia's training and long service as a Pakistani military intelligence officer.[5] The Pakistanis picked him out for such work quite early in his career. Four years after he was commissioned Zia was given special training and employed in military intelligence from 1959 to 1964. This experience would prove invaluable to him later when he assumed a political role in 1976.

As much as anything else, Zia was also a professional soldier—'a soldier's soldier' someone once call him. Otherwise this scion of a middle-class government science officer, born in Bogra in 1936, would not have opted to go to the Pakistan Military Academy at Kakul instead of the university of Dhaka in 1953. Zia did not shine at his military studies. He seems to have done well on the battlefield. The official life-sketch issued by the Ministry of Information (Bangladesh), without mentioning any decorations, records that 'he fought courageously in the Khem Karan Sector during the 1965 India–Pakistan war when he commanded a company of the 1st East Bengal Regiment.'[6] Zia was appointed an instructor in the Pakistan Military Academy in 1966. Among the cadets committed to his care were two other ambitious Bengalis, Farook Rahman and Khandaker Abdur Rashid who as majors nine years later would make him Chief of Army Staff in Bangladesh. Zia also attended the Staff College at Quetta and later spent three months with the British Army on the Rhine. It was his only overseas appointment.

Ziaur Rahman came into his own during the Bangladesh Liberation War, creating something of a legend surpassed only by General M. A. G. Osmani, the famous old 'Papa Tiger'. Zia may have been a late starter because of political immaturity in 1971, but once he joined the Liberation War he took an active role in pursuing Bengali nationalism. The glory of the independence broadcast helped immensely. Zia was quietly competent as head of 'Z (for Zia) Force', the 1st Brigade of the Bangladesh Army, operating from Roumari in the Sylhet district. For his prowess he was decorated with the Bir Utam, the second highest award for a freedom fighter. Zia was also abstemious and noted for his manners, personal honesty and lack of swagger. Unlike some of his comrades-in-arms, such as retired Lt. Colonel Abu Taher and retired Lt. Colonel Ziauddin, he was totally apolitical. All this made him a popular figure among the 'FFs' (freedom fighters) during the Liberation War and singled him out for advancement after independence in 1972. Promotions came quickly, even for the fledgling Bangladesh Army. He was made Colonel in February, 1972, Brigadier in the middle of 1973 and Major General on the 10th of October that same year. His appointments included Brigade Commander, Comilla (1972), Deputy Chief of Army Staff (1972) and Chief of Army Staff on 20th August, 1975, when he was only 39 years old.

It would be quite natural to assume that General Zia, having had such a fantastic military career, would be popular with his troops. Indeed he was—for a time, and until the real Zia emerged: vengeful, savage, authoritarian. THAT Zia was plagued by 20 mutinies, attempted coups and assassination attempts during the five and half years he ruled Bangladesh—a statistical average of one military uprising every 3.3 months and certainly a record no general could be proud of. It's ironical that the troops who literally carried Zia to power on their shoulders during the Sepoy Mutiny in November, 1974, would later try so many times to kill him. And Zia, as will be seen later, responded with incredible savagery. No general in the history of the sub-continent massacred his own troops the way that General Zia did after the aborted coup of 2nd October, 1977.

Although I had seen the evidence at first hand I found it difficult to believe that this quiet, well-spoken and well-mannered man whom I had interviewed on many occasions could be so brutal. Then one day I got a glimpse of the other Zia. It happened during a conversation with a man who had known him at close quarters in Chittagong and Agartala during the first two weeks of the Liberation War.

'What kind of a man was Zia?' I asked him.

My informant, who for the present does not wish to be identified, looked at me for a long time. Then almost in a whisper he said: 'Zia was a man who could kill with one hand and eat with the other.'

'Look here,' I told him angrily. 'That's a terrible thing to say about anyone. You had better stand it up.'

The man then recalled an incident at Kalurghat transmitter station that was seared in his memory. It happened on the evening of the 28th March, 1971, when the Pakistan army was battling to control Chittagong against stiff resistance from the East Pakistan Rifles under Major Rafiq and others. Zia was at Kalurghat providing military cover for the Shadin Bangla Betar Kendra broadcasts. At about sunset, my informant said, a group of Biharis, some 18 men and 12 women, were caught on the road while trying to slip into the city and the safety of the Pakistan army. These Urdu-speaking people were brought to Zia at the radio station since he was the senior Bengali military person in the area. 'Take the men out and shoot them,' Zia ordered. Then, pointing to the women he told his troops: 'You can do what you like with them.'

Although it had happened 14 years earlier, my informant was visibly upset, shaking with emotion as he talked about Zia and how the troops had dealt with those unfortunate people. 'How could he do it?' he wailed. 'I know war is war and that worse things were done to our own people. But doing such things ourselves polluted our cause. It undermined our moral right. After that I never wanted to see him again. What a tragedy for our country.'

'I, Abusadat Mohammad Sayem, because of my failing health, am unable further to discharge the function of the office of President. I do hereby nominate Major General Ziaur Rahman to be the President of Bangladesh and hand over the office of President to him.'

Thus did Major General Ziaur Rahman on the 21st of April, 1977, at the age of 43 become the seventh President of Bangladesh. Stripped of its imperial overtones, Sayem's proclamation was no different to a run-of-the-mill land deal with one man conveying title and possession to another; only in this case Sayem and Zia were playing about with one of the world's most populous Muslim states. Sheikh Mujibur Rahman, the Father of the 1972 Constitution, had himself perverted that eloquent document by the infamous 'Baksal' amendments. After his assassination, Proclamations entirely superseded the Constitution as the authority for government.

It started with Khandaker Moshtaque Ahmed's pompous declaration in August, 1975 that '. . . In view of the historical necessity the responsibility of the government has been devolved on me as the Head of State to perform, keeping trust in Allah the Merciful and the masses of Bangladesh, the holy and sacred duty of materialising in totality and collectively the true and real aspirations of the seven and half crore (75 million) people of Bangladesh . . .' In the three and a half years after that—until the National Assembly was reconstituted by general elections in 1979—everything was done by Proclamation. According to available records, between them Moshtaque, Sayem and Zia issued 23 proclamations; three by Moshtaque and ten each by Sayem and Zia. For them it was the most convenient form of 'legislation'. Sometimes, especially in the case of Sayem and Zia, it was taken to the extreme length of back-dating orders to a time when their authors were not even specks on the political horizon.

Sayem's last Proclamation wasn't the voluntary abdication brought on by some sudden infirmity that it was made out to be. He was forced out by Zia as surely as if the general had held a pistol to the President's head. What's more, the dethroning had in fact taken place five months earlier. Sayem was only formalising the fait accompli.

On the 28th November of the previous year General Zia had decided that it was too dangerous for him to allow President Sayem to continue to hold the supreme authority of Chief Martial Law Administrator (CMLA). Sayem, wearing both hats, had been an effective President, according to one of his aides. He asserted himself but always asked 'What does the Army Chief (Zia) say?' But then a week earlier Zia had forced the President, much against his will, to call off the elections to the National Assembly promised for the following February. The official excuse given was flimsy. The real reason was that Zia was preparing the ground for his own political career and did not want to be hampered by elections at that stage. This was a bitter pill for the former Chief Justice to swallow because he had staked his integrity on the elections and for a year had worked manfully to make them possible. Clearly Sayem was unhappy about the turn of events. Word got back to Zia from one of the President's own men that Sayem was having serious reservations about the Army Chief's professed dedication to the return of democratic government and might suddenly sack him and bring in a less ambitious man. I have not been able to ascertain whether there was indeed even a shred of truth in this allegation. The fact remains that it did prompt the ever-suspicious Zia to act quickly and decisively to emasculate President Sayem's authority.

Flanked by all the military brass he could muster, General Zia told the President that he would have to relinquish and hand over to him the role of CMLA. The confrontation took place at 7 pm that Sunday evening in Bangababan. Accompanying Zia were General Ershad, the Deputy Chief of Army Staff, General Manzoor, the CGS, General Mir Shaukat Ali, the commander of the 9th Division, and the Navy and Air Force chiefs who along with Zia had been designated Deputy CMLAs. Also present was Justice Sattar who had been appointed Special Assistant to the President.

One of those present on the occasion told me: 'Sayem refused General Zia's request. He fought bravely to prevent him becoming CMLA because, he said, he had undertaken the task of returning democratic government to the country and intended to see it through.' Zia was equally adamant and he made the others take turns to try to persuade Sayem. The argument went on till after midnight with the old man being denied food and rest. At one point Sayem turned to the Air Force Chief: 'Mahmud, you are my creation. Tell me, is it right that I should surrender the CMLA authority to this man?' Air Vice Marshal Mahmud was terribly embarrassed. He respected Sayem but couldn't oppose Zia. So he answered sheepishly: 'Sir, I'm very sorry but I'm not in a position to influence the course of events in any way. I must only support what he (Zia) says.' Finally Justice Sattar told Sayem: 'Brother, since he (Zia) wants to be CMLA let him have it.' It was nearing 1.00 am when President Sayem capitulated. He signed a proclamation transferring, 'in the national interest', the office of Chief Martial Law Administrator to General Zia so that he could 'do any act or thing or take any other action as he deems necessary in the national interest or for enforcement of Martial Law.' After that it was only a matter of time before Zia would entirely supplant President Sayem in Bangababan.

Before signing away his authority, the plucky President made one more grand gesture. He offered to promote the new CMLA to the rank of Lt. General.

I was told that Zia appeared to be gratified by the offer. Then once again the intelligence man in this complex personality surfaced and Zia declined the offer. 'They will say I wanted the job because I wanted to be Lt. General,' Zia told his men. But none of them, at least, would have accused him of such small opportunism. By then they were well aware that what interested Zia most was real power, only power, and not fancy titles.

Zia aimed high and took his opportunities seriously.

The decision to assume the role of President had grown on him in the same manner that Belal Mohammad's invitation 'to say something' over the radio in 1971 had prompted Zia to switch from an uninvolved spectator to a high-profile role in the freedom movement in the early days of the Pakistan military action. While others such as Major Rafiq and the gallant jawans of the East Pakistan rifles did the actual fighting in Chittagong against the Pakistanis, Zia after his first broadcast enthusiastically threw himself into the propaganda war over Shadin Bangla Betar Kendra. Belal Mohammad recalls that on the 28th March, the day after his 'independence' broadcast, Zia had come into the radio station with a new text claiming to be the Head of the Provisional Government of Bangladesh. Like Hanan's fabricated 'message' from Sheikh Mujib, Zia's 'Provisional Government' was a myth entirely of his own invention. But that did not stop him announcing it over the radio on the morning of the 28th and repeating it until the Pakistanis bombed the Kalurghat transmitter into silence.

Similarly when the jawans restored him as Army Chief during the Sepoy Mutiny, Zia seems to have accepted it as some kind of mission to rule. 'I did not capture power. I was made to assume power,' Zia told a press conference some years later.[7] It was almost an echo of the imperial theme of the 'White Man's Burden' and only Zia, with his exalted ego, could have put it quite that way. Zia's opportunism, however odious it may have been, was understandable. No general in his right mind would turn down the opportunity for the top job. But the problem was that there was no limit to Zia's ambition. Once he became President he wanted to remain President for life.

The 1978 Presidential elections were expertly tailored to effect Zia's transformation from the military President to the military President in mufti. 'A general in a safari suit,' is how one journalist described him. The image was patiently built up, layer upon layer, like some exotic piece of Chinese lacquerware. The role that Zia sought for himself required the broadest possible civilian support, while holding fast to the basic source of power, which is the Army. Direct control of the Army was ensured by his continuance as the Chief of Army Staff in addition to being Commander-in-Chief of the Defence Forces. A government spokesman underlined the point the day Zia replaced Sayem as President.[8] Zia's 'Proclamations (Amendment) Order, 1977', which gave the Constitution a distinctly Islamic tinge without really changing its broadly socialist and secular aspects, went a long way to win him public acclaim. It was a superbly-crafted operation executed with exquisite timing. First, the Proclamation decorated the Constitution's preamble with the opening acclamation: 'BISMILLAH-AR-RAHMAN-AR-RAHIM, In the name of Allah, the Beneficent, the Merciful. . . .' Next it stipulated that 'Absolute trust and faith in the Almighty Allah shall be the basis of all actions.' It will be recalled that Nationalism, Socialism, Democracy and Secularism—the Four Pillars of Mujibism—had been enshrined among the Fundamental Principles of State Policy. The Proclamation neatly excised all reference to 'secularism' and qualified the word 'Socialism' to mean 'economic and social justice'. It was cosmetic surgery at its best because the amendments did not really change any of the operative clauses of the Constitution. But they did answer an emotional need.

The Proclamation also stipulated that the citizens of Bangladesh would henceforth be known as 'Bangladeshis' instead of 'Bengalees' as hitherto. The changes seemed to echo an overwhelming public sentiment which is a blend of Islamic faith, personal piety and love of country. At the same time it deftly avoided making waves in neighbouring India. In 1972 Sheikh Mujibur Rahman had caused some irritation in New Delhi by his insistence on calling his people 'Bengalees'. The Indians felt this flaunting of Bengali nationalism by the newly-created Bengali state could at some time in the future have undesirable implications for their own West Bengal state. Zia's switch to the name 'Bangladeshis' was therefore welcomed in New Delhi and helped offset any misgivings it had about the new Islamic tinge given to the Bangladesh Constitution.

These popular changes were introduced the day after General Zia took over as President from Justice Sayem, giving Zia the benefit of maximum impact. It not only ensured a massive personal endorsement for him in the referendum held a month later, but also helped him to victory in the Presidential elections in June, 1978.

Despite this advantage Zia did not hesitate to rig the elections against his opponents, chief among them being General Osmani. Zia gave them only 40 days notice of the election and 23 days to campaign.[9] While he used the entire paraphernalia of the government in his own election campaign, he made it difficult for the opposition even to know who was entitled to vote. A complete set of the Voters' List was priced at US $60,000, well beyond the pocket of any opposition candidate.[10] The government-owned TV and radio was stacked against them; so also the compliant press. To top it, Zia was simultaneously President, CMLA, C-in-C of the Defence Forces, and Chief of the Army Staff. If nothing else, this ensured that the police and government officials would work on his behalf. According to retired General Khalilur Rahman, an Awami Leaguer, 'a senior general addressed senior police officers in the Dhaka Cantonment and asked them to ensure that Zia won the elections 'at any cost' but that Zia should not be shown to have polled more than 70 per cent of the votes.'[11]

The result was a predictable 'landslide victory' for General Zia. But in retrospect, and on the basis of new evidence now available, there is serious doubt whether Zia was in fact validly elected President in June, 1978. The evidence is strong that he did NOT qualify as a candidate.

The Presidential Election Ordinance, 1978, promulgated by Zia himself on 18th April, 1978, stipulated that a person shall NOT qualify as a Presidential candidate:

(1) If he is less than 35 years old.
(2) If he is not qualified for election as an MP.
(3) If he has been removed from the office of President under the Constitution.

For its part the Constitution lays down that a person shall be DISQUALIFIED for election as a Member of Parliament, 'who holds any office of profit in the service of the Republic, other than an office which is declared by law not to disqualify its holders.'

Zia had an active role in the army which clearly attracted the disqualifications imposed by the Constitution. To overcome them he promulgated the

Second Proclamation (Thirteenth Amendment) Order, 1978, on 29th April, 1978.

This order stipulated:

(1) The Chief Martial Law Administrator shall be the Commander-in-Chief of the Defence Services of Bangladesh and shall exercise his power of superintendence, command and control over these services either directly or through their Chiefs of Staff; and

(2) The CMLA shall NOT be deemed to be a person holding an office of profit in the service of the Republic for any purpose whatsoever.

By these two clauses Zia hoped to maintain his tight grip on the armed forces, particularly the army, while at the same time immunising himself against any penalties in the Presidential Election Order. The gambit was good so far as his roles as CMLA and, by implication, the C-in-C of Defence Forces were concerned. But on 2nd May, 1978, the last date for nominations and on Election Day itself Zia was also Chief of Army Staff and a serving officer on the current Army List. He had NOT been exempted in those capacities. Thus he was clearly employed or 'held office of profit in the service of the State' when he stood for election and in normal circumstances should have been disqualified.

It is a matter of record that General Zia did NOT relinquish the office of Chief of Army Staff till the 1st December, 1978, when he appointed General Ershad, the Deputy CAS, to the post—but back-dated the appointment by eight months to April, 1978. I understand that General Ershad had protested in November about the Constitutional impropriety of Zia simultaneously being President and CMLA and Chief of Army Staff. Zia had responded a month later by summoning him to his office on 1st December, 1978, and in the presence of the Defence Secretary, had hand-written his appointment as CAS, effective April, 1978. The back-dating, I was told, 'was to overcome a Constitutional problem.'

Zia is further exposed by a curious series of Gazette notifications issued in 1979.

On 28-2-1979 by Gazette notification No. 7/8/D-1/175-160 Zia promoted himself to the rank of Lt. General 'with immediate effect'.

On 9-4-1979 that notification was cancelled by another notification No. 7/8/D-1/175–270 which also promoted Zia to rank of Lt. General 'with effect from 28-4-1979.'

Again on 9-4-1979 by another notification, No. 7/8/D-1/175-271 Zia retired from service as Lt. General 'with effect from 29-4-1978'.

There could be no clearer evidence of malfeasance. The operative dates are the dates the notifications were issued, viz. 28th February and 9th April 1979. Both these dates confirm that Zia considered himself to be—and in fact was—a serving military officer up to 9th April, 1978. Zia back-dated his promotion and retirement because as CMLA he could do almost anything. But he could not backdate his qualification as a candidate for election as President. Not even the CMLA could do that once the last date for nominations had passed. So his election in June, 1978 appears to have been illegal and unconstitutional.

There was, understandably, at that time an uproar about Zia's involvement with the armed forces while putting himself forward as a candidate for President. The group supporting General Osmani demanded that Zia resign his posts as CMLA, Chief of Army Staff and from active service in the army. 'Not to do so,' they said, 'would be contrary to the Constitution and law and fundamental principles of democracy and would further imply a contest between the people and the armed forces which is contrary to the national interest.'[12]

Zia brushed aside these objections. 'Osmani was an MP and also held the office of commander-in-chief' he told a press conference: 'I am C-in-C exercising powers through the Chief of the Navy Staff, the Chief of the Air Staff and the Deputy Chief of the Army Staff. My resignation would not be good for the country.'[13]

There was some merit in Zia's contention that General Osmani had been both an MP and C-in-C. But it was hardly a precedent for the Presidential election. Nothing Zia said extenuated the basic falseness of his own position. By the rules he had himself made, he simply did not qualify as a candidate. Otherwise he would not have fudged the dates of General Ershad's appointment as Chief of Army Staff, his own promotion to Lt. General and his retirement from active service in the Army.

Unfortunately no one at that time could challenge this electoral sleight of hand. Martial Law regulations in force effectively prohibited any intervention by the Courts. This would not be the only occasion that General Zia fiddled the books. It happened again and again and Zia always had the Martial Law or rubber-stamp Parliament to do the needful.

The wide-ranging amendments to the Constitution prior to the general elections are another example of how Zia perverted the authority of Martial Law for his personal aggrandisement. His transformation to a civilian identity required that he 'restore democracy' and revive the National Assembly. This posed a serious problem for the general who was not quite satisfied that Sheikh Mujibur Rahman's 'Baksal' amendments in 1975 gave him enough power in exactly the way he desired it. Zia wanted a tighter hold on all the strings if the National Assembly was to be reconstituted. This was easily done, again by Martial Law proclamation on 18th December, 1978. The Second Proclamation (Fifteenth Amendment) Order, 1978, made a bluster about responding to the popular demand for the repeal of 'undemocratic provisions' of Sheikh Mujib's Constitution. General Zia's amendments, however, were even more undemocratic. They were a combination of Mujib's 'Baksal' philosophy and the system of Basic Democracies propounded by Field Marshal Ayub Khan, Pakistan's first military dictator. The main difference was that Zia allowed for a multi-party system. But he strictly limited its effectivness by concentrating overwhelming authority in an executive President.

Under the new arrangement the President, i.e. General Zia, would appoint the Prime Minister who would hold office at his pleasure and would not necessarily be the leader of the majority party in the National Assembly. The President could appoint one-fifth of his cabinet from outside Parliament. He could also withhold his assent from any bill passed by it. In such cases Parliament could overrule the President only if it won a national referendum on the issue. The amendments allowed the President to sign treaties with foreign powers without informing Parliament if he considered it to be 'in the national interest'. He could summon, prorogue and dissolve the National Assembly at will. And just as Sheikh Mujib had done before him, General Zia left himself an open-ended opportunity to be President for the rest of his life. There was no limit to the times he could have himself re-elected.

'This complete concentration of powers in the hands of the President makes him a virtual dictator,' General Osmani complained.[14] Khandaker Moshtaque said: 'Ziaur Rahman's democracy is worse than dictatorship. He has established a constitutional dictatorship to mislead the people. The role of dictator will not be sustained through slogans of Zindabad.'[15]

Having established himself as the uncrowned king of Bangladesh, General Zia went all out to transform the country and society. First he strengthened the military establishment which was his power base. He created new divisions, appointed a number of new generals and strengthened the para-military units such as the Bangladesh Rifles and the Ansars until he could muster approximately 150,000 under arms. The number of policemen was increased from 40,000 to 70,000 including a 12,500-strong elite Combat Police Force trained and equipped for counter-insurgency action. Backing them was the Village Defence Force consisting of 900,000 men and women volunteers organised on the lines of the boy scouts and girl guides. Every village had one platoon each of men and women to help mobilise resources and assist in the maintenance of law and order. Because they were locally recruited and entirely locally motivated, they became a uniquely successful organisation, one of the few of General Zia's innovations to survive his death.

The defence and internal security budget, a mere 13 per cent of the total revenue budget under Sheikh Mujib in 1974/75, almost trebled by 1981 when Zia died. All this, however, did nothing to dampen the unrest and opposition to Zia within the cantonments. The mutinies and coup attempts continued with dismaying regularity.

The President-General was at least cosmetically more successful on the civil side.

Central to Zia's political and economic philosophy was the belief that the salvation of Bangladesh lay in the uplift of its villages and that this could best be achieved through the total involvement of the people, particularly the youth, in the development process, by encouraging at all levels the work ethic and the habit of self-reliance. 'Bangladesh is what its villages are,' he said on one occasion.[16] 'The people of Bangladesh have been wasting their time . . . they have got to be organised and put to work,' he said on another.[17] And again he told the country: 'There is only one slogan: Work. Work. Work.'[18]

The basic good sense of this argument and Zia's appeal to the people's patriotism won him wide-ranging support. No one grumbled as he put them to work digging canals, building roads and embankments and filling-in marshes and swamp lands near the urban centres. Some of the work was done on a voluntary basis; some under the Food-for-Work programme; some for cash payment.[19] Gram Sarkars (village governments) began to proliferate. 3670 'Jubo Complexes' (youth cooperatives) with a total membership of 93,990 were registered in three years to 'galvanise' the youth. The President himself worked tirelessly. Some ministers recall being summoned to Bangababan at 4 am. Zia also visited each of the 414 thanas (village groupings) as much to harangue the people to greater effort as to canvas support for his BNP.

This remarkable effort had some dramatic results. Dhaka, Zia's show-piece for his many foreign guests, was quickly cleaned up. Dark, narrow streets were transformed into broad, well-lit and well-maintained roads. The inevitable 'juggis' (bamboo and sacking hutments) that once mushroomed everywhere were tucked out of sight. The markets filled with fancy goods, from colour TVs and quadrophonic music systems to elegant or hideously complicated wrist watches and British and American cigarettes. Japanese cars were everywhere. And where once the really wealthy could be counted on the fingers of both hands, the prestigious Dhaka Club alone, so I'm told, boasted at least 100 millionaires. There were said to be many more in Chittagong, Khulna and Sylhet.

But behind this glittering facade were the more sinister aspects of General Zia's regime. Corruption of a kind hitherto unheard of in Bangladesh ate deeply and irreversibly into the social fabric and everywhere there was a palpable undercurrent of violence.

These were not the inevitable by-product of ill-conceived and badly executed economic development efforts such as one often sees in other parts of the Third World. They were the direct result of serious character defects in Zia's immensely complex personality, a man who wanted to be President for life and surpass Sheikh Mujibur Rahman as the messianic Leader, the Father and the Friend of his people. According to some of his associates this was General Zia's all-consuming ambition. Everything else was subordinated to it. For this, Zia institutionalised corruption.

'For a time we all believed in him,' Dr. Zafrullah Chaudhury, the respected head of the social institute at Sawar, told me. 'We all believed that General Zia really wanted to change the country and make it a progressive, socialist and caring society. But we soon realised that Zia was only playing with words. He definitely did not have any serious commitment to change. He only wanted to secure his political ambitions.'[20]

Against this back-drop there was always a brazen dichotomy between the high morality of Zia's rhetoric and the sordid reality of his actions. Zillur Rahman Khan, the Bangladeshi academician living in America, underscored the point in a caustic commentary on Zia: 'A Machiavellian double standard, which preached the traditional morality of truthfulness, honesty, gratitude and fair play for the masses while reserving an 'end-justifies-the-means' approach for its leaders, became the rule rather than the exception during the Zia regime.'[21]

No one disputes that Zia was incorruptible as far as money and the trappings of wealth were concerned. He didn't own a house in Dhaka as did almost everyone in the higher echelons of government. It has been recorded that on one occasion he took an advance against his salary to buy furniture and paid it back in instalments. Zia was a teetotaller. He didn't gamble or have any of the other social vices. But he allowed and even tacitly encouraged all this and more in the people around him so that they would always be vulnerable and dependent on his grace and favour. Incredible instances of corruption during Zia's regime would fill many volumes.

'Zia polluted everybody and everything, the whole system,' retired Air Vice Marshal Abdul Ghafur Mahmud told me. 'He did more harm than Sheikh Mujib in compromising the nation. He belittled and pygmied every appointment except his own by appointing and sacking people on whim.' Mahmud is by no means the only one to feel so strongly about Zia. Even Zia's admirers admit that while he was personally honest, he tolerated corruption in others because it suited his purpose.

Clearly Zia operated on the assumption that everyone carried a price tag and he would meet that price if it suited him. Because of this motivation many of his highly publicised 'nation-building' schemes were perverted for political advantage. A case in point is the 'Jubo Complex' or organisation of Youth Cooperatives. On paper they had a wide-ranging role in promoting economic and social advancement of the youth. In practice the 93,990 members spread throughout the land were essentially groups of young toughs and thugs kept on leash for use in elections, demonstrations, referenda or simply to smash the opposition whenever Zia or the BNP required it. To finance their operation, i.e. to buy them up, Zia assigned them the government taxes normally recovered from 'hats' or weekly bazaars and fairs in the countryside. These were not inconsiderable sums. For instance, the annual licence to make the collection at Gabtali Hat, an important cattle market near Dhaka, was auctioned for 4,800,000 Takkas in 1982 when the Jubo Complex was wound up. So at least that much money had been going to the Youth Cooperative controlling Gabtali Hat. On a national scale the takings were even more phenomenal. According to official estimates the 3670 Youth Cooperatives in the Jubo Complex raked in 127,487,200 Takkas in the two financial years 1979/80 and 1980/81.

The government now admits that much of this money was extracted by 'zor zulum', i.e. by force by the young thugs who operated the scheme. It also now says that Jubo Complex kept no accounts. Since there is no evidence that anything was spent on the designated 'nation-building' schemes, it is officially admitted that the entire amount went into the pockets of the leading members of the Youth Cooperatives in return for the political support they gave Zia. The village people paid a terrible price in misery and harrassment for this form of Zia patronage.

One of the first things General Ershad did when he assumed power in March, 1982, was to disband the Jubo Complex. But the poison it had spread among the youth was beyond recall. 'General Zia corrupted an entire generation,' a Finance Ministry official told me.

Another example of Zia's perverse prodigality was the canal-digging programme, officially billed as 'The First Phase of the Revolution'.

Launched on 1st December, 1979, it was intended to provide 900 miles of new or renovated canals for enough dry season irrigation to grow an additional 6,000,000 tons of foodgrains. According to a government publication, an important aspect of the programme was for it to be executed by 'voluntary participation of the masses to create a sense of belonging among the people so as to ensure utilisation of the facilities . . .' Another key element was that 'it would involve the least expenses and the shortest possible time . . .'[22]

It was also done with the maximum fanfare. Thousands of men and women with pickaxes, spades and baskets for carrying earth turned up wherever General Zia and his advisers went to start a new canal. It was good holiday fun and sometimes several yards of canal were dug in a single day. Unfortunately, when Zia and the VIPs left, so did the 'volunteers', sometimes taking home with them the government-issue digging implements. This left the local organisers—both government officials and BNP office bearers—to complete the task by food-for-work or cash payment. Sometimes Zia had army units drafted in to do the work. In such cases the money budgeted for the canal digging invariably went to the BNP minions or local officials.

Billions of Takkas were sunk into this programme. There is no real count of it because the money was requisitioned from many different ministries and government organisations. The tragedy is that it was largely a wasted effort. Apart from the corruption that the vast amounts of unaccountable funds generated at the local level, the programme had an elemental flaw. Constructing un-lined canals in a delta area is as pointless as digging holes on the sea shore. They get washed away or clogged with silt by the rainy season floods. For these reasons the highly-touted canal digging programme was terminated when Zia died.

The general had a penchant for gimmicks that sometimes bordered on the ridiculous. In August, 1978, Zia got the idea of duplicating London's famous

'Speakers Corner' where political, religious and social views are freely aired, with a 'Muktangan' or free area in Dhaka. Accordingly a small park near the GPO was allotted for the purpose. The Home Minister, retired Lt. Col. Mustafizur Rahman, who opened the facility, exhorted the people 'to speak out your problems, complaints and grievances without fear'. He promised no one would be arrested for airing their views—'except for personal vilification and treason'. With 15,000 political detainees languishing in jail, these qualifications and the presence of intelligence officers in the park were enough to make the political smart set give it a wide berth. No one trusted Zia. The Muktangan became a laughing stock, the haunt of prostitutes and gamblers.

Another gimmick which got a lot of laughs was Zia's order that his ministers and party MPs take a written test on the 'ideology and philosophy' of the Bangladesh National Party. If no one else, Zia at least took it seriously. He was chief instructor at a series of 'training classes' where he lectured them on the intricacies of the great movement. On 12th of April, 1981, just six weeks before Zia was assassinated, 60 party stalwarts sat down for the written test at Bangababan. It was a disaster. Only 10 made the merit list. Prominent among the failures were Prime Minister Shah Azizur Rahman and Deputy Prime Minister Jamaluddin Ahmed. That was the BNP!

Zia's real contribution to Bangladesh was that he gave the people a distinctive identity and gave them pride in being Bangladeshis. There was the warming realisation that despite its crippling financial and economic disadvantages, Bangladesh did have and could play an important role among the nations of the world. This, for some time at least, anaesthetised the pain he inflicted by his dictatorial methods.

The Proclamations (Amendment) Order 1977 had stipulated that the people should be known as 'Bangladeshis' instead of 'Bengalees'. At first glance this seemed to be merely window-dressing. In fact it was a fundamental appreciation of the raison d'etre for the state. To his credit General Zia, more than any of the other FFs (freedom fighters), realised that the people had moved forward from the tremendous emotional upsurge of the Bangladesh movement and the Liberation War.

Bengali nationalism had been the essence of those events. But it was not a matter of the East Pakistanis' choosing. Rather it was the reaction to years of discrimination and second class status imposed on them by West Pakistan and particularly the Punjabis. The Bengalis of East Pakistan had fought for and willingly joined Pakistan in 1947. As a matter of fact it is freely admitted that Britain would not have accepted the demand for the creation of Pakistan without the massive pressure exerted by the Muslims of Bengal. Pakistan was the first state in history to be founded solely on the basis of religion and the equality of man is fundamental to Islam. Yet although the East Pakistanis outnumbered the West Pakistanis by 20 million souls, the latter would not accept the logic of numbers. Nor would they accept East Pakistan's distinctive language and culture. After 20 years of trying to live together, the East Pakistanis share of the central services was not more than 30 per cent (it was much less in the armed forces). The province also suffered terrible discrimination in terms of language and economic development. It reached the point where East Pakistanis realised that since they could not live within Pakistan they would have to make a life for themselves outside it. Thus the 1969 general election in Pakistan became a referendum on Bengali nationalism. In pursuing the idea against the concept of the religious statehood of Pakistan as a homeland for Muslims (which was the sole justification for its creation), the upsurge of Bengali nationalism quite inevitably got entwined with the idea of secularism. West Pakistanis did not accept it and answered with a massive military crackdown.

Sheikh Mujibur Rahman enshrined both Bengali nationalism and secularism in the Constitution of the new state in 1972. But in this he was clinging to already obsolescent concepts. After the creation of Bangladesh the people had mentally reverted to their separateness. They were not just Bengalis. They were MUSLIM BENGALIS i.e. Bangladeshis. Sheikh Mujibur Rahman blindly resisted the assertion of this unique identity. In time he became the symbol of its suppression and to that extent the pressures against him built up to bursting point. This would explain why after Mujib's assassination in August, 1975, there was widespread disappointment when Khandaker Moshtaque Ahmed failed to proclaim Bangladesh as an Islamic State. Remember the question asked of the Bangladesh Deputy High Commissioner in London? 'If it is not an Islamic State then why did you kill Sheikh Mujib?'

General Zia filled the emotional hunger of the people by conferring on them the title of Bangladeshis and giving the Constitution an Islamic tinge. He also wrote the country's name large on the international scene. Zia expended as much energy travelling abroad as he did on politicking at home. He seems to have set some kind of record for Head of State travel, visiting some 30 countries in five years. He was welcomed by the most prominent leaders in the world. Even more gratifying to the Bangladeshis was the fact that he brought most of these dignatories to Dhaka on return visits. Zia took an active role in the international Islamic conference and the Non-Aligned Movement. He won Bangladesh a seat in the UN Security Council against stiff competition from Japan. The emotional Bangladeshis saw all this as a heart-warming recognition of their true worth, not just the sympathy of the advanced countries for what Henry Kissinger once so insultingly called 'an international basket case'. President Zia is remembered for this.

In retrospect it will also be acknowledged that Zia, perhaps accidentally, made a lasting impression on the politics of Bangladesh by bringing into the mainstream powerful groups that could not be left out indefinitely. It came about as he manoeuvred to create and strengthen his Bangladesh National Party. The Awami League would not touch Zia because he was the main beneficiary of Sheikh Mujib's assassination. So Zia perforce turned for support to his men in the military/bureaucracy, to the Muslim League and other fundamentalist groups, and to the lower and middle-class leftists of the NAP-Bashani group. This melding of Islam and socialism in the BNP restored to national politics an influential section of the community that had been deprived of a political role since the creation of Bangladesh. Zia opened the doors to these right-wing 'collaborators'. During the 1979 general elections, one-eighth of the 2000 parliamentary candidates were people who had been accused or convicted of collaboration by Mujib. Three of Zia's ministers were from that group. The Prime Minister, Shah Azizur Rahman, had been detained and convicted for collaboration. There was understandably an outcry when, in Zia's first cabinet, 'die-hard loyalists to Pakistan sat with heroic leaders of the Liberation'.[23] But it had to happen at some time. Bangladeshis are reasonable people who know they cannot live indefinitely with the spirit of vengeance. However much it pained them, to deny the 'collaborators' a political role would have created dangerous pressures and perhaps led to even more bloodshed. Zia opened the safety valves. Zia claimed he was a 'concensus maker'. In a way he was. But concensus-making was clearly never his original intention, only a by-product of his efforts to maximise his own support.

President Zia's Government somehow miraculously escaped the ravages of weather and floods during the five and a half years of his rule. Even the devastating floods in the Ganges Delta region which brought ruin to parts of India in 1979 somehow by-passed Bangladesh. Despite such lucky breaks Zia left the economy in a shambles. Landlessness and the fragmentation of small parcels of land in the villages increased rapidly during his regime. So did unemployment, malnutrition among children and young adults, and social decline. The man who incessantly preached self-reliance to his people, left his country entirely at the mercy of its foreign donors. Food aid amounted to 10 per cent of actual consumption and counter-part funds generated by this food aid from the USA accounted for between 16 to 18 per cent of revenue. It created a Catch 22 situation because any measure to cut down food aid through increasing self-sufficiency would not provide for a compensating source of revenue.[24] Zia quite early in the day realised that his policies were not going to make any difference to the situation. Nevertheless he continued to preach the pipe dream of self-reliance. 'We are determined to remove forever this tendency of begging and open a new chapter where the people of the country are not only self-sufficient but are able to sell their commodities to the outside world and earn huge amounts of foreign exchange . . .'.[25] At the same time Zia was telling the international community that not only did it have an 'obligation to give' but the 'moral duty' to give more. He boasted that Bangladesh could absorb double the one billion dollars it was getting annually by way of aid. Such blatant hypocrisy did not go unnoticed. Zia's lack of credibility, like his promotion of corruption, began to alarm people.

M. B. Naqvi, a senior Pakistani journalist who visited Bangladesh for the first time a month before General Zia was asassinated, painted a harsh picture of what he saw: 'The bureaucracy, backed fully by an authoritarian regime and entrusted with ample funds, has become the purveyor and promoter of corruption. A new ruling elite . . . comprising traders, indentors, contractors, the civil and military part of the bureaucracy and a good number of political wheeler-dealers at district level, have become the inheritors of all that Bangladesh had . . . It was a sort of rapid deployment of corruption.'[26]

Marcus Franda, in his study 'Ziaur Rahman's Bangladesh', was equally critical. 'Authoritarian control of the foreign-related portions of the economy by a small elite class of nouveau riche has made possible a dual economy of the most extreme kind, with the modern enclave centred on Dhaka becoming increasingly affluent and the fetid rural sector continuing to grow and rot . . . It mercilessly accentuates the gap between the rich and the poor . . .'[27]

In these circumstances it was not surprising that tension, violence and lawlessness—promoted no doubt by the hot house corruption, the expanding misery and the President's declining credibility—led to the fading of the dream, both for Zia and for the people. There were a lot of political murders and dacoities. A judge was attacked in his court in Dhaka. A deputy commissioner (a powerful government officer in the districts) was beaten up by a police constable in Kushtia. A bank manager was assaulted in his office by his own staff in Dhaka. Women's groups expressed concern about the increase of incidents of rape involving policemen.[28] Such things had been unheard of in Bangladesh in the past. By the end of 1980 and early in the following year there was also disturbing evidence that the 'freedom fighters' and the 'collaborator' groups were heading for a showdown. There were violent clashes almost every week and clear indications that they were both collecting arms for a country-wide battle. This was the direct result of Zia's new efforts at 'concensus making'. He realised that he was fast running out of steam because his policies were coming unstuck. Instead of changing them, he apparently decided to change the complexion of his political support. Zia began to woo the Awami League and some middle-class leftist groups quite openly. Reporting on the 'influx' of Awami Leaguers and JSD workers into the BNP, the well-informed Dhaka weekly newspaper HOLIDAY noted: 'The veteran leaders (of the BNP) who joined Ziaur Rahman from the rightist political platforms, particularly have been feeling insecure. Some of them feel . . . this is to squeeze out the old Muslim Leaguers and the like who associated themselves with the President from the beginning of his political career. The ruling party is already divided among many factions.'[29] At the beginning of January, 1981, officially-inspired newspaper reports began to suggest some sort of deal was in the offing between General Zia and the Awami League. The weekly ITTEHAD in fact reported that the Indian Prime Minister, Mrs. Indira Gandhi, had urged President Zia to 'patch up' with the Awami League and Sheikh Mujibur Rahman's elder daughter, Hasina Wajid, who had taken up his political mantle from her self-exile in New Delhi.[30] ITTEHAD said the Awami League had made two conditions for the deal. One, that Sheikh Mujibur Rahman be fully restored to his historical position of Father of the Nation 'with full honours'. The second, that his assassination be investigated by an independent judicial commission. The paper claimed it had heard from 'reliable sources' that Zia was inclined to accept both of these demands. In this connection ITTEHAD also said Zia had decided that retired Lt. Colonel Pasha, one of the team that killed Mujib, who was being tried for another attempt to overthrow the government, would also be charged with Mujib's murder.[31]

Such reports brought hope to the Awami League and caused dismay among the 'collaborator' groups. The government did nothing to deny such speculation, although many people thought it unlikely that Zia would do such a thing. Apparently he was trying the usual tactic of divide and rule; in this case to split the Awami League and hive off a major portion of the party to his side.

Whether or not it was at the behest of the Indian Prime Minister, General Zia did make a gesture to Sheikh Mujib's daughter, allowing her to return home to Dhaka and a triumphant welcome on 17th of May, 1981. At least a million people turned out to greet her with the government doing nothing to discourage or hamper them in any way. The manner of Hasina's return convinced the 'collaborator' group and the other fundamentalists that Zia was preparing to dump them. They were determined not to let this happen. So the confrontation between fundamentalists and 'collaborators' on the one hand and the FFs and the Awami League and like-minded groups on the other, mounted. Political murders and 'secret killings' of political opponents proliferated, making the most disturbing aspect of Zia's last days. On the 7th of May, Abdur Rahman, president of the Jatiya Sramik League (Mizan group) who was a well-known trade union leader, and Ferdous Alam Dulal, senior staff reporter of the BSS, the Bangladesh national news agency, were travelling in a cycle rickshaw near the Central Law College, Dhaka, when they were gunned down by two men on a motor cycle. The cold-blooded killing outraged the nation. Whether or not the government party had a hand in it, the public outcry blamed the government for the outrage. There was a national shut-down of newspapers and newsagencies on 9th May, all opposition groups held public protest demonstrations and the Bar Association also had a public procession to condemn the killing. In all cases the government was accused of closing its eyes to such 'secret killings'. Zia himself was on the defensive at a press conference a few days later,[32] when he admitted that the law and order situation had deteriorated. When pressed about the non-publication of the reports of inquiry committees which had investigated many such 'secret killings', Zia said action on them would have to await the strengthening of the administration and this would take some time.

This was not the first time that Zia had talked about changing the administrative system. Just as Mujib before him, General Zia could not bring himself to admit the failure of his policies. Instead he, again like Mujib, blamed the administration and the constitutional structure for the mounting chaos. Addressing a meeting of the council of his ruling BNP, Zia said: 'The revolution cannot be successful with the present laws and statutes which we inherited from the colonial rulers. We have to revise and recast these laws, suiting our needs . . . we are going to reform the administrative structure in phases.'[33] A crisis was rapidly developing within the government itself with the ministers sharply divided and branding one another as 'reactionary' or 'infiltrator'.[34]

'Just as it was in Mujib's last days,' Dr. Zafrullah Chaudhury told me, 'reports and rumours began to circulate that something was about to happen. If Zia did not die as he did then there would have been serious disturbances throughout the country within six months. Zia's administration had become weak. It would have weakened further because he seemed incapable of corrective action.'[35] Zafrullah, who had a meeting with Zia about six weeks before he was killed, said he had left with the impression that Zia was 'going to do something drastic'. Zafrullah also noted that about that time there had been rumours that General Zia would soon declare a 'national emergency' and constitute a 'revolutionary council' to help him run the government. Even before this HOLIDAY, the news weekly, had reported: 'Some political circles feel that in the new phase of activities to be started by President Zia, the Cabinet in its present form may not exist. There may emerge some kind of "Revolutionary Council" including members of the military and civil bureaucracy with the reorganised BNP playing as its civilian-political wing . . .'[36]

Six years after Sheikh Mujib's assassination, the wheel had turned full circle. Ziaur Rahman's Bangladesh was coming apart at the seams. And Zia, like Mujib, was looking for more draconian extra-constitutional measures to control it.

In Zia's case the basic problem was his character flaw that would not allow him to let go even a semblance of the overwhelming power he exercised. It made him a prisoner of political convenience, quite unable to create the viable political institutions that alone could have saved him and Bangladesh. And his insanely suspicious nature in the end made no one trust him. In an ironic way General Zia did achieve his all-consuming ambition to be President for Life. But it was a short one.

Notes
1. Interview with Belal Mohammad, Dhaka, 12–12–84. Also see Major Rafiq-ul-Islam's 'A Tale of Millions', pp 98–99.
2. Rafiq-ul-Islam's 'A Tale of Millions', p 130. Rafiq confirmed that Zia made the remark to Khalid Musharraf.
3. ibid. Chapter 6, p 67.
4. ibid. Chapter 7, p 84.
5. Life sketch of Maj. General Ziaur Rahman, Bangladesh Info. Dept.
6. ibid.
7. General Zia's press conference, Dhaka, Bangladesh Observer, 8–5–78.
8. Bangladesh Times, 22–4–77.

9. Marcus Franda: 'Ziaur Rahman's Bangladesh'.
10. ibid.
11. ibid.
12. Bangladesh Observer, 3–5–78.
13. Bangladesh Observer, 7–5–78.
14. Marcus Franda: 'Ziaur Rahman's Bangladesh'.
15. Ittefaq, 14–6–81.
16. Speech to Chairmen of Union Parishads, Khulna, B. Times, 22–4–77.
17. Marcus Franda: 'Ziaur Rahman's Bangladesh'.
18. Speech at Kundipur, near Chuadanga. Bangladesh Times, 29–4–77.
19. Marcus Franda: 'Ziaur Rahman's Bangladesh'.
20. Dr. Zafrullah Chaudhury interviewed in London in summer of 1982 during Gen. Osmani's Presidential election campaign.
21. Zillur Rahman Khan: 'Martial Law to Martial Law'.
22. Revolution 1st Phase—Countrywide Canal Digging Programme. A booklet by Control & Coordinating Cell for Canal Digging Prog. published by Dept. of Films and Publications, Dhaka.
23. Marcus Franda: 'Ziaur Rahman's Bangladesh'.
24. Rahman Sobhan: 'Crisis of External Dependance'.
25. Speech at Darsana. Bangladesh Observer, 28–4–78.
26. Pakistan Economist, 27–6–81.
27. Marcus Franda: 'Ziaur Rahman's Bangladesh'.
28. Bangladesh Times, 24–2–78.
29. Holiday, (weekly), Dhaka 4–1–81.
30. Ittehad, 9–1–81.
31. Ittehad, 9–1–81.
32. Bangladesh Observer, 11–5–81.
33. BSS Bangladesh National Newsagency, 9–2–81.
34. Holiday (weekly) Dhaka, 11–5–81.
35. Interview in London, 1982, summer.
36. Holiday (weekly), Dhaka, 4–1–81.

XII

Coups, Mutinies, Executions

Hang them by the neck till they are dead.

General Ziaur Rahman

On Wednesday, 14th April, 1976, Lt. Col. (rtd) Khandaker Abdur Rashid, after a leisurely lunch, was at Heathrow Airport, London, checking in for Singapore Airlines Flight SQ 734-A to Rome, Bangkok and Singapore when he asked the girl at the counter: 'What time do we touch Rome?'

'Oh no sir,' the girl replied. 'We will be by-passing Rome this flight because of a strike at Leonardo da Vinci airport.'

Rashid was bound for Bangkok, but the sudden change of route seemed to upset him greatly. 'I want my bags back,' he told the girl in sudden panic. 'I've changed my mind. I'll have to catch another flight.'

Grabbing his bags, Rashid fled to the nearest bank of telephones and called the Hotel Jolly near Rome Airport, asking to be connected to 'Mr. Farook Rahman'. After what to Rashid was an age of waiting, the operator informed him that Mr. Rahman was not there. He had checked out a little earlier.

Swearing silently to himself, Rashid caught a taxi to Kensington Hilton hotel and checked into Room 1024. The he called Hotel Jolly again. Once more he got the same answer. Farook was not there. Rashid began to sweat profusely despite the cool spring air laced with the scent of cherry blossoms that was flowing through the window. He was sick with worry. Farook was to have joined him on the Singapore Airlines flight at Rome with a three-man 'hunter-killer' team. Now they wouldn't be able to make the rendezvous and two months of careful plotting to seize the government in Dhaka was in danger of going down the drain. And all because of a stupid little lightning strike by airport workers at Rome!

This second coup attempt by the former Majors—they had been promoted to Lt. Colonel by Khandaker Moshtaque—was the result of a series of events starting at the beginning of the year that inexorably put them back on the road to Dhaka. When they left the country on the 3rd November, 1975, after Khalid Musharraf's 'counter-coup', Farook, Rashid and the rest of the gang responsible for killing Sheikh Mujibur Rahman and his family had expected that their exile in Libya would be brief. 'About a month or two,' Farook told me. But by the end of December it had become evident to them that the Bangladesh government under General Zia wanted them out of the country indefinitely, if not permanently. All representations to Dhaka by the exiled group remained unanswered. They were completely ignored by the Bangladesh authorities to the extent that even their families in Bangladesh were not given the salaries and allowances due to them. Even more galling for Farook and Rashid was the discovery that they had been dropped from the Bangladesh Army List. Apparently the two of them had been compulsorily retired without notice or a hearing. Now they would not be able to command troops again or to rightfully wear the uniform they both so greatly prized. Farook and Rashid found themselves reduced to the ignominy of 'retired' officers and were now in the same situation as Dalim, Noor, Huda and the rest of the gang on whom they had once privately looked down.

Morale was at a low ebb in the middle of January, 1976, when the exiles got what seemed to be their first break. Air Vice Marshal Towab, the Chief of Air Staff, visited Libya in an effort to obtain supplies for the Bangladesh Air Force. He did not get anything. But while he was in Tripoli, Farook, Rashid and Dalim, through the good offices of the Bangladeshi Chargé d'Affaires, managed to get a meeting with him at which they requested his help to return to Bangladesh. Towab promised 'to do something'. But within a matter of weeks it became clear that the Air Force chief either could not or would not assist them. So on the 15th of February, Rashid wrote a two-page letter to General Ziaur Rahman requesting permission to return to Bangladesh. Sent through the diplomatic bag by the Bangladeshi Chargé d'Affaires Mohammad Zamir, the letter in part said:

'Due to unsuitable circumstances, there has been an accretion of personal problems. Our mental condition and morale have both deteriorated and dropped sharply. There is now a possibility that this might lead to serious indiscipline and other problems causing reactions, for which we should not be held responsible. We do feel that due to various personal reasons and embarrassing factors we cannot undertake to serve in the Libyan armed forces in any capacity. There are in addition to this other considerations both financial and mental which make it imperative that we should return to Dhaka immediately.'

Rashid stressed two other points. Should General Zia agree to their return he should immediately send them £15,000 for travel expenses. Alternatively, if the answer was in the negative, Zia should give them reasons for his refusal in writing. And, keeping the sting for the tail, Rashid ended up informing Zia that should they not get an answer by the 7th of March, i.e. within three weeks, the exiles would feel free 'to return to Dhaka individually or as a group'.

The ultimatum had the desired effect. On 23rd February, General Zia sent the Adjutant General of the Bangladesh Army, Brigadier (later Major General) Nurur Islam, popularly known as 'Shishu', to Benghazi to sort out the problem. Shishu met the exiles separately and as a group. Farook and Rashid say he promised them many advantages if they would remain outside the country. The offer included diplomatic assignments in Bangladesh embassies. When the offers were declined, Shishu said he would try to help them get back to Bangladesh but warned that this would take some time. Accordingly, Rashid acting on behalf of the group, gave him a hand-written note to General Zia in which he extended the time limit for Zia's response by two weeks i.e. to the 20th of March. Rashid also said:

'We sincerely place our loyalty and owe allegiance to you personally and to the government. There is no scope of any misunderstanding from our side. We genuinely feel disgraced regarding our coming out of the country on the night of 3rd/4th November, 1975. We are eagerly interested to go back to the country to wash off that unfortunate disgrace and to solve our problems. Once we are back to the country we place our devoted services at your disposal for the betterment and glory of our nation.'

The letter was a curious mixture of cringing servility and an admission of cowardice. It would be the one and only time that Rashid would admit that they had been cowards to run away during Khalid Musharraf's counter-coup, leaving their troops behind to face the music. For this reason Rashid and

Farook were all the more vengeful when General Zia didn't even bother to acknowledge receipt of the letter, spurning both the offer of fealty and the ultimatum. The two retired officers decided to press on. 'Since we didn't get any response by the 21st of March,' Rashid told me, 'We felt ourselves completely free to do all things possible to overthrow the government and eliminate General Zia.'

Once again Rashid and Farook began to plot in earnest. Long-distance plotting, however, wasn't easy especially when they were sitting in Benghazi and attempting to get things done thousands of miles away in Bangladesh. Telephone calls to and from Libya were invariably subject to tapping at both ends. Then Dhaka had a decrepit telephone system badly affected by rains. Numbers were not easy to get at the best of times within the city itself. So on the 24th of March, Farook flew out to Frankfurt from where he felt he could communicate more easily with his agents at home.

While he was away Rashid got a very welcome message from Bangladesh. The government, it said, had decided to allow him to return to Dhaka on a short visit to discuss their problems. Rashid could take his wife and children with him and also Farook's wife since her children had been left behind with her in-laws. But, the letter emphasised, neither Farook nor any others from the exiled group should try to come back for the present. Here was another lucky break! No more long-distance plotting. Rashid could now go back to arrange things on the spot.

Rashid immediately got in touch with Farook in Frankfurt. Before returning home Farook decided to pay a short visit to London when he discovered that Air Marshal Towab was temporarily lodged in the Portman Hotel. Farook got to London on the 29th, checking into the Churchill Hotel which is adjacent to the Portman in the West End. The Air Force chief was not at that time party to the plot the two colonels were hatching. But neither was Towab unaware that they were up to something sinister. Just as Zia had done before him, Towab apparently played along with Farook and Rashid for his own purposes. And Farook made no secret of using him. He wanted to milk Towab for all he could get by way of military information—the deployment of troops, army and air force postings especially in Dhaka, and every little titbit of information that could provide the clearest possible picture of the situation obtaining in the Bangladesh capital. Farook and Towab had three meetings. The first was in the morning of the 30th of March; the second later in the evening; the third next morning over breakfast. What simply delighted Farook was the news that 14 tanks had recently been deployed at Sawar Cantonment, about 20 miles from Dhaka.

Farook had been particularly concerned about the disposition of the armour of his old outfit. General Zia, as a matter of prudence after the Sepoy Mutiny, had split the Bengal Lancers, using half its strength—some 500 men and 14 tanks—to create a new regiment, the 1st Bengal Cavalry. Zia then transferred both units out of the capital. The Bengal Lancers were sent to Bogra in the North-West, a safe distance from Dhaka with the river in between. The 1st Bengal Cavalry was located at Sawar where Zia felt he could conveniently keep a watchful eye on them. Towab told Farook that it had recently become the practice for the tanks to be taken out between 5 and 9 o'clock each morning to train new recruits to the Armoured Brigade. Farook considered this to be a God-send. Because of the normal morning training exercises, the movement of tanks would not attract attention or create alarm. Thus they had considerable mobility in the area. Farook figured that once he got to Bangladesh and activated his men, he could early one morning take the tanks out of Sawar and well into Dhaka before the alarm was raised. After that, he thought it wouldn't be too difficult to get rid of General Zia and to seize the government.

Farook returned to Benghazi and with Rashid quickly worked out a plan of action. They would leave Libya separately for Bangladesh, but within a day or two of each other. Farook would go to Singapore with his 'hunter-killer' team. These were the three NCOs, Muslehuddin, Marfat Ali and Hashim who were among those responsible for killing Sheikh Moni, Mujib's nephew, and later Tajuddin and his companions in Dhaka Central Jail. In Singapore they would await a signal from Rashid who would go alone to Dhaka, not taking with him the wives and children because they didn't want to expose them to unnecessary risk.

While in Dhaka Rashid would secretly prepare the ground for the coup as he went through an elaborate charade of negotiating with Army Headquarters for the return of the exiled group from Libya. Rashid would have to activate their supporters among 2 Field Artillery, the Bengal Lancers and the 1st Bengal Cavalry and to prepare combat teams for action. Thereafter the two colonels gave themselves two options: Plan 1 called for 2 Field Artillery and the armoured units to seize Dhaka airport, the action being synchronised with Farook's arrival by commercial flight from Singapore. Farook and the troops would then proceed to 'eliminate' General Zia and key army officers and seize the government. Plan 2 was less dramatic. A 'watch party' of artillery and cavalry men would await Farook's arrival at Dhaka airport. Then before anyone was aware of his return, they would secretly whisk him off to Sawar and the safety of the tank regiment. At an appropriate time Farook would roll the tanks into Dhaka, 'eliminate' Zia and his officers and seize the government.

This action plan was incredibly simple—simple-minded or naive some would say—and one totally dependent on surprise. It required the utmost secrecy. Here they had a problem. The colonels were not happy with the group that had accompanied them into exile in Libya. Months of boredom and the basic indiscipline of this cavalier group had bred suspicion and quarrels among them. Some of the exiled ex-army officers had also begun to blame Farook and Rashid for their plight and were jealous of the preferential treatment that the Libyans accorded them. It had reached the point where the two colonels couldn't trust anyone apart from the three NCOs, Muslehuddin, Marfat Ali and Hashim whose loyalty to Farook was beyond doubt. So they decided that if the coup was to have any chance of success, it would have to be carried out without the knowledge of the others. Fortunately for Farook and Rashid they were able to draw on the help of their Libyan hosts in this matter.

They were on excellent terms with the two most important men in Benghazi. One was Major Salim Ebrahim, the elegant, erudite head of military intelligence for Benghazi who had the cover job of Port Director. The other was Major Suleiman, administrative head of the province of Syrenica which includes Benghazi. He was also a member of Ghadafi's Revolutionary Command Council. The two Libyan officers, especially Major Salim Ebrahim, had taken a keen interest in the colonels and had had lengthy discussions with them about their plans for Bangladesh. As the interest deepened, it was at one point suggested that a secret meeting could be arranged with Ghadafi. But this was abandoned for reasons of diplomacy. According to Farook the Libyans did not want to give the impression of formal interest or commitment should anything go wrong. It was, however, arranged that Salem and Suleiman should unofficially give them all necessary assistance. Thus Farook and Rashid were able to make several trips to Europe in secrecy, fully equipped with money and airline tickets. The colonels now appealed to them for help in keeping their exit from Benghazi secret. This was easily accomplished by their Libyan hosts. On the excuse that they were to observe Libyan army manoeuvres, the Bangladeshi exile group was split into small batches and posted out of Benghazi for two to three weeks. Farook, Rashid and the three NCOs were assigned to one group. When the others departed on their junkets, they were able to slip out of Benghazi unnoticed on their deadly mission to Bangladesh.

Farook and his team flew out to Rome and Hotel Jolly on the 12th of April, quickly establishing contact with an agent in Singapore who relayed messages to and from Dhaka. Rashid came to London a day earlier and checked into Room 726 at the Kensington Palace Hotel. Rashid came to London to make telephone calls to his people in Dhaka. But a major purpose of his visit was also to recruit their old friend ex-Major Sharful Huq Dalim. Dalim had gone to Paris for medical treatment at the end of March and had come on to London where he was living with his father-in-law R. I. Chaudhury. Rashid met Dalim at Chaudhury's house on the evening of the 13th. Evidently he got a positive response from him for late that night Rashid telephoned Brigadier Nurul Islam 'Shishu' requesting permission for Dalim to accompany him to Dhaka as he was 'a bit nervous' about returning alone. The ruse worked. Dalim was instructed to reach Dhaka by the 20th when he would be required by Rashid and Farook. Having accomplished his tasks, Rashid was ready to leave London on the 15th of April when the ground staff strike at Rome airport made him change his plans. He was finally able to contact Farook later that day to arrange another rendezvous. Next day, Thursday the 16th, Rashid took Singapore Airways Flight SQ 742-A out of Heathrow. Farook and his team joined the flight at Rome. They then proceeded as planned, exchanging the information each had gleaned on the telephone and refining their plans all through the long flight to the next stop, Bangkok.

Rashid flew into Dhaka from Bangkok on the 20th of April. He was met by some relatives, Farook's father and mother, and a number of friends. Also taking a keen interest in the arrival was a big turnout of officers from military intelligence and the civil NSI (National Security Intelligence). They made careful note of everything. Rashid went to live in his own quarters in the Cantonment which had been kept for him. Later that night, accompanied by the Adjutant General, Brigadier Nurul Islam 'Shishu', he had his first meeting with General Zia. Rashid recalled that the meeting was a long and friendly one, with a break for an informal dinner. Zia inquired about their welfare and Rashid responded with a litany of the problems the exiles were facing. Then, rather casually, Zia asked about Farook and his whereabouts. Rashid told him Farook was in Benghazi. 'Is that so?' Zia asked. 'Then why am I getting reports that Farook is in Singapore?' Rashid denied this vigorously, hoping he could bluff his way through. But after Zia told him that the reports had come from 'reliable sources, including Americans' Rashid realised that the cat was out of the bag. Somehow their security had been breached. The plans for a quick strike would have to be abandoned. They would now have to move with extreme caution.

Farook was due in from Singapore on Friday, 23rd April (Friday's Child was still banking on his lucky day). Rashid spent the next two days secretly preparing for his arrival. Working under the noses of the intelligence agencies he managed to activate his own 2 Field Artillery, elements of the Bengal Lancers at Bogra and the 1st Bengal Cavalry at Sawar. Rashid also got together a 'watch party' to receive Farook at Dhaka airport; even arranged to be on hand himself at Sawar when Farook was brought there. This remarkable achievement in such difficult circumstances underscores Rashid's cunning and ingenuity.

Farook's return went exactly as planned, despite Zia's prior knowledge of his presence in Singapore. He was given a tremendous welcome at Sawar by more than 2000 troops, not only those from his own cavalrymen, but also from among the infantrymen based at Sawar. They carried him on their shoulders chanting 'FAROOK ZINDABAD' (Long Live Farook). When the military intelligence reported that the 'troops were 100 per cent behind Farook', Zia had no option but to close his eyes to the colonel's defiant return and to allow him at least temporarily to remain in Dhaka.

Dalim turned up on the 25th of April, on the same plane that brought Air Vice Marshal Towab from Dubai. Towab insists that it was entirely coincidental that he and Dalim travelled together. Zia thought differently and later used the incident as an excuse to sack Towab. The presence in the city of these 'killer majors', as they were commonly called, sent political barometers plunging. Other storm warnings were seen in the mounting tension in Dhaka Cantonment and the brazen manner in which groups of soldiers, mainly from the cavalry and artillery, defied orders and left their barracks to call on Farook and Rashid. The colonels themselves played it cool. On the one hand they showed an apparent reasonableness during the endless rounds of talks they had with the army brass; on the other, they secretly stoked the fires of rebellion in Dhaka, Sawar and Bogra. Trouble finally erupted on the 27th of April when the NCOs and sepoys of the Bengal Lancers sent a message to General Zia which in effect said: 'Send Farook to visit us in Bogra or we will come to Dhaka with our tanks.'

The message caused consternation in Army Headquarters.

General Zia immediately moved an infantry regiment to the ferry terminal at Aricha Ghat to block the river crossing and the approach road to Dhaka. As he was not yet in a position to do much more, Zia temporised by authorising Farook to go to Bogra 'to pacify the Lancers'. This was, even to a layman, an incredibly stupid decision. Since his arrival in Dhaka Farook had been working up the Bengal Cavalry to fever pitch. Clearly he wanted to do the same to the Bengal Lancers, his old outfit. Now Zia played into his hand. Farook was delighted. With both units of the armoured brigade under his control he couldn't be in a better position to take on Zia.

Farook made a grand entrance into Bogra, turning up in a chauffeur-driven military jeep resplendent in a new, black Lancer uniform with Lt. Colonel's pips. It made the Lancer officers extremely nervous, but the troops were overjoyed and they mobbed him. Farook rallied them as a general would do his troops before battle: 'Bogra is not the place for us. Dhaka is where we belong. We will go there!' Colonel Momin, Farook's old CO, advised him not to do anything foolish where troops could get killed because they had already suffered terribly. Farook was in no mood to listen. However, for his own reasons he decided to stay put in Bogra with the Bengal Lancers until he got the green light from Rashid. Meanwhile the 1st Bengal Cavalry, secretly incited by Farook's NCO team, began acting up at Sawar. General Zia suddenly found himself confronted by the prospect of another major mutiny, perhaps not as widespread as November's sepoy uprising, but potentially as dangerous. Sending Farook to Bogra had been a mistake. Zia felt he must move quickly if the situation wasn't to get entirely out of hand.

On the evening of the 27th, Rashid discovered he was a prisoner in his own home. The house was entirely surrounded by military guards who wouldn't let him go out or allow anyone in. But he had astutely anticipated that something like this could happen and had prepared for it. Using pre-arranged secret lines of communication, Rashid sent messages to Farook in Bogra and to Muslehuddin who was with the 1st Bengal Cavalry at Sawar, warning them of the danger and to 'be alert and stand by for action'. They immediately prepared for a fight, but it was General Zia who made the next move.

Rashid was taken from his home to Army Headquarters next morning by four officers and some men from Zia's own bodyguard unit. They kept him isolated in a room for six hours before taking him to the General's office for the show-down. According to Rashid, Zia spoke quite candidly. He acknowledged his gratitude to them for making him Army Chief when Khandaker Moshtaque was made President. But he said he now felt it necessary 'in the national interest' to insist that all of them—Rashid, Farook and Dalim and the rest of the exiled group—should continue to live abroad for some time. Zia offered to accommodate them in jobs of their choice in Bangladesh embassies abroad. He made it clear, however, that on no account should they attempt to return home without permission. Zia also informed Rashid that he would have to leave the country by the first available flight. This happened to be a Thai Airways plane due to leave for Bangkok in less than two hours. Rashid protested loudly, but was otherwise quite helpless. He was taken under military escort to the airport where he found Dalim had also been brought. Both of them were packed off to Bangkok without further ado. For Rashid at least that was the end of the second coup.

Farook continued to hold out at Bogra with the tanks of the Bengal Lancers, defying all threats and blandishments to get him to return to Dhaka. He was entirely surrounded by the 6th East Bengal Regiment commanded by Col. Hanan Shah (he would later be made a brigadier), who had taken up offensive positions against the Lancers with recoilless rifles. The 11th Infantry Division under General Latif was also moving down from Rangpur to back up the 6th East Bengal. The situation was no different in Sawar where the Bengal Cavalry was encircled and pinned down by the 46th Infantry Brigade under General Shaukat Mir. Bangladeshis held their breath as the stalemate extended to the third day. After that it became clear that the infantry was holding firmly behind General Zia and the position of the mutineers was hopeless. By then Farook also knew he had run out of luck. So when General Zia sent his father and sister in a helicopter to Bogra to coax him to give up and avoid bloodshed, Farook quietly packed it in.

His departure from Bogra was as dramatic as his arrival, only this time the troops were distraught and disheartened, not cheering. A Lancer officer who witnessed the event told me: 'Farook told the troops he had to go to avoid bloodshed. But they knew he was dumping them for the second time and they didn't like it. Some even accused him of selling out to the Generals to get an ambassador's job. I have never seen such disheartened and disillusioned men,' the officer added.

The reason was obvious. The troops knew they had defied Army Headquarters and, unlike Farook and his team who had been guaranteed safe-conduct out of the country, they would have to pay for the mutiny. The prospect created a sharp division in the regiment. One group of sepoys wanted to surrender peacefully in the hope that it would mitigate the punishment. The other group made up of NCOs and sepoys argued that since they would anyway be hanged for the mutiny, they might as well go all-out for 'biplob' (revolution). As they argued through the night, Col. Hanan Shah managed to get a message to the terrified Lancer officers asking them to cross over quietly and join the infantry. This they did, depriving the regiment of its trained leadership. So next morning when the 'Biplobi' group took the tanks out they had only NCOs to lead them against the encircling infantry. As they moved towards the city, the 11th Division opened up with machine guns. The NCOs panicked and ran away, leaving the Lancer sepoys to be taken prisoner by the 6th East Bengal Regiment.

Thus the attempted cavalier coup ended in disaster—not for Farook and Rashid, the ring leaders, but for their poor, misguided troops. Some were tried and hanged for mutiny; others were sent to jail. Two months later, on the 15th of July, 1976, General Zia disbanded the Bengal Lancers, erasing one of the most famous cavalry names from the military list.

Zia was unaccountably partial in dealing with mutineers. He showed no mercy to Lt. Col. Abu Taher, a comrade-in-arms in the Liberation War, who he hanged for attempting to overthrow the government after the Sepoy Mutiny. Yet he let Farook, Rashid, Dalim and the three NCOs go scot-free, giving them safe conduct and airline tickets to return to Libya. It encouraged other groups to have a go. Eighteen months later a military commission investigating yet another major sepoy uprising noted regretfully: '. . . since strict action was not taken as per law in the earlier incidents it gave a general feeling that a group of persons can organise a mutiny and get away with it even if the mutiny fails.'

Farook and Rashid refused to accept diplomatic appointments offered by Zia. But 11 others of the exiled group that killed Sheikh Mujibur Rahman did accept Foreign Service postings. Sharful Huq Dalim and Abdul Aziz Pasha were appointed First Secretaries, the former in Peking, the latter in Buenos Aires. The others went as Second Secretaries, Noor to Teheran, Shariar to Jakarta and Bazlul Huda to Islamabad.

Although the evidence against him was circumstantial, the unsuccessful coup abruptly put an end to Air Vice Marshal Towab's military career. General Zia was convinced that he was deeply involved and sacked him on 30th April, the day after he deported Rashid and Dalim. Towab gave me a vivid account of his dismissal in an interview in London 12 days later. He said he had been instructed by Zia to be at Bangababan at 12.30 pm but had been kept waiting for 40 minutes in a reception room with Admiral M. H. Khan and some others before the General walked in with President Sayem. Zia took out a small note book from his pocket and proceeded to interrogate Towab. First he accused Towab of supporting the 'majors'; then of being involved with the 'Al Badar' (a fanatical pro-Pakistan group) and finally of corruptly making one and a half million dollars in a deal involving the purchase of a Boeing 707 for the national airline. Towab said he vigorously denied all three allegations. Zia then wanted to know why he had not brought his German wife and their children to Bangladesh. 'That,' said Towab, 'was the last straw. I told him: "General, you just stop there. What I do with my wife and children is none of your business. If they are in Germany or in Dhaka it's no business of yours unless I'm screwing around with someone else's wife. It seems that it's time that I should go. I'm prepared to resign."'

Zia: 'Yes, you had better resign since you and I are not pulling the same way.'

Towab: 'Do you want it now?'

Zia: 'Yes, now.'

President Sayem sent for pen and paper and Towab wrote out his resignation, noting the time (13.20 hours) below his signature. Zia then informed Towab that a Bangladesh Biman plane was due to leave for London at 6.30 pm and he should be on the plane. Zia added: 'I would like you to please stay here till about half an hour before the plane is due to leave and then you may go to your quarters and take your things. If anything is left I will arrange to send it off to you.'

Towab: 'Are you arresting me?'

Zia: 'No, not that. But I think you should stay here.'

There was an angry exchange between the two men. Towab insisted that he be allowed to go to his quarters to pack. Zia was adamant that he should not leave Bangababan until just before flight time. Finally it was agreed that Admiral Khan accompany Towab to his quarters, allow him to pack and then personally put him on the plane. The airman never forgave Zia this humiliation.

When General Ziaur Rahman visited President Anwar Sadat in Cairo on 25th September, 1977, he had only one thing in mind. Bangladesh would next year be contesting a seat in the UN Security Council against strong Japanese competition and Zia wanted Egypt and the Arab League to support him. But the Egyptian President had something else to say which, to Zia at least, turned out to be infinitely more important—literally a matter of life and death. By a lucky break the Egyptian intelligence services had uncovered a left-wing plot to assassinate General Zia and Bangladesh's top military command in a re-run of the Sepoy Mutiny. The conspirators planned to strike at an Air Force Day celebration in Dhaka on the 28th, just three days away and also the day after Zia was due to return home. The conspirators—NCOs and sepoys, allegedly instigated by the JSD and the Communist Party—would then proclaim a Marxist revolutionary government. It was suggested to Zia that the Libyans and the Soviet Union had a hand in the plot, but I have not been able to ascertain whether this was just speculation or whether any proof of their involvement was made available to Zia.

Sadat's bombshell shattered Zia. Since taking charge in November, 1975, he had been plagued by no less than five mutinies and attempted coups. Now Sadat was warning him of yet another uprising, one which indicated a foreign hand and was potentially more dangerous than anything since the last Sepoy Mutiny.

The function at the centre of the plot was the formal opening of the new Officers' Mess in the Farm Gate area of Dhaka on Air Force Day. Zia had agreed to be Chief Guest. All the top military brass would also be present. According to Egyptian intelligence it was planned that they should all be gunned down by the 'revolutionary sepoys'. While they were certain about the targets, Anwar Sadat's men were not able to identify the units involved in the conspiracy. This was maddening for Zia because he did not have enough time to make his own inquiries as he would have liked to do. Nevertheless it is typical of the man that he played it cool.

On returning to Dhaka as scheduled on the 27th of September, Zia sent Air Vice Marshal Abdul Ghafur Mahmud, the Air Force chief, a brief hand-written note regretting his inability to attend the function. No reason was given: nor did Zia even vaguely pass on Sadat's warning. This suggests that Zia wasn't sure about the Air Chief's loyalty (a suspicion that was belied by the events) and did not want to risk tipping off the conspirators about the discovery of their plot.

Zia's 11th hour cancellation without any explanation put Air Vice Marshal Mahmud on the spot. Clearly the President was upset about something. Mahmud couldn't decide whether he should get someone else to stand in for Zia—and risk his further displeasure—or to postpone the opening of the

Officers' Mess to a later date. Mercifully for him fate intervened in a totally unexpected way and took the decision to postpone out of his hands.

A Japanese Air Line DC-8 bound for Bangkok with 156 passengers was hijacked soon after it took off from Bombay. The five hijackers, a 'Hidaka Commando Unit' of the Japanese Red Army Faction, which is a notorious terrorist group, forced the plane to land at Dhaka airport. They demanded a ransom of US $6,000,000 and the release of nine of their comrades serving jail sentences in Japan or they would start executing the hostages after the midnight deadline.

Dhaka was in an uproar because the authorities were not equipped to deal with such a dicey international problem. After a hurried Cabinet meeting, General Zia put AVM Mahmud, who was also minister for aviation, in charge of the negotiations with the hijackers. Mahmud immediately stationed himself in the airport control tower where, with the help of Vice President Sattar and two senior civil officers, he spent the next four days negotiating by radio with the hijackers. Inevitably that led to the indefinite postponement of the opening of the Officers' Mess.

The cancellation of the function on the 28th upset the conspirators to the extent that they lost control of the troops who had been assiduously worked-up for the uprising. As a result, the sepoys of the 22 East Bengal Regiment mutinied at Bogra two days later (on 30th September), killing two young army lieutenants and taking prisoner the 93 Brigade Commander and a number of his officers. They also tried to incite the sepoys of the 4 Horse, a new cavalry unit built around the loyal elements of the Bengal Lancers who had been disbanded in July, 1976. When this failed, the infantry sepoys looted some banks and shops in Bogra city and broke open the jail to release 17 ex-army men serving rigorous imprisonment for the 1976 Bogra mutiny.

Tension ran high in Dhaka Cantonment next morning when the body of Lt. Hafizur Rahman was brought from Bogra for burial in the military grave yard. During the burial ceremony, his father and brothers hurled verbal abuse at the sepoys and cursed them and the army for the young officer's death. This caused an angry reaction among some jawans who were at the graveyard and an ugly scene was averted only by the tactful intervention of some senior officers. By then reports were coming in through military intelligence of imminent trouble at Jessore where troops were said to be agitated and in a defiant mood.

As the storm gathered, Zia hurriedly called a meeting of all senior officers in Dhaka. He alerted them to the possibility of a mutiny and told them to be vigilant and to ensure that the armouries were secure. The officers were also instructed to remain with their units at all times during the alert and to control their troops. Zia then slipped out with a few aides to a secret hideout which he temporarily made his headquarters. This probably saved his life.

The uprising was coordinated by troops of the Army Field Signals Battalion. The Dhaka Signals complex gave the lead. The pre-arranged signal was a cracker burst followed by a single rifle shot fired by the sentry on duty, Signalman Sheikh Abdul Latif. On hearing it hundreds of soldiers rushed out of their barracks and looted the unit armoury. Firing wildly in the air and screaming 'SEPOY BIBLOB' (Sepoy Revolution) they swarmed out of the lines to rally the other units. They seemed to have been well prepared with vehicles and loudspeakers.

The signalmen were quickly joined by several hundred men of the Bangladesh Air Force from the nearby Kurmitola air base. They went about looting unit armouries. At around 02.45 hours a group of about 700 army and air force personnel in 25 trucks and jeeps stormed the Central Ordnance Depot and made off with the weapons and ammunition. As the uproar developed, leaflets began to appear in the cantonment telling the soldiers what to do and listing demands which were a carry-over from the earlier Sepoy Mutiny. Again the call was for continued armed revolution, an army without officers, and the inclusion of troops in the decision-making process. But where previously General Zia had been proclaimed the hero, this time the sepoys called him a 'traitor' to their cause and wanted his 'elimination'.

At about 5 am a heavily armed column of soliders and airmen in seven trucks raced through the city and occupied the radio station. Once in control, they interrupted a running commentary on the hijack drama, still going on at the airport, to proclaim 'SEPOY BIBLOB' and the formation of a 'revolutionary government'. The announcer spoke in strident bazaar language. After chanting a number of slogans he asked the people to 'stand by for our leader'. A Sergeant Afzar of the Air Force, declaring himself Head of State, said a revolution had taken place, a revolutionary council had been formed to run the country and he was head of the council. He didn't get much further because the radio transmitter at Sawar was abruptly switched off on instructions from the 9th Division Headquarters.

Meanwhile the sepoy mutiny had taken a savage turn at the airport with the unprovoked killing of officers. The first to die were two young Air Force pilots who were caught and killed in cold blood just outside the airport hangar. Nine other Air Force officers were similarly gunned down when several hundred frenzied airmen occupied the terminal building and control tower just as the negotiations with the Japanese hijackers for the release of the hostages had entered a crucial phase. Group Captain Raas Masood was shot and killed in front of the Air Force chief. It's a miracle that Air Vice Marshal Mahmud himself escaped death. He was found later hiding in one of the downstairs rooms dressed in lungi and under-shirt. The others killed were Group Captain Ansar Ahmad Chowdhury, Wing Commander Anwar Sheikh, Squadron Leader Matin, Flt. Lts. Shaukat Jan Chowdhury and Salhauddin, Flying Officers Mahboobul Alam and Aktaruzzaman, and three Pilot Officers: M. H. Ansar, Nazrul Islam and Shariful Islam. Also killed by the mutineers was Mohammed Enam, the 16-year-old son of Squadron Leader Sirajul Hoq. In a moment of savagery the mutineers cut by half the Air Force's effective flying strength.

The mutiny did not progress beyond that point because the ring leaders failed to bring out the troops from the fighting units in Dhaka. It was mainly an Air Force and Army Signal Corps affair, with a good measure of jawans from the Supply and Transport battalion. Few infantrymen actively joined in. General Zia and the Army Staff were able to call on the services of the infantry units to rapidly bring the situation under control. The 46th (Dhaka) Brigade and the 9th Division based at Sawar were extensively used for this purpose. It was in fact elements of the 29th East Bengal Regiment, which formed part of the 9th Division, that was most successful in squelching the uprising. One company under Major Mostafa fought its way into the airport terminal building and cleared it by 7 am after killing at least 20 Air Force mutineers and taking another 60 prisoner. Another company of the 29th East Bengal regained control of the radio station within an hour of it being taken over by the mutineers. And in an encounter at Farm Gate near the airport, 30 men from the same regiment intercepted and routed 200 armed mutineers driving into the city in trucks.

General Zia escaped death only because the mutineers were unable to find him. The mutiny was effectively over by 8 am on the 2nd of October. It only remained for the loyal troops to mop up isolated pockets of mutineers and to recover the weapons and ammunition. Three truck-loads of guns were collected from the Kurmitola air base. By then the Japanese terrorists had fled Dhaka in the hijacked plane after releasing two-thirds of the hostages. General Zia went on the radio just before mid-day to reassure the country and to rally the people and armed forces 'to unite and resist any violent actions against the independence and sovereignty of the country'. He said: 'For some time past some misguided soldiers have been trying to create disorder in the armed forces at the instigation of interested quarters.' Later he would also accuse them of 'terrorism', of aiding 'foreign infiltration' and of undermining the government by 'crippling the armed forces'. Zia did not name the 'interested quarters' but it soon became obvious who he was referring to when he banned the JSD, the Communist Party and the Democratic League 'for activities prejudicial to the national interest'.

Later that day Zia received a single congratulatory message from abroad. It came from Cairo, from Egyptian President Anwar Sadat who almost tongue in cheek congratulated Zia on crushing the military rebellion.

The mutiny was a water-shed in President Zia's life. After that he realised he could not depend on the army alone, as he had been doing, and must broaden his support on the civil side. But first he took harsh and often the most vindictive measures to crush the opposition within the armed forces. He summarily sacked Air Vice Marshal Islam, the Director General of Forces Intelligence, for failing to warn him about the mutiny. Then in quick succession he disbanded the 22 East Bengal Regiment for the mutiny in Bogra, and four army units for the uprising in Dhaka. They were the Army Field Signal Battalion, the Army Static Signal Battalion, the Corps of Signals Centre and School, and the Army Supply and Transport Battalion.

Zia also wanted to disband the Bangladesh Air Force for its leading role in the mutiny.

Air Vice Marshal Mahmud told me the fate of the Air Force hung in the balance for more than two months as Zia toyed with the idea of a 'Unified Service' in which the Air Force would be replaced by an Army Aviation Wing. The idea was the brain-child of General Manzoor, Chief of General Staff, who secretly nursed his own ambitions for the top Army job. However, wiser councils prevailed and the Air Force was reprieved. But Zia made no secret of his distrust. For several weeks he banned the Air Chief and his Staff from their own operational area at Dhaka Airport! Mahmud himself was under a cloud till the middle of December, while a Judicial Commission investigated the mutiny. Zia suspected that the Japan Airlines hijacking had been expressly timed to distract attention from the planned uprising and that Mahmud had deliberately strung out the negotiations. His escape while the officers in the airport were killed by the mutineers also lent credence to the suspicion. Mahmud was cleared by the Judicial Commission but he found it impossible to continue in service under Zia. He resigned in December, 1977.

Zia took the opportunity to reshuffle the army command, sending out of Dhaka two fractious generals who were constantly jostling to succeed him as Chief of Army Staff. He posted General Mir Shaukat Ali to Jessore. General Manzoor, the CGS, was sent as General Officer Commanding, Chittagong, where three and a half years later he master-minded Zia's assassination.

General Ziaur Rahman reserved the full venom of his vengeance for the troops and airmen who had been involved in the mutiny. According to official records he hanged 1143 men in the two months from 9th October, 1977. He also gave several hundred other men jail terms ranging from 10 years rigorous imprisonment to 'life'. It was the most brutal, devastating punishment exercise in the history of Bangladesh, carried out with the utmost speed and with total disregard for justice and the legal process. Men were tried in groups of three or four, were sentenced to death, had their sentences confirmed by Zia and were hanged—all within the space of 48 hours. I have been told by one of his aides that General Zia, wearing the double hat of President and Chief Martial Law Administrator, spent several hours each day grimly confirming in his own handwriting the sentences of these unfortunate men. He hanged them three and four at a time on specially-extended gallows in the jails at Dhaka, Comilla and Bogra. Civilian prisoners recall how for several weeks the nights were made hideous by the screams of servicemen protesting their innocence as they were dragged to the gallows.

It was death by murder by Zia!

Officers who witnessed the proceedings still shudder when they talk about them. The men were not dealt with by established procedures, neither the Bangladesh Army Act nor the Air Force Act. According to regulations, only General Courts Martial can award the death sentence in peace time. Strict procedures governing this form of military court are designed to ensure a fair trial before mature and responsible army officers. Accordingly, a General Court Martial has at least five military judges, with one of them at least a Lt. Colonel and the others NOT of lesser rank than Captain who have held commissions 'for at least three whole years'. The accused are also given adequate opportunity to defend themselves. General Zia found these regulations too irksome for the task he had in mind. So he promulgated a Martial Law order creating 'Special tribunals' where JCOs and NCOs down to the rank of Havildar could sit as judges and where court procedures were 'streamlined' i.e. cut to the minimum to ensure the rapid disposal of cases.

Nothing like this had happened before in the sub-continent, either in Bangladesh, in India or in Pakistan. Thus by the stroke of the pen Zia created more than two dozen kangaroo courts which tried and executed the mutineers virtually by assembly-line methods. There was no question of justice. Men were convicted and executed on the flimsiest evidence, by a judicial licence to murder. A vivid example of this is given by the proceedings of Martial Law Tribunal No 18, Dhaka; Case No 1 of 1977, dated 8th October, 1977.

The five military judges were:

1. Lt. Col. Quazi Salimuddin Mohammad Shariar.
2. Subedar Mohd. Abdul Halim.
3. Naik Subedar Abdul Hakim.
4. Havildar Anwar Hussain.
5. Havildar M. Faroogiera Ahmed.

Charged with mutiny on the night of 1st/2nd October, 1977 were:

1. 6274028 Naik Enamul Haq.
2. 6284854 Signaller Kazi Shaid Hussain.
3. 6281186 Naik Abdul Mannan.
4. 6284736 Signaller S. K. Javid Ali.

They all pleaded NOT GUILTY but had no access to counsel and had to defend themselves as best as they could—if defence it could be called in the circumstances. The complainant, Junior Officer Subedar Serajul Islam doubled up as one of the three prosecution witnesses. The other two were 6271646 Naik Abdul Bashar and 6276435 Lance Naik Abdul Ali.

There were no defence witnesses.

If it did not have such tragic consequences, the 'evidence' recorded by the Tribunal would have been more appropriate for comic opera.

One witness deposed that he had seen the 'culprits' break into the armoury and take rifles and drive off in an army vehicle. Another saw the accused running about the barracks verandah. Someone had called out 'Revolution has started'.

One of the accused, Naik Enamul Haq, said he was the last to wake up in the barracks and that he was absolutely innocent. Another, Kazi Shahid Hussain, said not only had he never fired the weapon he was accused of looting, but that he did not even know how to load it. The third accused, Abdul Mannan, said he heard shouting and along with others had taken a rifle from the armoury. But then he had discovered there was no war and subsequently returned the weapon on the orders of the OC.

On the basis of this 'evidence' and statements by the accused, the Special Tribunal unanimously found all four guilty and awarded each the death sentence. Next day, the 9th of October, General Zia confirmed the sentences with the remark: 'THEY BE HANGED BY THE NECK TILL DEATH'. The four unfortunate men were hanged in Dhaka Central Jail on the 10th of October, just two days after being brought to trial and only eight days after the mutiny. Such was General Ziaur Rahman's vengeance.

Early in May, 1979, retired Lt. Colonel Anwar Aziz Pasha, First Secretary of the Bangladesh embassy in Ankara who was returning home on vacation, stopped off at Islamabad to meet retired Major Bazlul Huda, Second Secretary of the Bangladesh embassy in Pakistan.[1] They were not only good friends, but were also closely related by marriage for Pasha had married Huda's sister. More importantly, they had both been part of the team that killed Sheikh Mujibur Rahman and his family in August, 1975, With temperatures soaring above 100 F, Islamabad was hardly the place for a holiday, even a brief one. But Pasha had important matters to discuss with Huda and they were quickly joined by another member of the killer team, retired Lt. Col. Sharful Huq Dalim. He was First Secretary in the Bangladesh embassy in Peking.

Thus a thousand miles away from Dhaka were planted the seeds of another attempt by the 'majors' to violently overthrow the Bangladesh government, only this time the second string of the killer team would make the running and Farook and Rashid would follow. Though they had been repeatedly pardoned by the government and were living it up in cushy Foreign Service postings which many Bangladeshis would give their eye-teeth for, this cavalier group remained unrepentant and thirsting for power.

Pasha, Dalim and Huda quickly agreed on a plan of action which included the formation of a political party with underground and overground branches and cells within the armed forces. Dalim, who made a quick trip to Teheran, also worked out with retired Major Noor, another of the killer team who was posted as Second Secretary in the embassy there, a system of codes by which the conspirators could communicate with one another from their places of exile.[2] The objective, according to Pasha,[3] was to 'change the incumbent government. Not only to take over power but also to distribute justice to society.' Clearly they had a left-wing government in mind. But Pasha warned his friends: 'Communism divorced from religion will be of no use to Bangladesh. Socialism with an Islamic tinge will be acceptable to us since the majority of the people are Muslims.'[4]

The scene then shifted to Dhaka where Dalim and Pasha began a search for like-minded people in the army and among the political parties. Lt. Colonel Didarul Alam, an artillery officer, and Lt. Colonel Nurunabi Khan of the Corps of Engineers were recruited to build up a secret organisation within the army by capitalising on 'the frustrations of the jawans and NCOs.' Two civilians, Mosharraf Hossain and Kasi Munir Hossain, were brought in as contacts with left-wing political groups which Dalim and Pasha hoped to unite and rally for the coup. Munir was a left-wing student leader of Jaganath College, Dhaka; Mosharraf a trainee officer with the Agriculture Bank who had connections to the JSD. Dalim also volunteered to bring in retired Lt. Colonel Mohammad Ziauddin, the legendary underground leader of the Maoist Sharbohara party.[5] He failed to do so apparently because Ziauddin did not buy the killer majors' new-found love of socialism even though Dalim insisted that they had learned their lessons and would not repeat the mistakes made after they killed Sheikh Mujib. Dalim and Pasha did manage to meet several prominent left-wingers, including some from the JSD and Sharbohara party. At one such meeting held behind an ancient tomb near the new airport, a man posing as the 'representative of Col. Ziauddin' suggested it would be a long haul to their objective since their party 'had insufficient cadres to run the state after the capture of power'. Dalim thereupon said other leftist groups could be counted on to help. 'At this hour we require unity of the leftist groups,' he declared.[6] At another meeting Dalim told them: 'If you maintain your identity as small factions you cannot bring about socialism in the country.'[7]

Before they returned to their posts apparently well-satisfied with their initial success, Dalim and Pasha gave some money to their leftist friends and promised Lt. Colonel Didarul Alam that they would help to finance the purchase of a printing press which he wanted to print leaflets 'to educate the people', and for a bus which would be hired out to generate funds for their underground work.

Between the 26th and the 29th of December, 1979, some members of the killer group gathered in Ankara to consider the next step and to raise funds for the work being done in Bangladesh. Apart from Pasha who was resident in the Turkish capital, the meeting was attended by Khandaker Abdur Rashid from Libya, Bazlul Huda from Islamabad, and Noor from Teheran. Dalim, who was in Peking and Shariar who was posted in Tokyo, were supposed to attend but at the last moment failed to obtain leave of absence. Farook, of course, was unable to attend since he was in jail serving a five-year sentence for a solo attempt to overthrow the government in January, 1977. Significantly Rashid brought along with him to the meeting a senior Libyan government officer.[8] Although he was not identified at the subsequent trial, this man clearly was Farook and Rashid's old friend and confidant, Major Salim Ebrahim, a senior member of the Libyan intelligence service. His presence at the Ankara meeting would indicate that the Libyans had moved from their public 'see no evil, hear no evil' stance to a policy of active involvement, albeit still secretly, in Farook and Rashid's attempts to overthrow the Bangladesh government.

According to evidence given by Pasha, Rashid, obviously backed by his Libyan friend, assured the group that the money required for the work in Dhaka would be forthcoming. This was duly reported to Didarul Alam in Dhaka and to Shariar in Tokyo whose turn it now was to visit Bangladesh to promote the conspiracy. The Ankara meeting did not go unnoticed by the Bangladesh Ambassador, retired Major General Mamoon. He promptly informed the Foreign Office in Dhaka about the gathering of the clan and was in turn instructed to keep a close watch on them. Unfortunately for him,

Pasha intercepted these instructions and in the course of a row is reported to have assaulted the Ambassador.[9] It is a matter of shame that this unprecedented act of violence and indiscipline against the person of a Bangladeshi ambassador went unpunished by the Foreign Office and Anwar Aziz Pasha remained in his post to host another meeting of the group in Ankara five months later.

The meeting was held on 27th May, 1980. This time Dalim flew in from Peking, Shariar from Tokyo and Huda from Pakistan via London. Noor was unable to get leave and did not attend. Rashid stayed away for unreported reasons. In his place came Farook Rahman who had only recently been released from jail in Bangladesh and returned to exile in Libya.[10] The main purpose of this second meeting was to keep the group informed about the progress being made in Dhaka. Didarul Alam and his group were anxious to launch the coup in June because they feared they could not maintain secrecy for long since their secret organisation had expanded in different cantonments.[11]

The group was not to know that by this time military intelligence had tumbled to their plans for the commonest of reasons: the jawans and NCOs on active service in the army who they had been trying to subvert, had taken over the conspiracy and decided to make their own bid for power. According to the trial record, Lt. Colonel Didarul Alam, while maintaining contact with the exiled majors, had apparently also established a close working relationship with some JSD leaders to organise secret revolutionary cells within the armed forces. The cry of 'Sepoy Biplob' had once more been raised by them. Using serving and recently-released soldiers, Didarul Alam and his group were able to make extensive contacts in Dhaka, Comilla and Sawar cantonments. Out of this had emerged a plan to seize control of the government on 17th June, 1980, by the use of artillery units supported by elements of the East Bengal regiments. First, the officers would be held prisoner in their messes and residences. Since President Zia was away on one of his many foreign tours, the Chief of Army Staff (General Ershad) would next be arrested and killed and the radio station seized. Any opposition from other units would be squashed by concentrated fire by the artillery and infantry. Thereafter a Revolutionary Council would be established to rule the country and to implement the unfulfilled demands of the Sepoy Mutiny of November, 1975.[12]

Although on paper this appeared to be a well-conceived plan of action, in fact it was a blotchy, uncoordinated effort by uneducated men who hardly knew what they were doing. Jawans kept telling each other: 'Let's do revolution' as though they were suggesting a picnic. At the end of May an exasperated Didarul Alam confessed to Kazi Munir Hossain that the 'troops are about to get out of control'.[13]

On the 26th of May an intelligence NCO intercepted one of the leaflets being circulated by the conspirators and the cat was out of the bag. When they became aware that their security had been compromised the jawans became panicky and tried to get Lt. Colonel Didarul Alam to bring forward the date of the coup. But Didarul Alam couldn't make up his mind. He seemed to be having second thoughts. On one occasion he told his men that they should 'forget about the revolution for some time' because he wanted to educate the troops politically and get them better prepared. On another occasion he told them that because of a split in the JSD they would not be able to implement the 'revolutionary programme', to take charge of State affairs and to run the government. On hearing this one of the men retorted that if a sergeant could run the revolutionary government in Liberia, why couldn't a Lt. Colonel run

Bangladesh for them.[14] Didarul Alam had no answer. The jawans decided to strike on the night of the 17th June. The officers, however, pre-empted them and the soldiers ran away. Didarul Alam fled to India and on returning to Bangladesh was arrested on 11th November, 1980, from the Ambassador Hotel in Kushtia. Anwar Aziz Pasha was summoned back from Ankara by the Foreign Office 'for consultations'. When he reported in Dhaka on 18th November, he was immediately taken into custody. The others were picked up soon afterwards.

Five men were originally charged with conspiracy to overthrow the government and with subverting the loyalty of the armed forces, but only three were brought to trial before a military court on 10th March, 1981. They were Lt. Colonel Didarul Alam, Lt. Colonel Nurunabi Khan and Mosharraf Hossain, the probationary officer with the Agriculture Bank. Anwar Aziz Pasha and Kazi Munir Hossain, the 'student leader', pleaded guilty and turned State's Evidence against the others. Although he was the man who started it all, Pasha made a star witness for the prosecution as he blithely shopped his mates. Mainly because of his evidence, the prosecutor asked for the 'highest sentences' i.e. death for the accused. But when the trial ended on 20th May Didarul Alam was sentenced to 10 years imprisonment, Mosharraf Hossain got two years and Lt. Colonel Nurunabi Khan one year. Kazi Munir Hossain was pardoned. So was Pasha, the killer major, who returned to his post as First Secretary in the Ankara embassy as though nothing at all had happened. Such was the whimsicality of General Ziaur Rahman, the Bangladesh President. He would be killed in another military uprising nine days later.

Notes
1. Pasha's confessional statement and evidence as an 'approver' in the trial of Lt. Col. Didarul and others by military court in Dhaka reported in HOLIDAY, the news weekly, on 22-3-81.
2. ibid.
3. ibid., 29-3-81.
4. ibid., 22-3-81.
5. ibid.
6. ibid.
7. Holiday, 5-4-81.
8. Holiday, 22-3-81 and 12-4-81.
9. Cross-examination of Pasha by defence lawyer Aminul Huq reported in Holiday, 29-3-81.
10. Holiday, 22-3-81.
11. ibid.
12. Holiday, 19-4-81.
13. Holiday, 5-4-81.
14. Holiday, 19-4-81.

XIII

The Killing of General Ziaur Rahman

*Now is the time to act. How you do it, with
what you do it, I don't know . . .*

—Maj. General Manzoor

Fate intervened twice to make sure that General Ziaur Rahman died in
Chittagong. In the third week of May, 1981, President Zia and his wife Khalida, nicknamed 'Putul' (doll), played host to Baudouin, King of the Belgians,
and his charming Queen Fabiola. It was not every day that a real life king and
queen visited the country, although any number of presidents and prime
ministers had made the trip before this. So when they arrived on a four-day
visit Zia put on a royal show for them, an act that was reflected in the warm
public interest even though many of the people who gathered to cheer had
only a vague impression of what Belgium was all about. The royal couple left
on the 23rd. Zia should have flown next day to Jeddah to attend a meeting of
the Peace Committee of the Organisation of Islamic Conference which was
helping to bring about a settlement of the Iran-Iraq conflict. The Committee
was to have met on the 25th. Had it gone through its intended course of visits
to Teheran and Baghdad, Zia would have been out of the country for at least
a week, well beyond the 29th which events were conspiring to make a day of
destiny for him. The Jeddah meeting, however, was called off at the last
moment for unexplained reasons. Accordingly Zia cancelled his own trip
abroad. He decided instead to tour the Rajshahi district and asked his Military
Secretary Major General Sadiqur Rahman Chowdhury to make the necessary
arrangements for the 29th. But that visit had also to be called off because of
more pressing need of his presence elsewhere. Zia's Bangladesh National Party
(BNP) was being torn apart by the intense rivalries of the two Chittagong
factions. One was led by Jamaluddin Ahmed, the Deputy Prime Minister. The
other by Sultan Ahmad Chowdhury, the Deputy Speaker. Things had reached
a stage where Zia felt it necessary to visit Chittagong personally. If he couldn't
bring peace to the Gulf War, he would try to bring peace between the warring
factions of his own party. On the 25th of May Zia told his Military Secretary
to cancel the trip to Rajshahi. He would go instead to Chittagong on the 29th.

The decision created a problem for the security services because on the day
that Zia decided to go to Chittagong, he also passed orders transferring Major
General Mohammad Abul Manzoor, the ambitious and insubordinate GOC
of Chittagong, to Dhaka as Commandant of the Defence Services Command
and Staff College. The youngest general in the Bangladesh army was being
removed from command of troops for the first time in his military career.

Manzoor did not take kindly to the transfer although he had held the post
of GOC Chittagong for six months more than the routine three years. Adding
insult to injury, President Zia sent word to Manzoor that he should NOT attend
his arrival at Patenga Airport on the 29th, a protocol duty which would

normally have been required of the local garrison commander. The excuse given was that the President was making a purely political visit and he did not want the GOC to be involved in it. But Manzoor took the instructions as a calculated public snub. Indeed, he had good reason to feel so. The other military commanders would be on hand as usual. Rear Admiral M. A. Khan, the Chief of Naval Staff whose principal base was at Chittagong, was expressly accompanying Zia. Air Vice Marshal Sadruddin, Chief of Air Staff, would also be present at Patenga Airport to receive the President. All this made Manzoor furious and he made no bones about his fury. The general and his aides repeatedly telephoned the Military Secretary at Dhaka demanding to know why he was being kept out of the reception committee at Patenga Airport. Finally the exasperated Major General Sadiqur Rahman Chowdhury is reported to have snapped back at Manzoor: 'Can't you understand? If he (Zia) doesn't want you there why do you want to go?'

Major General Mahabbat Jan Chowdhury, Director General of Forces Intelligence (DGFI), which is the top military intelligence body, repeatedly advised General Zia to postpone his visit until after the 1st of June. That was the date by which Manzoor had been ordered to join his new post at Dhaka. I understand that the National Security Intelligence (NSI), and the Director of Military Intelligence also made similar recommendations. Zia ignored them all. He also ignored the DGFI's request, made on the eve of his departure, that he should at least not spend the night at Chittagong but should return to Dhaka the same day. It seems that Zia was confident that he could handle Manzoor and, in the final analysis, he did not think that the Major General was a threat to his life. This was a major blunder by the otherwise overly suspicious and cautious President. It would cost him his life.

Zia and Manzoor had been on a collision course for many years as their careers entwined and the former got all the breaks and honours while the latter took second place. Manzoor's father was a relatively poor clerk who had moved from the family home in the Noakhali district to Krishnanagar, in West Bengal (India). Manzoor was born there. His mother died at an early age and his hankering for maternal affection is advanced as one reason why Manzoor would in later years allow himself to be dominated by the ambitious woman who became his wife. The Judicial Commission that investigated Zia's assassination described Mrs. Manzoor as the 'driving force' and said that in the pursuit of high office of State she was 'a little more itchy' than Manzoor.[1] After obtaining an intermediate degree from the Pakistan Air Force College at Sargodha, Manzoor joined the Pakistan Military Acadamy at Kakul where he is said to have been a brilliant student.[2] He was commissioned in 1960 at the age of 20 and among the milestones in his career it is recorded that he attended the Defence Services Staff College in Canada.

Like many other Bengali soldiers, Manzoor found himself caught up in West Pakistan during the Bangladesh Liberation War. But unlike the others, he was conveniently located near Sialkot, not far from the border with India. Prodded by his wife, Manzoor tried to defect to India where the 'Mujibnagar' government was spear-heading the resistance to the Pakistanis. After one unsuccessful attempt, Manzoor and his family crossed over the Kashmir border into Jammu with two other Bengali officers whose names are also carved in the history of the Bangladeshis. One was retired Lt. Colonel Abu Taher, who led the Sepoy Mutiny in November, 1975, and was subsequently hanged by Zia. The other is retired Lt. Colonel Mohammad Ziauddin, the legendary underground leader of the Sharbohara (Maoist) Party. All three were majors at that time and even then Manzoor was insufferably arrogant. An Indian government officer who received Manzoor and his companions at Jammu and escorted them by train first to New Delhi and then to Calcutta, vividly remembered how Manzoor threw a tantrum when they were served their first meal on the train in 'thalis', the round, flat brass utensils used as plates in India. It was also a vegetarian meal—two varieties of 'dhal' (pulses), some vegetables and some 'puris', the hand-rolled bread cooked in deep oil. Manzoor took the thalis and threw them out of the window of the speeding train. 'We are army officers,' he told his startled Indian escort. 'We will be served proper food, not this rubbish. And it will be on plates with knife and fork.' So the train made a longer than scheduled stop at the next station to allow the railway catering staff to rustle up some chickens, crockery and cutlery for these special passengers. My informant did not tell me—and I must confess that I failed to ask him—how Abu Taher and Mohammad Ziauddin reacted to the incident. But Taher is on record during his trial of criticising his fellow officers for their affectation, extravagance and greater interest in comfort than in fighting during the Liberation War. Ziauddin was even more Spartan. When they finally got to Calcutta, the 'Mujibnagar' government appointed the three majors as Sector Commanders, Manzoor getting command of Sector 8 (Jessore). Promotion followed rapidly after independence until Manzoor was made Brigadier and sent to New Delhi as Military Adviser in the Bangladesh High Commission.

Manzoor became prominent after the Sepoy Mutiny and Abu Taher's arrest. Zia summoned him back to Dhaka in November, 1975, to become Chief of the General Staff (CGS). They were good friends at that time and Zia trusted him, or else he would not have been given that most sensitive job. But even then Manzoor was nursing his own ambition. I remember meeting him in his new office in Army headquarters on several occasions in the second week of December of that year. Manzoor was as cocky and garrulous as ever. He was dismissive of President Sayem and his bureaucratic advisers. 'Don't you believe a word you hear from them,' he told me. 'Every decision is being taken within a 30-yard radius from where I sit.' Two days later he confided: 'I can't say much just now but in the next two or three weeks I'll be better placed to talk and then you will see how we are going to change the country.' The implied improvement in his status was obvious. I did not let the hint go unnoticed. 'Don't tell me the coups and killings have not ended,' I exclaimed. 'You mean to say we are going to see some more changes?' Manzoor backtracked quickly. 'You misunderstand me,' he replied with a grin and in his smoothest manner. 'I meant we will have taken our decisions by then.' I did not forget Manzoor's slip and began to watch him closely.

After the second Sepoy Mutiny in October, 1977, Zia undertook a wide-ranging reorganisation of the army. As CGS Manzoor was at the centre of the exercise. But then suddenly in the course of a reshuffle of the top army command, he found himself transferred out of Dhaka and the centre of power and posted as GOC of the 24th Infantry Division and Area Commander of Chittagong. Manzoor resented the change. He considered it an exile to the backwoods. Zia refused his request to be allowed to remain in Dhaka as Commandant of the Defence Services Command and Staff College. He began to fret and fume and became openly resentful of Zia. When the general gave a farewell dinner for his departing CGS, Manzoor and his wife caused a sensation by failing to turn up. (Ironically, three and a half years later when Zia posted him to that job Manzoor would resent his transfer from Chittagong so much that he caused Zia's death.)

Using the opportunity of the tribal insurgency in the Chittagong Hill Tracts, Manzoor built up a small empire for himself in the area. New units were raised, more equipment procured, and some of the brightest and most outgoing young officers in the army were slowly gathered to his command. In time Manzoor could justifiably boast that he commanded one-third of the Bangladesh Army and had under him the most well-trained Brigade Commanders and Staff Officers.[3] Among them were two men who would have a deep influence on Manzoor. One was Lt. Colonel Motiur Rahman, his GSO-1 or Principal Staff Officer. The other was Lt. Colonel Mehboobur Rahman, CO of 21st East Bengal Regiment which formed part of the 24th Infantry Division. Mehboob was Manzoor's nephew. The officers were both freedom fighters, having fought side by side in Sector 6 in 1971. They hated President Zia and the army brass in Dhaka, holding them responsible for the political and economic rot that was devastating the country. On the other hand they adored Manzoor and looked to him for leadership. Just as Majors Farook and Rashid at another time and another place had decided that a change was necessary, so did Lt. Colonels Moti and Mehboob now feel strongly that the national interest demanded the removal of Zia and the senior military echelon under him. They found a sympathetic response from General Manzoor.

It's not known exactly when the germ of rebellion began to sprout. But clearly Moti and Mehboob were conspiring actively as early as September, 1979, when they found themselves posted together with another Liberation War colleague, Lt. Colonel Dilawar Hussain, in the Chittagong Range. Mehboob was at Dighinala, Moti at Rangamati, and Dilawar, who was Assistant Director of Ordnance Services, at Chittagong Cantonment. Moti visited Dilawar in Chittagong and during a cordial lunch sounded him out about 'the wrongdoings of the government and BNP—high prices, social injustices, corruption.'[4] Moti said he had discussed these matters with General Manzoor, the GOC, and found him 'appreciative'. Moti added: 'A collective effort by like-minded officers is required to solve the problems once and for all.' When Dilawar told him that, as an ordnance officer he had his limitations, Moti retorted: 'That should not bother you. What is important is that you should be with us.'

Moti and Mehboob also recruited Major S. M. Khalid, Brigade Major of the 69th Infantry Brigade. The four of them with Manzoor's patronage became the driving force of the rebellion that eventually killed Zia.

They started a campaign to win over young officers by a mixture of paternal interest in their welfare and by harping upon the 'wrongdoings' of Zia and the army command in Dhaka. Major Khalid was given the task of suborning majors and officers of lesser rank, the JCOs and NCOs. Manzoor, Moti and Mehboob concentrated on the seniors. Mehboob also thought of buying a small press to print leaflets for circulation among the troops but abandoned the idea because it was too costly. In the middle of 1980 Manzoor opened up Flag Staff House, his official residence, to all ranks of officers. The junior ones, including some NCOs, were invited on specific occasions. The senior ones such as Brigade Commanders, colonels and the COs were brought in once a fortnight for cards, tea and a chat. At the same time Manzoor opened up the channels so that the GOC was accessible to the maximum number of officers. The objective of all this rubbing of shoulders was to influence as many as possible of the officers so that they would spread the word to the other cantonments when they were transferred and thus the moment of 're-volution' would be brought closer.

Manzoor established links with civilians through an organisation called the 'Trend Setters'. It was started by a student of Chittagong University by the name of Ziaur Rahman with the objective of 'educating the people' i.e. opening their eyes to the national problems. Manzoor became its Patron-in-Chief. All these doings did not go unnoticed by the military intelligence. Manzoor countered their snooping by virtually barring Lt. Colonel Abu Lais Chowdhury, OC of the local detachment of the DGFI in Chittagong, from entering the Cantonment in February, 1981. He also quietly won over the Divisional Field Intelligence Unit and its CO, Major Mujibur Rahman, for his own purposes.[5]

The first attempt by the group to topple Zia was planned for the 19th December, 1980, during the Bangladesh Military Academy passing-out parade. General Zia, the top Army brass from Dhaka and a number of other VIPs were expected to be present. According to the plan, Manzoor, as GOC, would host a dinner for them in the East Bengal Regimental Centre (EBRC) mess at which they would all be arrested. Alternatively one group would raid the Circuit House, where Zia would be staying, and another the EBRC officers mess and bring the VIPs to the parade ground where they would all be 'dealt with'. The plan required the support of the 10th East Bengal Regiment then stationed in the Chittagong Hill Tracts. Manzoor ordered it to move to Chittagong by 18th December. It failed to turn up because the Brigade Commander of the 65th Brigade, Col. Rashid, refused to let it be withdrawn from the operational area at such short notice. The attempt was therefore abandoned. There was nevertheless a sensation at the dinner when it was discovered that some officers, including the Brigade Major, were carrying hand guns in the presence of the President. On being questioned, they said that they were doing so on the orders of the GOC 'because he thought there may be an attempt on the President's life'. Zia was not amused by this unforgivable breach of protocol and security regulations. However, he allowed the officers to return to the dinner after they had deposited the guns in the armoury.

The conspirators decided to have a second try in February, 1981. The occasion was 'EXERCISE IRONSHIELD', an amphibious landing at Cox's Bazaar, a popular beach resort south of Chittagong. President Zia and the top VIPs would be there—the three service chiefs, all Formation Commanders, Principal Staff Officers and, on the civil side, the Prime Minister Shah Azizur Rahman and some other ministers. The 27th East Bengal Regiment was assigned to carry out the exercise during which all other units of the 24th Infantry Division would also be armed. This gave the plotters the excuse they needed to carry arms for their own deadly purpose. Lt. Colonels Moti and Mehboob and Major Khalid told the others that the plan was to 'lift' (seize) General Zia and the army brass during the lunch and hold them hostage until six demands were conceded. These were: (1) The dismissal of General Ershad, the Army Chief of Staff, Major General Mir Shaukat Ali, GOC 9th Infantry Division, Major General Amjad, Major General Amin and some other senior officers. (2) The suspension of the Constitution and the formation of a 'Revolutionary Government' to run the country. (3) No elections or political activity for three years. (4) Efficiency to be the only criterion for promotion to the higher military ranks. (5) Improved law and order. (6) Social justice for all and the removal of financial hardship suffered by the officers and men of the armed forces.

Nothing was said about killing General Zia. But I have learned that the inner group of conspirators in fact intended to kill the President and the assembled VIPs by concentrated automatic fire. The talk about 'lifting' the President and holding him hostage was only a ruse to get the widest possible support from the officers who would not have agreed to the assassination. Major Khalid revealed this to a friend who passed it on to me during an interview in Dhaka. 'They all kept waiting for Manzoor's signal to open fire,' my informant said, 'but it seems that he changed his mind at the last moment because such a massacre would have totally discredited them.'

A third attempt to assassinate General Zia was made 20 days before he was finally killed on the morning of 30th May, 1981. According to Marcus Franda,[6] explosives were found in a switch that Zia was to throw open while inaugurating a dry dock in Chittagong. A senior military officer confirmed that something like that had happened but would not give details, nor would he say who was suspected for it.

On the 25th of May, Lt. Colonel Motiur Rahman went to Dhaka for an interview for a foreign military training course he had applied for. Moti had been one of the principal plotters against Zia in Chittagong for more than two years but apparently had got fed up with their many aborted coup attempts. So he decided to go abroad for some time 'to get away from it all'. Accordingly he had applied to go abroad for training and there was a good chance of him doing so. But fate intervened again against Zia. While in the capital Moti called as he normally did on his old friend Lt. Colonel Mahfuzur Rahman, Personal Staff Officer (secretary) to President Zia. They were accustomed to chit-chat about current developments and the latest Army gossip. What Mahfuz had to tell him this time would change the course of history in Bangladesh.

Zia had just decided to transfer Major General Manzoor out of Chittagong to the Command and Staff College at Dhaka. Although the transfer orders were to have been kept secret till they were formally announced and conveyed to Manzoor, Mahfuz thought he should tip off his friend about the posting orders since they also affected Moti as Manzoor was his immediate superior. Mahfuz may also have wanted to forewarn Manzoor about the orders since he had come under the general's spell when he served under him for two years before joining President Zia's staff. The news angered Moti very much. His immediate reaction was that it was another demonstration of the 'anti-freedom fighter attitude' of Zia and the Army Headquarters. Something had to be done about it. When Mahfuz also informed Moti that Zia had decided to visit Chittagong for a day on the 29th, the idea for another assassination attempt was born.

According to the evidence produced at the subsequent trial, Moti and Mahfuz discussed the outlines of an assassination plot that day. With Mahfuz's help Moti also visited Bangababan to personally check the security arrangements there and to inspect the helicopter landing pad. On returning to Chittagong next day he got together with his other chums, Lt. Colonel Dilawar Hussain and Major Khalid in the latter's office in 69th Brigade Headquarters. After breaking the news of Manzoor's transfer and Zia's visit, Moti told them they would have to raid the Circuit House and grab Zia. They would then fly him to Dhaka by helicopter, landing at Bangababan where by subterfuge they would have already assembled General Ershad, the Army Chief, General Mir Shaukat Ali, the 9th Division Commander, and all the PSOs. They would then all be forced to resign or be 'eliminated'. 'We need 30 officers for the task,' Moti told Khalid. 'I've seen Bangababan carefully this time and I tell you it can be done'. Major Khalid immediately counted off 20 names on his fingers, but then gave up. 'It's too risky,' he told the others. 'It can't be done that way.'

The three officers discussed the matter for a long time. While they could not agree on a concrete line of action, they were in complete accord that they had to do something quickly. They wouldn't get another opportunity once

Manzoor was transferred out of Chittagong. Zia had to be killed and it would have to be done on the 29th when he visited the city. Thereafter they would play it by ear. The conspirators were well placed to make the strike. Night training exercises being held at that time in the Cantonment would provide excellent cover for the movement of the strike teams bound for the Circuit House. Then there were four infantry battalions in the area: the 1st, 6th, 11th and 21st East Bengal Regiments. The entire 6th East Bengal had come to Chittagong for EXERCISE IRONSHIELD and had been kept there minus only two companies which had been drafted for special duty outside the city. At the same time there was a preponderence of FF officers. All but two of the 24th Infantry Division Headquarters staff were freedom fighters; so also were the COs or 2nd in charge of the infantry battalions. Rightly or wrongly the conspirators thought they could call upon the sympathy of these FFs for what they had in mind. To make sure of this, Moti began spreading a story that during his visit to Dhaka he had personally obtained evidence of a plot to 'eliminate' all the freedom fighter officers in Chittagong. To back up his story he produced what was purported to be a list of names. Those with stars against them, he told the others, were the officers who had been marked for killing. One of the listeners, Major Abdul Qayyum Khan, Brigade Major of the 65th Infantry Division, was so panicked by the information that he immediately set about telephoning other FF officers to warn them about the 'plot'. By the 28th Chittagong cantonment was agog with the rumour of the impending decimation of the FFs. The announcement of Manzoor's posting out of Chittagong was seen as confirmation of these rumours. After that it was not difficult for the conspiratorial group to manipulate the others for their purpose.

There was some consternation that day when it became known that General Manzoor had been ordered not to be present at Patenga Airport when Zia arrived. Moti immediately telephoned the Military Secretary in Dhaka. When he found it to be correct, the conspirators feared that their plot had been exposed. This confirmed the need to strike at Zia before action was taken against them.

The 29th of May was perhaps the worst day that Major General Abul Manzoor had ever experienced. Zia had arrived that morning from Dhaka to be received by the Air Force Chief and the senior officials of the city. The Navy Chief was also at the airport, having arrived on the same plane as Zia. Manzoor had not only been publicly snubbed by being ordered to stay away, but he was also required to prepare himself immediately for transfer to Dhaka. He had to be there by 1st June. On that day he would be reduced to the status of a glorified college principal. It was all too galling for this ambitious man who gloried in the command of troops.

After Jumma prayers Manzoor summoned his confidants to his office. Present were Lt. Colonel Mehboobur Rahman, Lt. Colonel Dilawar and Major Khalid. Moti, the fourth member of the inner team had made a sudden dash to Rangamati. Manzoor was irritated by his absence and kept asking for him. He was assured by the others that Moti would return shortly. After a brief pep talk, Manzoor told them in peremptory tones: 'Now is the time to act. How you do it, with what you do it, I don't know. No troops are to be deployed. Only selected persons will go to the Circuit House to lift the Head (Zia). In the morning KPIs (key point installations) and VPs (vulnerable points) will be guarded'.[7]

The hounds of death had been ordered to get Zia!

*

According to the available evidence, General Zia's last day on earth was an unspectacular one. He got off to a good start at 9 am from Dhaka by a special flight of Bangladesh Biman accompanied by the Navy Chief, Rear Admiral M. A. Khan, and senior members of his BNP party's Standing Committee. They were Dr. Badruddoza Chowdhury, Secretary General; Syed Mohibul Hasan, Minister for Manpower Development and Social Welfare; Dr. (Mrs.) Amina Rahman, Barrister Najmul Huda and Mr. A. Razak Chowdhury. A staff of seven also accompanied the President. Landing at Chittagong 50 minutes later, they were greeted by Air Vice Marshal Sadruddin, the Air Force Chief, senior officials and members of the BNP. Saifuddin Ahmed, the Commissioner of Chittagong, was returning to the city by train and did not make it to the airport in time. But he managed to join the party shortly afterwards.

On reaching the Circuit House, a colonial-style mansion in the middle of the town which he had made his temporary headquarters, Zia was offered some light refreshment. But before he sipped the tea and nibbled on the biscuits, they were tested by his personal physician, Lt. Colonel Mahtabul Islam. The President's doctor, according to security regulations, was also his personal food taster!

There followed a two-hour political discussion with party members on the first-floor verandah of the Circuit House. The meeting broke up for Jumma Prayers at 12.30 pm. Zia, dressed in white kurta and pyjamas, was enthusiastically greeted when he went to the Chandanpura Mosque in Chawk Bazaar. After prayers he spent a few minutes chatting happily with the crowd and then returned to the Circuit House for lunch with some party members. Lunch, taken on the verandah, was a simple affair because Zia did not like oily food or heavily-spiced curry. Thereafter he rested for 90 minutes, was awakened with a cup of tea at 5 pm and went on to address an elite group that had gathered in the conference room downstairs. The 45 people included the Vice Chancellor and professors of Chittagong University, members of the Bar, distinguished citizens and journalists. They talked for about two and a half hours when Zia called a break before going on to the main purpose of his visit to Chittagong: knocking heads together to bring peace to the warring factions of the BNP.

Between 9 and 11 pm Zia talked separately to at least nine party men. In between these meetings, Saifuddin Ahmed, the Commissioner of Chittagong, accompanied by the Metropolitan Police Commissioner, A. B. M. Boiduzzaman, was ushered in to see Zia for a few minutes. Saifuddin told me[8] they had gone to discuss a law and order problem posed by some members of the BNP party. Apparently the police wanted about 40 of them for extortion, land-grabbing, carrying arms and for involvement with well-known city thugs. And Zia promised to clean up his party.

Dinner was served a little after 11 pm with the President's doctor once more testing and certifying that the food was safe to eat. When he called it a day at midnight, Zia telephoned his wife in Dhaka and spoke to her for about 15 minutes. It would be the last time they talked. When he turned out the lights half an hour after midnight a massive monsoon storm was raging over Chittagong, filling the air with thunder and lightning and a heavy unbroken curtain of rain. Zia went to sleep blissfully unaware that they were portents of disaster. He had ordered a wake-up call and 'bed tea' at 6.45 am and hoped to leave for Dhaka an hour later if the storm had subsided by then. At that very moment in the cantonment outside the city his assassins were preparing to strike.

*

Once they got the signal from General Manzoor the other officers gathered in Lt. Colonel Dilawar Hussain's house to draw up a plan of action. It was 6 pm and Lt. Colonel Moti had returned from Rangamati. Others present were Lt. Colonel Mehboob, Lt. Col. Fazle Hussain, Major Khalid and two majors who had been coopted into the inner group: Major Mohammad Latiful Alam Chowdhury, GSO-2 (intelligence) of the 24th Infantry Division, and Major Rawshan Iazdani Bhuiyan, Brigade Major of the 65th Infantry Brigade. According to Lt. Colonel Fazle,[9] two propositions were discussed at Dilawar's house that evening. The first was to snatch General Zia from the Circuit House. Using him they would then get Vice President Sattar, the Army Chief General Ershad and his senior staff officers to Chittagong where they would all be 'eliminated'. Alternatively, if that failed, they would kill General Zia. Clearly Moti, Mehboob and Khalid were still dangling the idea of kidnapping Zia, not killing him, before the other officers to get their support for the operation. The group then worked out troop requirements and how the teams would operate.

Each of the leaders was assigned a specific task. Major Maruf Rashid, OC of the 112 Signals Company who came in late, was instructed to cut all communications links with Dhaka early next morning. The conspirators had already made arrangements for support from within the Circuit House. In the course of the day, Col. Moti had made telephone contact with his friend Lt. Col. Mahfuz, the President's principal staff officer. Moti confirmed the decision to strike that night and in return had been promised all possible help.[10] Thereafter Mahfuz had withdrawn the two armed police guards normally posted outside the President's suite.[11] He has also obtained from the Nazarat Deputy Commissioner (the local government protocol officer) a copy of the accommodation arrangements for the President and his party.[12] Apparently this was made available to the conspirators through Major Mujibur Rahman, OC of the divisional 515 Field Intelligence Unit who without reason had called on Mahfuz at the Circuit House earlier in the day.[13]

Despite Manzoor's orders that no troops were to be used, Major Khalid was given the task of obtaining troops for the strike. He was Brigade Major but was having difficulty in getting the soldiers. At about 9 pm he summoned Subedar Abul Hashim, an NCO of the 1st East Bengal, and ordered him to get together a detachment of soldiers, to arm them and prepare to take them to Kalurghat later that night.[14] Khalid held out a bundle of notes which, he said, should be used to hire a truck to transport the men. Subedar Hashim immediately became suspicious. Declining the money he asked Khalid: 'What shall I tell the men it's for?' Khalid: 'Tell them anything . . . Say it's punishment for going to the cinema during parade hours'. The Subedar, now even more suspicious, began to prevaricate. Khalid turned on him angrily. So the NCO went off seemingly to obey the Major's orders, but instead he went home to hide after dispersing the troops.

Half an hour later Major Khalid approached Major Mohammad Mostafa, DQ of the 69th Infantry Brigade,[15] with a request for troops. Mostafa went to the Brigade Commander's house to inform him that 'Major Khalid wants to move troops of the 1st East Bengal to lift and bring the President from the Circuit House'. Brigadier Mohsinuddin Ahmad: 'Has Khalid gone mad? Ask him to see me immediately'. He issued orders that no troops should move out of their barracks. When questioned about it later, Brigadier Mohsinuddin said he tried to report the matter to the GOC, General Manzoor, but failed to locate him. He then sat back instead of alerting the President's security staff or the intelligence agencies.[16] There is also no record of the Brigadier actually talking to Major Khalid to dissuade him.

It soon became evident to the conspirators that they wouldn't be able to get soldiers and would have to depend on officers alone for the strike. At about 10 pm Lt. Col. Mehboob sent two officers to reconnoitre and observe the Circuit House and report any significant movements. Major Shaukat Alley, 2nd in charge of the 15th East Bengal, and Major Latiful Alam Chowdhury took up positions on the compound wall of the Chittagong Club from where they had an uninterrupted view of the Circuit House. They remained there till the strike was completed.

The pace of the action in the Cantonment began to quicken as it approached midnight. At 11.30 pm Moti and Mehboob summoned all available officers of the 11th and 28th East Bengal for a meeting in the office of the 2nd in charge of 28th East Bengal. Six turned up. They were Major Momin, Major Gia-suddin, Captain Munir, Captain Jamil, Captain Mainul Islam and Captain Ghyasuddin Ahmed. Moti locked the door and brought out a Holy Koran. 'Gentlemen,' he told the assembled officers, 'This is the Holy Koran. Whatever we are doing we are doing in the interest of our country, our people and for justice. Those of you who are with us will touch the Holy Koran and promise to do what is necessary. Those of you who are not with us may leave the room. But my only request to them is not to tell about this thing to the others.'

No one demurred. They each in turn took the oath. Then they changed into uniforms and armed themselves with sub-machine guns and ammunition clips.

A similar drama was conducted a little later in the 6th East Bengal Head-quarters by the regiment's CO, Lt. Colonel Fazle Hussain. Fazle summoned Lt. Mohammad Rafiqul Hassan Khan and asked him: 'Will you go anywhere that I go?' Rafiqul replied: 'If you order me Sir.'[17] Fazle then called in the other officers who were in the lines. They were Major Dost Mohammad, Captain Ilyas, Captain Areefin and Lt. Muslehuddin. Fazle told them: 'You know that the country's condition is bad and that the army is corrupted to a great extent. The President is here today and tomorrow and we have to do something about it. We have decided to go to him, talk to him and make him aware of certain things. Who will go with me?' When they all agreed Fazle made them swear on the Holy Koran that they would stay together and do everything necessary till the mission was accomplished.[18]

The strike group began to rendezvous at Kalurghat around 2.30 am on the morning of the 30th of May, not far from the radio transmitter that was the scene of General Zia's first rise to prominence. It was raining heavily with thunder and lightning. They came in groups of three and four, in jeeps and pick-ups. Lt. Colonel Mehboob, accompanied by three others, was the first to arrive in the colonel's white Toyota car. Within an hour 18 officers and two JCOs had assembled there. Quite unexpectedly Major Fazlul Huq, 2nd in command of 1st East Bengal, turned up with two platoons (40 men) of his regiment. But when Major Khalid briefed them about the impending opera-tion, he got a strong negative response. The conspirators therefore thought it advisable to leave the soldiers behind in charge of Lt. Matiur Rahman. To keep them occupied they were instructed to take Mehboob's Toyota car and the extra military vehicles along the Bandarban road and park them on the other side of the bridge.

The refusal of the common soldier to get involved in the mutiny and Zia's assassination was the outstanding feature of the Chittagong events. The uprising failed principally because the soldiers refused to join in and the rebel officers were left without an army. In doing so the jawans to a great extent retrieved the reputation of the Bangladesh armed forces which was disgraced by the cowardly acquiescence of some officers in Chittagong to the dictates of the mutineers or the equally disgraceful tacit acceptance by others of the fait accompli.

The movement of armed men out of the Cantonment went largely unnoticed because of the night training exercises that were going on at that time. But there were also some glaring security lapses. The officer in charge of the Army Security Unit in Chittagong, Captain Rafiqul Hassan, had informed the Director of Military Intelligence at Dhaka on 29th May about the strong adverse reaction among the FFs to Manzoor's transfer. With the President in the city he anticipated there might be some trouble. But instead of personally keeping watch, Capt. Rafiq sent his intelligence Havildar to the Cantonment after dinner. The man returned four hours later to report all's well when in fact anyone keeping a proper watch would have noticed the unusual movements of officers in uniform arming themselves and preparing for the strike. Thus the opportunity of a timely warning was lost. The luck was continuing to run against Zia.

Lt. Col. Moti took charge of the strike force. They had 11 sub-machine guns, three hand rocket-launchers and three grenade firing rifles. He ensured that they were all properly loaded and ready for action. Then he crowded as many of the 16 remaining officers as he could into a single pick-up with the overflow standing outside. Moti briefed them on the action plan, using a sketch of the Circuit House and the living quarters. He passed around a Holy Koran so that they could renew their oaths and then, more as an affirmation than an exhortation, he declared loudly: 'We are going to get the President today.'

There were to be three teams. The first two would constitute the strike force going into the Circuit House. The third would act as a cut-off party near the Almas Cinema behind the Circuit House and shoot anyone trying to escape. When Moti called for volunteers for the first team, the officers vied with each other for the privilege of going for Zia. Moti chose six men: Mehboob, Fazle, Khalid, Captains Jamil Haq and Abdus Sattar and Lt. Rafiqul Hassan Khan. Fazle would be in charge and Mehboob would drive. The privilege of assaulting Room 9—where Zia was supposed to be sleeping—was given to Fazle and Captain Sattar.

Moti placed himself in the second team along with Major Mominul Haque, Major Mozaffar Hussain, Captains Ilyas and Salahuddin Ahmed and Lt. Moslehuddin. This team would provide the back-up and block interference while the first went for the President. Majors Giasuddin and Fazlul Huq and Captains Ghyassuddin Ahmed and Syed Munir, riding in a jeep, made up the cut-off team.

The three teams left Kalurghat a little after 3.30 am driving slowly in the heavy downpour that severely restricted visibility. Young Lt. Rafiq, riding in the lead pick-up, asked Fazle tremulously: 'Are you going to kill the President?' 'No', Colonel Fazle told him. 'We will only get him.'[19] Apparently at that late stage there were still some among the strike force that believed that it was only intended to seize and hold Zia hostage.

The two strike teams entered the Circuit House unchallenged. The main gate, a huge iron thing, was inexplicably left open that night. The four sentries guarding it allowed the killers to go through unopposed. As they approached the building, Lt. Colonel Fazle Hussain fired his hand rocket-launcher twice in quick succession. The rockets blew out huge chunks of masonry just below

Zia's bedroom. The explosions were intended to frighten the occupants and also be a signal for the others of the strike group. They immediately opened up with grenades, rockets and machine guns, completely demolishing the opposition, what little there was of it. One of the pair of 'watchers' who had earlier been posted on the Chittagong Club wall marvelled at what they saw. 'The whole thing was so spectacular,' one of them later told a friend. 'It was just like the commando strikes you see in the films.'[20]

The first to die among the security staff was Police Constable Dulal Miah who was on sentry duty in front of the portico. He was hit in the head by the first salvo fired by the attackers. The 44 other armed policeman on guard duty at that time offered no resistance whatsoever. Some of them even ran away and hid themselves. The Commission of Inquiry headed by the judges noted that apart from Dulal Miah, only three policemen received bullet injuries. This it put down to 'indiscriminate firing by the intruders' and not the result of active resistance to them.[21] The injuries sustained by 12 other policemen were caused by 'splinters, abrasion, friction and crawling'.[22]

Even the soldiers of the President's Guard Regiment in the Circuit House were caught napping. Two of them, who should have been standing outside the President's bedroom, were found downstairs, one of them dead, the other uninjured, in their quarters. These men were to have been relieved from sentry duty at 4 am and apparently had gone down well before their replacements arrived.[23] When the firing broke out the soldiers did try to rally to Zia's defence. They didn't get very far. Four of them were killed and two severely wounded in the opening minutes of the raid while still on the ground floor. General Zia's bedroom on the first floor was completely unguarded.

Significantly, none of the raiders was killed or wounded by the Circuit House security guards. The two who were wounded were accidentally shot by their own men. Lt. Col. Fazle Hussain was badly wounded and put out of action by bullets fired by the back-up team. Captain Jamil was another such casualty. Despite his injuries, Jamil managed to climb to the first floor verandah where he shot and wounded Naik Rafique Uddin, the President's personal bodyguard, as he came running out of a corner room. Lt. Colonel Moinul Ahsan, Chief Security officer to the President, and Captain Ashraful Khan, of the President's Guard Regiment, were sleeping in back rooms on the first floor when they were awakened by the exploding rockets. They reacted immediately as they were expected to do, coming out with their guns to defend the President. They were shot dead in the corridors by the attackers before they had a chance to use their guns.

Five members of the back-up team, including Moti, had by this time joined the others on the first floor in the hunt for Zia. According to the information they had been given, the President should have been in Room 9. When Captain Sattar kicked in the door of that room he found Dr. (Mrs.) Amina Rahman, the BNP Standing Committe member, cowering inside. As the killers went down the corridor hammering on the doors, Captain Salahuddin was heard calling out: 'Where is the President? Where is the President?' They soon realised that Zia was in Room 4. It was the one closest to the staircase and had two doors. One faced the stairs. The other opened onto the verandah and was bolted from the outside. Sattar tried to kick down the bolted door. Suddenly someone shouted: 'President is coming out'. A moment later someone else exclaimed: 'Here is the man'.[24]

Zia in white pymam pyjamas with his hair tousled, emerged from the other door. Standing with his hands slightly raised in front of him, the President boldly called out: 'Tomara ki chao?' (What do you want?)

The men who happened to be nearest to him were Major Muzaffar, who was visibly shivering, and Lt. Muslehuddin. Muslehuddin tried to reassure the President. 'Don't worry. Nothing to be afraid of, Sir.'[25] Incredibly these two officers were still labouring under the impression that Zia was to be abducted, not killed. Moti, who was also close by, however had no mercy for Zia. He didn't give the President a chance. Hardly had the reassuring words passed Muslehuddin's lips when Moti opened fire with his sub-machine gun, hitting Zia many times on the right side of his body. Zia twisted around as he fell near the door, face down and bleeding profusely. The sight seemed to trigger a madness in Moti. He went berserk. Turning the body over with the barrel of his gun, Moti emptied the magazine into Zia's face and upper torso. The bullets tore away a part of the head. You have to hate somebody very much to do such an awful thing. I can't imagine what Moti's grievance was; but it is evident from the record of mutinies against him that Zia was a man who made violent enemies. Having killed Zia, the killers withdrew quickly, taking their two wounded comrades with them. The whole dreadful business had taken less than 20 minutes.

Riding back to the Cantonment in one of the jeeps, Major Muzaffar, who was still shaking with shock, whimpered to Lt. Muslehuddin: 'I didn't know we were going to kill the President. I thought we were just to bring him out.'[26]

Zia's personal physician, Lt. Colonel Mahtabul Islam, who came out of his room after the firing had stopped, gave a vivid description of the dead President: 'I saw his body lying in front of the door riddled with bullets ... His one eye was completely destroyed and the neck muscles stripped off. There were lots of bullet marks on the chest, abdomen and legs ... There was a pool of blood on the carpet ... His specs were lying on the staircase.'[27]

Long after the raiders had departed and the firing had stopped (apparently the police had begun firing after they left), the other occupants of the first floor bedrooms began to emerge like frightened rabbits from their burrows. None of them had done anything to help Zia at the critical moment. The civil Commission of Inquiry noted: 'Lt. Colonel Mahfuz (personal staff officer) and Captain Mazhar (ADC) did not come out of their rooms until their doors were knocked and they were called out by Naik Abul Bashar, the wireless operator, well after the killers had left ... These two army officers were busy with their telephones inside their rooms and never cared to come out for a long time.'[28]

The ADC was in the bedroom adjoining Zia's. He did not try to reach the President personally, but instead telephoned the President without success.[29] Commenting on his actions, the civil Commission of Inquiry said: 'There is a connecting door between the two rooms. It was the easiest thing for the ADC to reach the President or at least to have made an attempt in that behalf through that door at the time of the occurrence. While the killers were banging on the doors of the President's room, one of the escape routes available was through the room of the ADC. One would have expected that the ADC would bang on that door even if it was bolted from the other side and urge upon the President who was in imminent danger to sneak into his room ... We are surprised to hear from the ADC that he did not even know that there was a connecting door ...'[30]

Col. Mahfuz told a dramatic story of how he had been fired at by an armed man in uniform as he tried to go to the President's aid. Mahfuz had then slammed the door shut and prostrated himself upon the floor until the firing had stopped. He pointed to bullet marks on the bedroom wall to support his story. But many days later when the marks were examined by experts, it was found that they could not have come from outside the room but were in fact made by Mahfuz himself. That gave the investigators the first clue to his involvement with the mutineers. When he was interrogated, Mahfuz broke down and confessed and was later hanged for his part in the mutiny.

The 60-year-old Dr. (Mrs.) Amina Rahman, who narrowly escaped death when her bedroom was mistaken for President Zia's, showed commendable courage when she came out of her room 45 minutes after the incident. But Dr. Badruddoza, the BNP secretary general, and State Minister Mohibul Hassan, who shared the other VIP room with him, by all accounts seem to have been afflicted by paralytic terror and did not leave their room till much later in the morning.

President Zia's body lay unattended for a long time on the floor of the verandah where it had fallen. Lt. Colonel Mahtabul Islam, his personal physician, had pronounced Zia dead but did nothing about the body. None of the BNP leaders or the Commissioner of Chittagong, senior civil and police officers and the Navy Chief who visited the Circuit House early in the morning, did anything to protect it. The did not even have the grace to place the President's body on a bed, but let it lie on the floor like some odious piece of baggage.[31]

Only Mizanur Rahman Chowdhury, the BNP leader, had the good sense to bring a white bedsheet from his own bed and place it over the slain President. Admiral Mahmood Alam Khan, Chief of the Naval Staff who had travelled with Zia from Dhaka, turned up at the Circuit House at about 5.30 am. He spent a few minutes talking to some of the officials on the porch. But despite being pressed to do so by some of the officers, he did not go up to the first floor to see the President's body. Statements made by him subsequently have not entirely explained away this odd behaviour.

I asked Saifuddin Ahmad, the Commissioner of Chittagong,[32] in particular why he as the senior-most civil officer had not protected the President's body or treated it more reverently. Saifuddin was obviously embarrassed by my question. He said: 'I would rather not talk because I would like to put all that behind me.' When pressed for an answer, he began to prevaricate: 'I was not sure what to do. I was about one hour in the Circuit House. By that time we knew that the killing had been done by the army. They killed the President and they would do what they wanted. We felt helpless.'

I asked again: 'Why didn't you recover the President's body?'

Saifuddin: 'I didn't know what to do. It was purely a police matter. Under the rules they were responsible for the body.'

I looked at him unbelievingly. Saifuddin was silent for a moment, then he added: 'I didn't have the heart to lift up the bed cover and see President Zia.' Such is the calibre of the officer who as Commissioner of Chittagong Division controlled one-third of both the land mass and population of Bangladesh.

By 7.30 am all the BNP leaders and senior civil and police officers had departed, leaving two junior functionaries in the Circuit House to keep an eye on the President's body which was still lying on the floor of the verandah.[33] Commissioner Saifuddin took Lt. Colonels Mahfuz and Mahtab and the ADC Captain Mazharul Hoq to his house for breakfast which he got his wife to cook for them.[34]

An hour later, three rebel majors—Muzaffar, Shaukat Alley and Reza— and about a dozen sepoys, all fully armed and in a convoy of two jeeps and an army van, turned up at the Circuit House. They ransacked the President's bedroom looking for 'secret papers' and Zia's personal diary in which he is known to have recorded his private thoughts. There is no indication that they found them. The rebels bundled Zia's personal effects into an old suitcase.

Then they wrapped Zia's body in a white bed sheet. They did the same to his two dead security officers, Lt. Colonel Ahsan and Capt. Hafiz. The three bodies were taken away in the van for burial at 9.30 am.

Major General Abul Manzoor acted swiftly after his boys reported back that they had killed President Zia. It was 4.45 am. Dressed in civies, Manzoor drove himself to the 6th East Bengal Headquarters (the wounded Lt. Colonel Fazle Hussain's regiment) and quickly ordered a number of defensive measures. All telephone lines out of the city were to be disconnected immediately. The guard at the Cantonment gates and the Army Signals Centre were strengthened. He ordered two companies of the regiment to take position at Shuvapur bridge to guard against an attack by loyal troops coming down from Comilla. Later Manzoor entrusted the defence of the area to his three brigades: the 65th to protect Chittagong; the 69th to secure the airport, seaport and Kalurghat radio transmitter; the 305 Brigade to defend the Shuvapur-Sitakunda-Chittagong axis and prevent landings at Kumira beach.

Manzoor then drove to his own office in the 24th Division Headquarters and summoned all available Brigade commanders, Divisional Staff Officers, and the Commandants of the various Army centres in Chittagong. Most of them had assembled in Manzoor's office by 6 am. Among those present were Brigadier A. S. M. Hanan Shah, Commandant of the Bangladesh Military Academy; Brigadier Mohsinuddin Ahmad, Commandant of the 69th Infantry Brigade; Brigadier Azizul Islam, Commandant of the East Bengal Regimental Centre; Colonel Abdur Rashid, Commander of the 65th Infantry Brigade; Colonel S. M. A. Hassan, Commandant of the Artillery Centre; Lt. Colonel Ataur Rahman, CO 12 Engineering Battalion; Lt. Colonel Shafiqur Rahman, CO 18th Field Ambulance; Lt. Colonel Shafat Ahmad, GSO-1; and Lt. Colonel S. A. Joarder, CO 12th Field Regiment Artillery. Also present were Manzoor's men from the killer team, Mehboob, Dilawar, Moti and Major Muzaffar Hussain.

In a brief address, Manzoor announced that the President had been killed by some young officers and he was with them. The administration, he said, was riddled with corruption and it had crept into the army. Zia had not taken corrective action despite repeated warnings. Manzoor then announced that a 'Revolutionary Council' had been formed to run the country, to restore Islam and to remove corruption. He held up the Holy Koran and asked each of them to touch it and swear allegiance and support to himself and the Revolutionary Council.

The White Paper records that each of the officers present took the oath. Not one of them demurred. Apparently they were all taken in by Manzoor's confident manner and were bowing down to what they thought was the fait accompli. It was only later when the realisation dawned that the rebellion was a localised affair that they began to have second thoughts and some of them actually crossed over to the government side.

It's also noted in the White Paper that later in the morning of the 30th of May several other senior civil, military and police officers called at the GOC's office at his request and took the oath of allegience to Manzoor and the Revolutionary Council after touching the Holy Koran. Among them were the Commissioner of Chittagong, Saifuddin Ahmad; the Deputy Commissioner Ziauddin M. Chowdhury; the Metropolitan Police Commissioner A. B. M. Boiduzzaman; the Base Commander of the Bangladesh Air Force Group Captain Nurul Islam; and the Sector Commander of the Bangladesh Rifles, Lt. Colonel Abdullah Azad.

Saifuddin Ahmad, the Chittagong Commissioner, told me about his own experience in Manzoor's office. 'I got a call from the Cantonment saying Manzoor wanted to see the Commissioner and DC (Deputy Commissioner). An officer came along to pick us up. I picked up the DC in my car and followed by an army jeep went to the GOC's office. We were told to wait. We waited 10 to 15 minutes. When we went inside they were listening to (Acting President) Sattar's speech ... We realised it was a mutiny, a localised affair, not a military coup. It was quite different to what Chittagong Radio was saying ... that Martial Law had been declared and a Revolutionary Council had taken power.'

Nevertheless Saifuddin did what Manzoor told him. He found Manzoor in uniform, sitting at his desk. There was a pistol on one side and the Holy Koran on the other. 'We have taken over power,' Manzoor told him. 'Certain things have to be done. You will carry on according to our instructions.' Manzoor then pointed to the Holy Koran. Saifuddin and Ziauddin touched the holy book and swore allegiance to Manzoor and the Revolutionary council.

'I went home,' Saifuddin added, 'and read the Holy Koran continuously. We knew things were not in our hands.'

Manzoor made a rambling, disjointed broadcast over Chittagong Radio in which he attempted to explain the reasons for the 'revolution'. 'As a result of unprecedented corruption,' he said, 'prices of commodities have gone beyond the purchasing power of the people. They are suffering enormously for want of food, clothing and housing ... The last government has patronised imported foreign culture ... Gambling, drinking and shameless body-exposing dances have been organised ... The youth community has been isolated ...' Claiming that 'anti-liberation forces have again raised their heads,' Manzoor said 'more than half of the council of ministers were opponents of Independence. They have defiled the posts of Vice President and Prime Minister ...'[35]

Chittagong Radio broadcast 11 'declarations of the Biplobi Parishad' (Revolutionary Council).

The first said a 'revolution' had taken place and a 'Revolutionary Council' of the armed forces had taken over the government. It would rule by Martial Law. The Constitution was suspended; the National Assembly dissolved and all political activities banned. All newspapers and magazines were being taken over by the government. The borders were sealed. All travel was prohibited. So were gambling and alcoholic drinks. 'The unequal 25-year Treaty of Friendship and Cooperation' with India was abrogated and the Revolutionary Council pledged itself to secure for Bangladesh its just share of the waters of the River Ganges basin. Dusk to dawn curfew was imposed on Dhaka, Chittagong and Rajshahi.

These orders were utterly meaningless—like straw in the wind—because the rebels had no power to enforce them. Still they persisted in the charade. Other declarations broadcast by Chittagong Radio 'demoted and dismissed' several senior military officers, including Lt. General Hussain Mohammad Ershad, the Chief of Army Staff. Major General Mir Shaukat Ali was named to 're-place' him. Manzoor sent a signal to Shaukat through the military com-munications system saying 'will contact you over the telephone as soon as line is through'. All this deeply embarrassed Shaukat who was sitting next door to General Ershad in Army Headquarters and was not involved in any way in the Mutiny. Similarly embarrassed was Major General Moinul Hussain who received a message from Manzoor: 'Will contact you over telephone as soon as line is through'.

Manzoor also sent signals appealing for support from the Air Force, the

Navy, the 46th Infantry Brigade at Dhaka, the 33rd Infantry Division Comilla, the 55th Infantry Division, Jessore and the Bangladesh Rifles. He said their cooperation was required 'for greater interest and integrity of the country'. All these appeals fell on deaf ears.

It was announced that 'Revolutionary Councils' had been set up in other military cantonments and that they had pledged support to the rebels in Chittagong. The rebels were trying an audacious bluff but it didn't work. Curiously never once during the two days of the mutiny did either Manzoor or any of his men disclose the composition of the 'Revolutionary Council'. There has been considerable speculation about the identity of its members. So far nothing is known with any certainty because all the ring leaders are either dead or absconding. Now I have been told by a retired army officer who had it from Major Khalid, the last of the ring leaders who is absconding, that the 'Revolutionary Council' had in fact not been constituted. It was to have consisted of 11 members based on rank: one general, one brigadier and one full colonel; two Lt. Colonels, two majors, two captains and two lieutenants. Manzoor, Dilawar, Mehboob, Moti and Khalid formed the nucleus of the 'council'. It was to have been formally constituted, Khalid told my informant, 'when we get to Dhaka'. When asked how they expected to capture power in Dhaka, Khalid told my informant: 'We expect all the FFs (freedom fighters) to rise up when they hear that charismatic name, Manzoor!'

The arrogance of the rebel leaders was matched only by their stupidity. Chittagong is hardly the place to launch a coup when the seat of government and the bulk of the Army and Air Force is far away to the north. Although they had been plotting President Zia's overthrow for at least two years, the mutiny itself was an impromptu affair brought on by Manzoor's sudden transfer to the Command and Staff College at Dhaka and the opportunity offered by President Zia's chance decision to visit Chittagong. Having started with an assassination, the rebels tried to develop a coup. In doing so they totally misread the mood of the Army.

They banked on the camaraderie of the Liberation War. It was a highly fanciful assumption. Since they were all freedom fighters, the rebels should have known better than anyone else that that camaraderie was now a dated and totally illusory concept. Hammered by Sheikh Mujib's insensitivity and lack of statesmanship during the formative days of Bangladesh and subsequently by the waywardness of Khandaker Moshtaque and General Ziaur Rahman, the people had long since abandoned the dream of Sonar Bangla (Golden Bengal) for the reality of frustration, corruption and selfish grasping in the effort to survive. The FFs—the few who were left in the armed forces where the instruments of power lay—were not immune to these changes. Thus if the cry that 'FFs are in danger' was enough to stampede some of this disparate group into a panicky reaction, it was not enough to rally them for a last concerted effort. The FFs had been beguiled too often. They were in no mood to ride again to the sound of trumpets. Apart from failing to win over the freedom fighters in the other cantonments, Manzoor and his men failed even to win the loyalty of their own troops. And in the end they were no match for the superior, more professional military tacticians in Army Headquarters in Dhaka.

The first information about President Zia's assassination was given to Dhaka over the telephone more than an hour after the killing. There was at that time no direct-dialling facility between the two cities. Captain Mazharul Hoq, the ADC who seems to have been in a state of shock, could have used the President's 'rover' wireless set specifically provided for emergency communication.

Instead he went through the involved process of booking a call through the long-distance operator. It was 5.30 am before he was able to talk to the President's Military Secretary, Major General Sadiqur Rahman Chowdhury, in Bangababan. The Military Secretary asked to speak to Lt. Colonel Mahfuz, the senior officer in the President's entourage, but the line went dead before he could be summoned from another room. The rebels' disruption of the telephone exchange had taken effect.

The Military Secretary immediately contacted Army Headquarters. Ten minutes later Major General Nooruddin, the Chief of the General Staff, was woken up. Nooruddin had been Director of Military Operations when Sheikh Mujib had been killed by the majors six years earlier. He had gained much from the experience of that crisis. Now on hearing the bad news from Chittagong, Nooruddin's reaction was positive and far-reaching. He also immediately informed Lt. General Ershad, the Army Chief. By 6.20 am Army Headquarters was functioning like a well-oiled machine. General Ershad had with him in his office the four PSOs (Principal Staff Officers—the CGS, Adjutant General, the Quarter Master General and the Master General of Ordnance), and other senior staff officers. The immediate problem was the lack of information: who was involved? How extensive was the mutiny? Did the mutineers have support in other cantonments?

Some confusion was caused when Lt. Colonel Mahfuz came over on the President's wireless at 7 am to ask the Director of Military Operations to send a helicopter to Chittagong with the Chief of Army Staff, the Home Minister and the Military Secretary to the President, to collect the President's body. Mahfuz said they must make sure that the helicopter landed in the Circuit House compound before he went off the air. Apparently Mahfuz was trying to lure them into a hostage situation according to the plan he had discussed with Moti in Dhaka on the 25th of May. Army Headquarters was not gulled so easily and Mahfuz's request, which raised eyebrows, was disregarded.

Despite the lack of information, the crisis management by Army Headquarters from the start was superb. The defensive and precautionary measures instituted by General Ershad proved invaluable in containing the mutiny in Chittagong and thereafter in quickly squashing it.

The army authorities were understandably reluctant to go into details for security reasons. I have, however, had it on good authority that apart from the customary protective measures taken in all cantonments, Army Headquarters discreetly boxed-in some senior officers as a matter of prudence. Some had a reputation for criticising the government. Some were known to be ambitious and indisciplined. Others had connections with Manzoor. All these officers were effectively isolated before the rebel leader could influence them. When I asked if any had been arrested, I was told: 'Not at all. It wasn't necessary. Once we had kept them in check there was no chance of anyone trying anything funny and none did.'

By far the most important action taken by General Ershad on the morning of the 30th May was to ensure that the Constitutional procedures were scrupulously observed. The President was dead. The Vice President would take over. Had the generals in Dhaka taken the opportunity to seize power for themselves they would have divided the army and precipitated a civil war. By adhering to the Consitution, General Ershad gave the defence services and the country as a whole a clear direction of the line of duty. It had a salutory effect everywhere. For one thing, it encouraged the overwhelming mass of troops and officers in the Chittagong area—even those who had mistakenly sworn allegiance to Manzoor at the start of the mutiny—to abandon the rebel group and bring a quick end to the mutiny. For another, it discouraged fence-sitting in other cantonments of the kind witnessed during previous crises. Once General Ershad had ensured the orderly succession as the Constitution stipulated, the crisis was reduced to manageable proportions.

Vice President Abdus Sattar was lying ill in hospital when General Ershad informed him about President Zia's assassination and told him to take over as Acting President. I understand that Justice Sattar at first demurred on the grounds of infirmity and old age. Sattar's reluctance is understandable. The killing had been an army affair and anyone who had experienced at close hand the trauma and unpredictability of the previous coups and counter-coups would not like to be caught in the crossfire. But his misgivings were overcome when General Ershad assured the old man of his fullest support. The Army Chief then personally escorted the Vice President to Bangababan and had him sworn in by the Chief Justice as Acting President of Bangladesh.

Helped by the Army, President Sattar's first act was to restore public confidence in the government. This he did in a 90-second broadcast. After announcing Zia's 'martyrdom' the new President appealed for peace, discipline and a display of patriotism. He said the government departments and Cabinet were functioning normally and that 40 days of mourning would be observed for the dead President. As an oblique sop to India, Sattar also reaffirmed that Bangladesh would adhere to 'all regional and international agreements.' Then he added: 'You will soon be informed of the detailed account of the situation on behalf of the government.' Clearly the government had not yet decided on a course of action.

A Cabinet meeting followed soon afterwards. A suggestion that Martial Law should be promulgated was quickly discarded. The civilian government had been agreeably surprised that the Armed Forces were following Constitutional procedures. So it was not at this stage going to cut its own throat by handing over authority to the military as Martial Law implied. Instead the government decided to proclaim a National Emergency which, under the Constitution, gave it extraordinary powers to deal with a crisis of this magnitude. They included the suspension of Fundamental Rights, but excluded the dissolution or suspension of the National Assembly. Public meetings were banned along with rallies and processions.[37] The Acting President directed the Chief of Army Staff and the Chiefs of the two other services 'to take immediate, stern action' to suppress the rebellion. The rebels were ordered to surrender forthwith.[38]

The civilian government with its new-found confidence made a great flourish of authority. But it was really the Army Chief, General Ershad, who was making most of the running. Apart from Chittagong, he had all the rest of the cantonments and military installations under control. There had been no overt support for the rebels anywhere. At the same time, General Ershad moved a strong force southwards from Comilla to block any attempts by the rebels to break out of Chittagong. The situation in that city was confusing. Army Headquarters was still not sure who was leading the rebellion and how extensive it was. Then around midday General Manzoor, in a surprising development, telephoned Army Headquarters in Dhaka to talk to Major General Mir Shaukat Ali who was Principal Staff Officer to the C-in-C i.e. the President. Manzoor briefed him about the formation of the 'Revolutionary Council' to run the country and some other details about their plans. He also advised the Army not to send troops against Chittagong unless it wanted to provoke a fight.

Manzoor's telephone call and other messages that were coming from Chittagong through the military signals system gave General Ershad the information he wanted. He was now able to home in on the source of the rebellion. In a radio and TV broadcast on that memorable Saturday, General Ershad asked the armed forces not to be misled by a small group of 'miscreants' who had killed President Ziaur Rahman. They claimed to be members of a Revolutionary Council, he said, but were a mere handful while the majority of the forces in the area were loyal to the government. The Army Chief also ordered the loyal troops to cross over to the government side at Shuvapur, north of Chittagong. He offered a General Amnesty to all those who did so by noon next day, Sunday the 31st of May. General Ershad also ordered Major General Manzoor and his group to surrender immediately and unconditionally or 'face the consequences'.

The Army Chief's directives were repeated over Radio Dhaka first at half-hour intervals and then every hour for the rest of the day. They had a telling effect on the officers and troops in Chittagong. President Zia's assassination and Manzoor's boasting about the formation of 'revolutionary councils' and support from other cantonments had led many to believe that a sea change had taken place in Bangladesh. General Ershad's broadcast and directives shattered that impression and promoted the realisation that the rebels were indeed a small group of adventurists completely isolated in Chittagong and that the legitimate government continued to function in Dhaka. After that it was only a matter of time before the mutiny collapsed.

Next day, Sunday, the Army Chief stepped up the pressure. He gave Manzoor and his men an ultimatum to surrender by 4.30 pm or face a strike by the Bangladesh Air Force. Unfortunately for General Ershad, Chittagong was hit by another heavy monsoon storm an hour before his ultimatum was due to expire. The Air Force was not able to operate in such extreme conditions. So rather than see his deadline pass without action, General Ershad extended it to 6 am the following morning (Monday, 1st June). He also directed the loyal officers and men in Chittagong 'to disarm the few misguided officers and soldiers' and to take control of the Chittagong Radio station so that it could relay broadcasts by Dhaka Radio.

Ershad was encouraged to extend the deadline by the flood of soldiers who were crossing over the Shuvapur Bridge to the government side. Manzoor had sent two companies of the 6th East Bengal to guard the bridge and prevent government troops coming down from Comilla. But once they heard General Ershad's broadcast, the troops defected en masse to the government. Other troops crossing over came from the 305 Infantry Brigade, the 12 Field Regiment Artillery led by Lt. Colonel Joardar, the 26th, 28th and 36th East Bengal Regiment and other units from Chittagong cantonment.[39]

The mood in the Cantonment itself had in 36 hours swung sharply from euphoria to deep depression.

Manzoor spent most of Saturday afternoon and Sunday morning trying to drum up support among the troops. Visiting each of the units, he harped upon the low pay, poor quality of uniforms and boots and how insecure the soldiers' families were because of the mounting violence in the countryside. He blamed corrupt military officers and ministers for their problems and promised that the Revolutionary Council would redress them. The troops, who were also listening to General Ershad's broadcasts over Dhaka Radio, did not respond to Manzoor's blandishments. He got the message and became increasingly depressed. On Sunday morning Manzoor called a meeting of senior civil officers, bank managers, newspaper editors, the Port Commissioners and leading members of the business community in the Deputy Commissioner's office. He lectured them for 90 minutes on the 'revolution' and issued a number of directives intended to enforce an economic blockade of the government in Dhaka. He ordered that no oil, petrol or lubricants would move northwards from Chittagong. There would be no ship movements in and out of the port. The local branch of the Bangladesh Bank would control the flow of foreign exchange and funds in other banks to prevent them going to Dhaka.[40] Later Manzoor would also threaten to cut the supply of electricity from the Kaptai hydro-electric power station, Dhaka and Bangladesh's main source of supply.[41]

By some perverse logic, Manzoor thought he could starve the government in Dhaka into submission. An indication of his thinking is given in a letter he sent by hand on 30th May to Major General Samad, GOC of the 33rd Infantry Division based at Comilla. Manzoor told him 'My earnest desire is to avoid civil war. If people insist, they are welcome and things will not be very pleasant. Chittagong as you well realise is in a better position economically and militarily. Economically the rest of the country will suffer . . .'[42] General Samad was not impressed. He immediately turned the letter over to the Army authorities in Dhaka.

By Sunday evening as troop defections mounted and General Ershad threatened a strike by the Air Force, Manzoor in some desperation sought the advice of senior army officers during a meeting in his office. Brigadier Hanan Shah, Commandant of the BMA, suggested that the only way to avoid bloodshed was to immediately start negotiations with Dhaka for a settlement. Most of the others agreed. The only standouts were Moti and Dilawar. The latter is reported to have shouted: 'What negotiations? March to Dhaka.'[43]

Manzoor himself favoured talks and nominated Brigadier Hanan, who made the suggestion in the first place, to make contact with Army Headquarters in Dhaka. The Brigadier got the CGS on the telephone and started the conversation by carefully reading out a message that Manzoor had dictated. It said: 'I feel there is scope for negotiation. You have to send two negotiators to Chittagong and announce it over the radio. Bangladesh (Dhaka) Radio should also stop anti-revolutionary broadcasts'. Major General Nooruddin, the CGS, made no comment. He only wanted to know if they had anything else to say. Hanan wasn't sure and Manzoor, who was monitoring the conversation, made a sign indicating that it should be terminated.

Two hours later Hanan was instructed to talk to the CGS again and pass on Manzoor's four demands for a 'peaceful settlement'. They were: (1) the promulgation of Martial law; (2) the Chief Justice be appointed President; (3) the dissolution of the National Assembly; and (4) recognition of the 'Biplobi Parishads' (revolutionary councils) which should be allowed to operate in the cantonments.[44] Major General Nooruddin's answer was that the government would accept nothing less than unconditional surrender. He also said the anti-rebel broadcasts would continue. At this point Lt. Colonel Moti began to get impatient. He wanted to start random firing at government troops and to arm civilian FFs in the area. Manzoor denied both requests and managed to calm him down.

The negotiations with Dhaka continued till after midnight with the CGS insisting on unconditional surrender. Finally at one o'clock on Monday morning, Manzoor personally spoke to General Nooruddin. The conversation was brief and it's not known what transpired. But when he hung up the telephone the rebel leader looked completely shattered. He quietly ordered the officers to return to their brigades. Then, accompanied by Majors Muzaffar and Reza, Manzoor got into his car and left for home. He promised to return shortly to his office. He never came back. By 2 am—46 hours after Zia's slaying—the mutiny was over and the rebels were on the run.

Manzoor and his group left the Chittagong Cantonment in batches between 2.30 and 3 o'clock in the morning of Monday, 1st June. Before leaving, Manzoor asked Major Khalid: 'Shall we take your Bhabi (your sister, my wife) with us?' Khalid made a derisory retort.[45] They were fleeing for their lives and the women and children would only hamper their escape. Manzoor, however, was too closely tied to his wife's apron strings to leave her behind. So Begum Manzoor, her two sons and two daughters, and her best friend, Begum Dilawar Hussain and her three daughters, were taken along. Curiously—and this has not been explained by anyone—Lt. Colonel Dilawar did not himself join the escaping group.

As they drove northwards, the batches joined up along the road leading from Hathazari to Fatikchari. Eventually there were 11 officers, two women and seven children in a convoy of three jeeps and a military pick-up. Lt. Colonels Moti and Mehboob, Major Muzaffar and Captain Munir were in the lead jeep. Majors Gias and Reza rode with General Manzoor in the second jeep. Major Iazdani drove the women and children in the third jeep. In the last vehicle, the military pick-up driven by Major Khalid, were Lt. Colonel Fazle Hussain and Captain Jamil Hoq, the two who were wounded during the assault on the Circuit House when President Zia was assassinated. Although they were in no condition to travel, the two officers had been forcibly taken from the Combined Military Hospital in Chittagong in a bid to remove them to a place of safety. But the journey was too much and they were abandoned at Fatikchari where they were arrested by Abdus Sattar, an officer of the NSI, at 8.30 am.

When asked by Major Reza where they were going, General Manzoor said they were bound for a safe area near Guimara where the 21 East Bengal was located. Manzoor obviously was not telling the truth. He couldn't by any chance have hoped to find sanctuary with the 21st East Bengal. The probable destination was the soft international frontier with the Indian state of Tripura which they could have reached with another few hours driving. Meanwhile they could hide out in the dense jungles of the Chittagong Hill Tracts. It was not to be.

As they drove out of Fatikchari in the general direction of Manikchari, Manzoor and the others got separated from Moti and Mehboob in the lead vehicle driving at high speed along the winding road. To their bad luck Moti and Mehboob suddenly came upon a column of soldiers from the 12 Engineers Battalion under Major Mannan who were on their way to the rally point for loyal troops. The two Lt. Colonels tried to bluff their way past the Engineers. But Mannan wasn't taken in. He had been listening to Dhaka Radio which by then was broadcasting the news of Manzoor's escape from Chittagong and realised that he had come upon the fugitives.

'You are under arrest,' Major Mannan told them rather nervously. Moti tried to talk him down; then suddenly picked up a sten gun and fired at Mannan from point blank range. The major miraculously escaped injury. Naik Subedar Shamsul Alam, who was sitting in the jeep next to him, took the full force of the sten gun burst and was killed instantly. The engineers then opened fire killing Moti and Mehboob. Captain Munir, who was riding the jeep with them, was arrested. Major Muzaffar, the other passenger, somehow managed to escape in the confusion and is still absconding with a price on his head.

On hearing the sound of firing, Manzoor halted and turned back the convoy in the direction of Fatikchari. When they were a couple of miles from the town, the rebel general unaccountably split the group. Sending the others off in the vehicles, Manzoor took his wife and children and Dilawar's wife and children and Majors Gias and Reza and set off walking through the countryside of the Khamar tribal area. No one knows where they were going and why. But they walked all through the morning and part of the afternoon in the scorching sun, stopping occasionally for water, rest and a change of guides.

When they reached the Asia Tea Gardens, tired and worn out, at about 2.30 pm they got some bad news. A tea garden employee told them he had seen in the town two army men bound and blindfolded and lying in a military vehicle. Manzoor was not to know that they were the unfortunate Lt. Colonel Fazle Hussain and Captain Jamil Hoq. He decided to hide. Taking the women and children and the two majors, Manzoor sought refuge in the coolie quarters of the tea garden. They were having a frugal meal in the home of a coolie named Manu Mian when the police turned up. The rebel officers ran out through the back door. They didn't get far because the house was surrounded by armed policemen. Manzoor had an SMG but realised his situation was hopeless. He surrendered without a fight and was taken into custody along with the two women, seven children and Major Reza. For the moment Major Gias could not be found although the police combed the tea bushes for him.

Sheikh Maruful Huq, Superintendent of Police, Chittagong, takes up the story:[46] 'The information of the capture of Major General Manzoor spread like wildfire and people started gathering from the villages. When the police party reached Hathazari there were about 10,000 people assembled there and it was impossible to proceed further (to Chittagong). The police force with the prisoners therefore went inside the police station for safety of the prisoners. By that time about 13,000 people had assembled around the police station and wanted to snatch away the prisoners and shouted repeatedly to tear Major General Manzoor to pieces ... By 7.45 pm the crowd had swelled to 30,000 ...'

Police reinforcements were summoned from Chittagong. By the time they arrived orders had been received from Acting President Abdus Sattar through Saifuddin Ahmad, the Commissioner of Chittagong, that all the prisoners should be handed over to the army officers deputed by Brigadier Abdul Aziz of Chittagong Cantonment.[47]

Manzoor protested the decision. He said he was no longer an army officer (he had been dismissed in a radio broadcast from Dhaka) and should be held by the civil authority and not handed over to the military. The police did not agree. They handed him over to Captain Emdadul Huq of the East Bengal Regimental Centre who had come to Hathazari with a military escort. Captain Emdad tied Manzoor's hands and feet with rope. blindfolded him with a piece of cloth and 'practically dragged him from the police truck to the army vehicle'.[48]

The final act took place where it all started, in Chittagong Cantonment. And one must depend on the authenticity of the Government White Paper and the civil Commission of Inquiry for what transpired. Captain Emdad brought his prisoners to the cantonment at about 10 pm in three closed jeeps. The one carrying the women and children went straight to Flag Staff House, Manzoor's official residence. Major Reza in the next jeep was taken to the East Bengal Regimental Centre. The third jeep in which Captain Emdad personally escorted his bound and blindfolded prisoner was a little behind the other two. The White Paper notes that Captain Emdad found troops with arms who were moving around in small groups along the road. As he neared the VIP house the escort officer found more troops so he took a round-about route. The White Paper goes on:

'As soon as the jeep reached near the tri-junction in front of the Canteen Stores Department Shop a group of about 20 to 30 armed troops stopped the vehicle and asked the officer to allow them to search it. Before he could say anything, they opened the back door and found the general. They started shouting 'KHUNIKAY PAIYACHI' (We have got the killer) and dragged him out of the vehicle . . . The agitated troops instead of listening to the escort officer pushed him inside the vehicle and threatened to kill him if he did not leave the place . . .'

When Captain Emdad returned to the spot a little later with two other officers, they found Major General Manzoor lying face-down in a drain with a gaping hole in the back of his head. A post mortem carried out next morning in the Combined Military Hospital indicated that the 4 × 2 inches jagged hole had been caused by a single bullet. 'There was no other injury on the body.'[49]

The ultimate humiliation for the rebel officers came next day (2nd June) after Manzoor's wife and children were flown to Dhaka by helicopter for their own safety. No one claimed Manzoor's body and that of his nephew, Lt. Colonel Mehboob. Lt. Colonel Moti's relatives wanted to take his body away to their home village for burial. But no one would provide transport to carry the body nor would any graveyard accept it for burial. The reason given to them was that the body of the rebel officer would 'desecrate' the graveyards. So they left it in Army custody. In the end, Manzoor, Mehboob and Moti were buried without fuss in unmarked graves in the Chittagong Cantonment graveyard much against the wishes of the troops.

After the collapse of the mutiny early in the morning of Monday, 1st June, the civil and military authorities began a frantic search for President Zia's body. An earlier attempt by the government to bring it to Dhaka under the aegis of the Red Cross in Chittagong had been turned down by General Manzoor. Now with the rebels on the run, military teams fanned out from the cantonment into the countryside to locate it.

Zia's body and those of his slain aides, Lt. Colonel Ahsan and Captain Hafiz, had been last seen two days earlier being taken from the Circuit House by a burial party of soldiers led by Majors Muzaffar and Shaukat Alley. They had proceeded along the Kaptai Road and indications were that the bodies had been buried somewhere near Rangunia, 17 miles from Chittagong where the Engineering College is located. It was in this area that the authorities directed their search. Lt. Colonel Khaleque, CO of the 28th East Bengal Regiment, was the first to set out. He was followed closely by a group composed of Brigadier Hannan Shah, Lt. Colonel Mahfuz (Zia's secretary, still posing as innocent), and Captain Mazharul Hoq, Zia's ADC. Both parties travelled swiftly but they were beaten to the discovery of the grave by the police acting on information supplied by a student of the Engineering College at Rangunia.[50]

Mohammad Bashiri, the young student, had become inquisitive when at about 1.30 pm on the 30th of May he had seen three army vehicles carrying 10 men and three bodies passing through the college campus. Their curious movements aroused his suspicions so he followed them to a market place not far from the college. He saw the soldiers take three labourers from the market and proceed slowly to the nearby village of Pathargata. There the labourers were made to dig a shallow grave. When Bashiri approached them to get a closer look, he was shooed away by the soldiers. So he hid himself on a convenient hillock nearby from where he watched the proceedings.

According to Bashiri the grave was dug and the three bodies were laid out alongside it. Then an Imam (priest) was brought from the nearby 'dargah' (shrine) to perform the Namaz-e-Janaza or prayers for the dead. The bodies were hastily buried without formality and a sentry was posted to guard the grave. Bashiri kep the secret for two days. Then early in the morning of 1st June when he heard that the rebellion had collapsed and found the guard over the grave missing, he reported the matter to the Rangunia police station. Bashiri took a police party led by a sub-inspector to the site and they began to dig. Soon they discovered three bodies covered by a single bed-sheet. One of them clearly was President Zia.

By then the military officers had also arrived. They took charge of the bodies and brought them to the Combined Military Hospital at Chittagong where they were handed over to the CO, Col. Mozammel Hossain. An autopsy on President Zia's body was carried out by Lt. Col. A. Z. Tufail Ahmed, specialist in pathology, who noted: 'The body was partially decomposed but the configuration was intact to be identified as the body of the late President Ziaur Rahman. There were about 20 separate bullet wounds on the body . . .' [51]

Zia's body was prepared for burial with formalin, eucalyptus and cedar oils and 'attar' (perfume) and placed in the coffin scattered with green tea leaves to keep it sweet. Then the coffin, draped with the National Flag, was placed in a helicopter to be flown to Dhaka at 1 pm. But the late President's ordeal was not yet over. A monsoon storm overtook the helicopter near Feni, forcing it to return to Chittagong. The coffin was transferred to an Air Force transport plane and three hours later was flown to Dhaka where it lay in state. More than one million people attended the funeral the next day.

Although there was no love lost between Zia and most of his BNP ministers during his life-time, once he was dead the successor BNP government of Acting President Sattar seems to have gone overboard in conferring honours and favours on Zia and his family. A 'hasty decision', which I'm told many of his ministers now privately regret, was taken to bury Zia near the National Assembly building. Accordingly an enormous stretch of land in this prime New Capital area was dedicated to a mausoleum for him. So far only a portion of this land has been used for a simple monument around Zia's lonely grave. Sadly it gets little attention from officialdom, the politicians and the public at large except on the occasion of his death anniversary when prayers are said at the tomb. Many acres of the mausoleum land remain unutilised and it's not clear what eventually will be done about it.

The government, according to Mirza Golam Hafiz, speaker of the National Assembly, had also decided to preserve Zia's ancestral home in Bagmare village in Bogra district as a national shrine. [52] Here too interest seems to have faded after the first emotional outburst. The late President's erstwhile political companions seem to be distancing themselves from his shadow as the public becomes increasingly aware of the seamier side of Zia's role in the troubled history of their country.

But at that time the Sattar government made a stupendous outpouring of cash, property and life-time perks on President Zia's widow, Khalida, and her two minor sons. Apparently they were left impoverished by his sudden death and the government moved rapidly to make handsome provision for them. By a Cabinet decision (No. 35/81) dated 12th June, 1981, the Sattar government approved the following grants and life-time perks for Begum Khalida Zia and her family:

1. An immediate cash grant of 1,000,000 Takkas.
2. The allotment of full ownership of a large modern bungalow in a privileged area of Dhaka for the nominal price of one Takka.
3. The government will bear the entire cost of educating the two sons in Bangladesh and abroad until they are 25 years old. During this time they will also receive an allowance of 1500 Takkas each per month in cash.
4. The government will bear the entire cost of medical treatment for Begum Khalida Zia and family in Bangladesh and abroad.
5. The government will give them a car and will bear the cost of a driver and all petrol requirements.
6. They will be provided with a free telephone.
7. The government will pay Begum Khalida Zia's gas, electricity and water bills. It will also provide guards for her home.
8. The government will pay for her personal secretary and for FIVE domestic servants—two 'bearers' or valets, a cook, a gardener and a sweeper.

Begum Khalida Zia in fact ended up with not one but two magnificent bungalows. The one in the posh Gulshan area of Dhaka (estimated market value 5,000,000 to 6,000,000 Takkas) she obtained for a nominal one Takka, has been leased to a foreign mission for what is said to be a handsome monthly rental. Meanwhile she and her sons continue to live at government expense in the sprawling bungalow in the Dhaka Cantonment which the family occupied when Zia was President.

Curiously, the Sattar government kept these arrangements secret. Only the cash grant of 1,000,000 Takkas was officially confirmed by Prime Minister Shah Azizur Rahman after an opposition Awami Leaguer, Shudhansu Sekhar Haldar, caused a sensation by revealing it in the National Assembly two weeks later. Haldar, in a snide reference to the transfer of funds by ministers, disclosed that Begum Khalida Zia, by cheque No. 447932, had withdrawn 1,000,000 Takkas from the Bangababan branch of the Sonali Bank on 16th June and next day had deposited it in her account, No. 3733, in the Bank of Credit and Commerce International (BCCI).[53]

The implication of Haldar's remarks—that the reputedly honest Zia had somehow left his wife a nest egg of 1,000,000 Takkas which she was attempting to hide away in a foreign bank—was an outrageous slander of the dead President. Nevertheless it inexplicably took the Sattar government all of two days to refute the allegation and put the record straight. On 29th June, Prime Minister Shah Azizur Rahman told the National Assembly that the government had made an 'ad hoc' grant of 1,000,000 Takkas to President Zia's widow, Khalida, and her two sons because Zia had not left anything for them.[54] Payment had been made by the President's secretariat and it was this money that Begum Khalida Zia had transferred from the Sonali Bank to her account in the BCCI. The Prime Minister, however, on that occasion made no mention whatsoever of the other grants and life-time perks given to Begum Khalida and her family.

Haldar's disclosure in the National Assembly was clearly intended to take the pressure off Sheikh Hasina Wajid, Sheikh Mujib's daughter and President of the Awami League. who was then smarting over a new scandal about corruption and the illegal storage of arms and ammunition in her late father's household.

Hasina had been living in self-imposed exile in India since her father's assassination in August, 1975. With Zia's permission privately given, she had returned to Bangladesh in the middle of May—just 12 days before Zia himself was killed. In keeping with the late President Zia's assurances to her, the Sattar government on 12th June, 1981, handed over to Hasina, as the legal heir, all Sheikh Mujib's property which had been held in government custody. This included the three-storeyed family home and its contents—the famous landmark on Road No. 32 Dhanmandi in Dhaka. The transfer had been affected at a private ceremony with Hasina in the presence of three witnesses signing a receipt for the family belongings listed on a 71-page inventory. Next day the fat was squarely in the fire when someone in the government leaked it to the press that the inventory included a large amount of gold, diamond and platinum jewellery and silverware (estimated value at that time 2.5 million Takkas), and an armoury of assorted weapons. They ranged from a Chinese-made sub-machine gun to high-velocity rifles, revolvers, three grenades and a quantity of ammunition.[55] The news that all this had been recovered from Sheikh Mujib's Dhanmandi residence caused an uproar and set tongues wagging again with stories of Mujib's corruption and misuse of power. Hasina was severely embarrassed by the disclosure. She tried to explain it away by saying that the jewellery was in fact the property of four or five families and the guns, disabled souvenirs given to her father by Freedom Fighters.[56]

Although it had been squashed in a remarkably efficient and bloodless manner, without the clash of arms, by General Ershad, the Chittagong Mutiny had devastating implications both for the Bangladesh armed forces (particularly the Army), and for the civil authority. Section 31 of the Bangladesh Army Act stipulates that anyone subject to the Act (i.e. members of the armed forces) who:

'(1) begins, incites or conspires with any other person to cause or joins in any mutiny in the military, naval or air forces of Bangladesh or any forces cooperating with it; or
(2) being present at such mutiny, does not use his utmost endeavour to suppress the same . . . Shall on conviction by Court Martial be punished with death or with such less punishment as this Act mentioned.'[57]

Civilians joining a mutiny fall within the ambit of Chapter VII of the Bangladesh Penal Code. According to the White Paper this chapter makes clear that 'when a person not subject to the Army Act commits an offence which may be military as well as civil in nature (i.e. abetting mutiny, seducing soldiers from duty or harbouring deserters) then in line with Section 139 of the Penal Code he is absolutely liable to be tried under the Army Act.'[58]
Had these civil and military regulations been strictly adhered to then several thousand Army, Navy, Air Force, Bangladesh Rifles and senior civil and police officers should have been tried by military court for 'being present' at a mutiny or not actively attempting to suppress it. I understand that a high powered Army Court of Inquiry headed by Major General Muzammel Hussain, which investigated the affair immediately after it ended, did in fact record that all the commanders and staff officers present in Chittagong at that time could have been charged under military law. This was not practicable and those not directly involved were given the benefit of a General Amnesty. Apparently after Zia's assassination, the general run of officers took the rebellion as a fait accompli and routinely complied with the orders of General Manzoor, the rebel leader. None of the army units or military installations in Chittagong area—or for that matter the Bangladesh Navy, Air Force and Bangladesh

Rifles based in Chittagong—resisted or attempted to suppress Manzoor's rebellion. In fact I understand that it is on record that some army officers failed to rise to the occasion when their juniors approached them to have a go at countering Manzoor. This is surprising indeed.

First, there were at that time in Chittagong vast numbers of troops and officers who with courageous leadership could have been used to mount a successful counter to the rebellion which was essentially by a small group of officers. It was evident from the start that the soldiers had refused to get involved in the affair. They had in the past suffered terribly because of the bonapartism of their officers and now wanted no part of it. The refusal of the common soldier to back him was the essential ingredient in Manzoor's failure. He was aware of this from the start, having received a chill reception when he spoke to the troops to win them over within hours of Zia's killing. Unfortunately, there was no one among the loyal officers to grasp this idea, to rally the troops and turn the tables on Manzoor.

Secondly, there were also in Chittagong several important military installations independent of Manzoor's command. These were the East Bengal Regimental Centre (1800 men), the Artillery School (1000 men), the Military Academy, the Bangladesh Rifles, the Navy and the Air Force which could between them have assembled another 4000 men. They could have joined to defeat Manzoor. Instead, apart from the Navy which seems to have been isolated, we have the spectacle of the senior officers of these establishments and most of the fighting units in Chittagong swearing allegiance to Manzoor and the 'Revolutionary Council'. Many other officers, to use a term that's become popular in Dhaka, 'remained fence-sitting'.

One of these men, now a Lt. Colonel, when talking privately to me about his experience in Chittagong during the ill-conceived rebellion, frankly said: 'I did not join the mutiny or support it or oppose it. In fact I didn't even surrender as we were supposed to do at Shuvapur.'

'What then did you do?' I asked him.

The man appeared to be surprised at my question. 'Why, I didn't do anything. I had to look after myself.'

This confession underscores the devastation wrought in the Defence Forces by the policies of Sheikh Mujib, Khandaker Moshtaque and Zia and by the many coups and attempted coups between 1975 and the middle of 1981. Discipline and the chain of command had been undermined. Morale was almost non-existent.

The military Court of Inquiry, the civil Commission of Inquiry into President Zia's assassination and the White Paper suggest that an underlying factor for no action being taken in Chittagong by loyal troops to counter the mutiny was that it would have inevitably led to bloodshed. This is no excuse at all. A soldier is paid, fed, clothed and his family cared for at public expense expressly to fight and risk his life when required to do so. It is the raison d'etre for his existence. The demand is seldom made but when it is, a soldier's failure to fight is an unacceptable dereliction of duty. General Ershad did well to use a heavy broom to clean out the Army after the Chittagong rebellion.

I understand that about 60 fairly senior army officers considered to be 'suspect', indisciplined or 'bad officers' were removed from service. General Ershad, unlike his predecessors, also made sure that all those directly involved in the mutiny and President Zia's killing were brought to trial. The Military Court of Inquiry under General Muzammel recommended that 33 army officers (three of them in absentia) and two JCOs be charged and 10 officers retired from service. Ultimately 30 officers were tried by General Court

Martial. The court was headed by Major General Mohammad Abdur Rahman and had six other senior officers—a brigadier, two colonels and three Lt. colonels.

Thirteen officers involved in the mutiny were convicted and executed by hanging. Seven others were sentenced to death but later had their sentences reduced to life imprisonment. Six officers were sent to prison for terms ranging from seven to ten years. Four were honourably acquitted. The last to be hanged was Lt. Colonel Shah Mohammad Fazle Hossain, CO of the 6th East Bengal Regiment who was badly injured by his own side during the assault on the Circuit House. Under Military Law an injured or sick person cannot be brought to trial. So, I'm told, the wretched man was given all the necessary treatment for a quick recovery. Then he was tried, convicted and hanged.

The trials and the clean-up of the Army, I am told, caused some rumbling. It was not so much because of the severity with which they were carried out, but because the civil and police officers in Chittagong who got snarled in the affair remained untouched. I understand that after he had prosecuted the army men and punished the others for dereliction of duty, General Ershad asked Acting President Sattar to do the needful on the civil side. Sattar chose to do nothing. I'm told there wasn't even an inquiry into how some officers came to swear allegiance to Manzoor and carry out his orders faithfully for two days. But Sattar did transfer one officer out of Chittagong. He was the Divisional Commissioner, Saifuddin Ahmad. The lucky man was posted to London in the privileged position of Minister, Economic Affairs, in the Bangladesh High Commission.

Acting President Sattar also unaccountably failed to make public the official report of the Commission of Inquiry into President Zia's killing. The successor BNP government of Sattar moved with commendable speed to get the inquiry going quickly after the assassination. But subsequent events suggest that it was perhaps only a sop to the public. Two Supreme Court judges—Justice Ruhul Islam and Justice A. T. M. Afzal—and Syed Serajuddin Ahmad, district and sessions judge of Khulna, were given two months to complete their inquiry. They did so in September, 1981, but the report was never published.

Sattar in the course of an interview in Dhaka in March, 1981, confirmed that he had not placed the Commission's report for Cabinet consideration. He would give no reasons for this anomaly. He did, however, say 'I gave it to the Home Minister (retired Lt. Col. Mustafizur Rahman) to follow up.' He said he did not know what transpired thereafter. Sattar also confirmed that 'the party (Zia's BNP) opposed it being made public. There was a lot of trouble in the party at that time and they didn't want it published.' Sattar would not elaborate or explain the reasons for the party's 'pressure'. A senior BNP minister of Sattar's cabinet, who for the present does not wish to be identified, told me privately: 'There was immense pressure from the party to bury the report.' Again no credible reason was given for it.

All this understandably has raised questions in the public mind about the real truth of the events in Chittagong on that fateful night in May, 1981, and the circumstances surrounding President Zia and General Manzoor's deaths. But I can find no reason for the Sattar government to suppress the Commission's report. I have a copy and find it innocuous; at times illogical and certainly very prodigal in handing out excuses. This is particularly so in the matter of the failure of the civil and police authorities to secure and reverence the body of the slain President which lay for hours unattended on the floor of the Circuit House verandah. On the whole the Commission's conclusions are little different from the government White Paper on the subject. This in turn is an edited version of the report of the military Court of Inquiry headed by Major General Muzammel.

The Commission's report uncovers no dark secrets. It focusses on General Manzoor and his small group for the conspiracy and the killing. It notes that the forces on duty at the Circuit House for the protection of the President 'failed to put up any resistance whatsoever to the raiders and the security system completely melted away in the wake of the attack.' It blames the civil and military intelligence agencies for their failure to forewarn. This, the Commission said, 'was the primary reason which caused grave insecurity to the person of the President and ultimately cost his life.' The Commission also confirms that General Manzoor was killed by irate soldiers who seized him when he was brought to the Cantonment in a jeep by Capt. Emdadul Huq.

There is nothing sinister or earth-shattering about all this, certainly no reason for not publishing the report. In these circumstances one is led to suspect the frailty of the BNP's own ministers and a Bangladeshi Rasputin among them who engineered the suppression of the innocuous report. The object, it seems, was to make insidious rumours fly to besmirch the reputation of innocent men perceived as potential rivals for power. Machination and murder have been the curse of Bangladesh—its legacy of blood. It will not end until public accountability and the sequence of crime and punishment is firmly established.

Notes
1. Report of the civil Commission of Inquiry on the killing of President Ziaur Rahman, 1981, pp 18 and 53.
2. Marcus Franda, 'Ziaur Rahman's Bangladesh'.
3. White Paper on assassination of President Ziaur Rahman, 1981.
4. Evidence given by Lt. Col. Dilawar Hussain.
5. White Paper. Also civil Commission of Inquiry report.
6. Marcus Franda, 'Ziaur Rahman's Bangladesh'.
7. Lt. Col. Dilawar Hussain's evidence. Also White Paper.
8. Interviewed in London, 4–1–85.
9. Lt. Colonel Fazle Hussain's evidence.
10. White Paper.
11. ibid.
12. Civil Commission of Inquiry.
13. ibid.
14. Trial evidence.
15. ibid. (DQ is the abbreviated form of Deputy Assistant Adjutant and Quarter-Master General).
16. ibid.
17. ibid.
18. ibid.
19. Rafique's evidence.
20. Ex-army officer interviewed in Dhaka in March, 1985.
21. Civil Inquiry Commission's report, pp 51–52.
22. White Paper.
23. Civil Inquiry Commission's report.
24. Rafique's evidence.
25. Muslehuddin's evidence.
26. ibid.
27. Lt. Col. Mahtab's evidence.
28. Civil Inquiry Commission's report, p 57.
29. White Paper.
30. Civil Inquiry Commission's report, pp 56–57.
31. ibid (Report says: 'We have it in evidence that none of the more responsible persons who happened to be there at the Circuit House at the time, namely two State Ministers & the Chief of Naval Staff, did even think of giving any suggestion or instruction to the local officials with regard to the security and protection of the dead body of the late President . . .')

32. Interviewed in London, 4-1-85.
33. Civil Inquiry Commission's report, p 11.
34. Interviewed in London, 4-1-85.
35. The only time Manzoor personally broadcast over Chittagong Radio on 31-5-85, reported in Weekly Ittehad, Dhaka, 4 6 81.
36. Ittehad, Dhaka, 4-6-81.
37. Government spokesman quoted by Bangladesh News Agency, BSS, 31-5-81.
38. Bangladesh Times, 1-6-81.
39. White Paper.
40. ibid.
41. Trial evidence.
42. ibid.
43. ibid.
44. ibid.
45. Ex-army officer interviewed in Dhaka in March, 1985.
46. Supt. of Police, Chittagong, evidence.
47. ibid (Sheikh Maruful Huq's evidence stated: '. . . the Divisional Commissioner, Chittagong, conveyed the decisions of government through police wireless to DIG & myself that he had discussed the matter of handing over the captured prisoners to the army authorities with the Hon'ble Acting president and Brigadier Aziz of Chittagong Cantonment. He told us that as per instructions given by the Acting President all the rebel prisoners, including the females and children, to be handed over to the army officers deputed by Brigadier Abdul Aziz of Chittagong Cantonment . . .')
48. Civil Commission of Inquiry report, p 23.
49. Post mortem report (also see appendix).
50. Bangladesh Observer, 3-6-81.
51. Post mortem report—also see appendix.
52. Bangladesh Observer, 26-6-81.
53. Sangbad, Dhaka, 29-6-81.
54. Bangladesh Observer, 30-6-81.
55. Bangladesh Times, 14-6-81.
56. Bangladesh Observer, 16-6-81.
57. White Paper.
58. ibid.

Index